MAGNA CARTA
TO THE
CONSTITUTION

LIBERTY UNDER
THE LAW

★

By
Caroline P. Stoel
and
Ann B. Clarke

Published jointly by Magna Carta in America and Graphic Arts Center Publishing Company, Portland, Oregon

STAFF

★

TEXT:	Caroline P. Stoel Ann B. Clarke
TEXT EDITOR:	Philippa Brunsman
PICTURE EDITING, CAPTIONS:	Paul St. John Parker
PHOTOGRAPHY:	Gail J. Parker
DESIGN:	Marra and Associates Graphic Design
TYPESETTING:	Paul O. Giesey/Adcrafters
PRINTING:	Graphic Arts Center
PRODUCTION:	Douglas A. Pfeiffer Graphic Arts Center Publishing Company
EDITOR IN CHIEF:	Paul St. John Parker
CONSULTANTS:	A. E. Dick Howard White Burkett Miller Professor of Law and Public Affairs, University of Virginia Stanley N. Katz Bicentennial Professor of the History of American Law and Liberty, Princeton University Paul L. Murphy Professor of American History and American Studies, University of Minnesota

★

Overleaf. Display cabinet for the Lincoln Magna Carta, by Sam Bush, Portland, Oregon.

ILLUSTRATIONS

★

PAGE 1 Gail J. Parker (GJP). **4** Paul St. John Parker. **5, 6** GJP. **7** Woodmansterne, England. **8** GJP. **13** Foundation charter of New Minster, Winchester, dated 966, Cotton Ms. Vespasian A VIII fo. 2V, British Library. **14, 15** Bayeux Tapestry, Scenes No. 25 and 57, with special permission of the town of Bayeux. **16** The Chronicle of John of Worcester, by permission of the President and Fellows of Corpus Christi College, Oxford. **19** Cotton Ms. Claudius 1D 70, fo. 116, British Library. **20** GJP. **21** Marianne Fellner. **22** by John Hamilton Mortimer, from the Art Collection of the Folger Shakespeare Library. **23, 24, 25** GJP. **26** Woodmansterne, England. **28** by Frederigo Zuccaro, Colonial Williamsburg Foundation. **29** by Marcus Geeraerts, by permission of Viscount Coke and the Trustees of the Holkham Estate. **30** by Van Dyck, The National Gallery, London. **32** by Robert Walker, courtesy of the National Portrait Gallery, London. **33** courtesy of the National Portrait Gallery, London. **35** eng. Simon van de Passe, Colonial Williamsburg Foundation. **36** Woodmansterne, England. **37** by Edward Percy Moran, Courtesy of the Pilgrim Society, Plymouth, Mass. **38** by John D. Woolf, Copyright Magna Carta in America. **39** GJP. **40** The Quaker Collection, Haverford College Library, Haverford, Pa. **41** by Edward Hicks, Abby Aldrich Rockefeller Folk Art Center, Williamsburg, Va. **43** by Paul Revere, Yale University Art Gallery, the John Hill Morgan Collection. **44** by John Trumbull, Copyright Yale University Art Gallery. **45 top,** courtesy of the John Carter Brown Library at Brown University. **45 bottom,** by Charles Willson Peale, Colonial Williamsburg Foundation. **46** by James Gillray, New York Public Library, Art, Prints and Photographs, Samuel J. Tilden bequest. **47** by Alonzo Chappel, Collection of the Heckscher Museum, Huntington, New York. **49** by Junius Brutus Stearns, Virginia Museum of Fine Arts, Gift of Colonel and Mrs. Edgar W. Garbisch. **50 top,** by Joseph Wright, The Corcoran Gallery of Art. **50 bottom,** National Archives. **51** by Louis M. D. Guillaume, Virginia Historical Society. **52** University of Minnesota. **53** by Thomas Sully, Virginia Historical Society. **55** GJP. **56** Nick Cerulli, SOL/EIF. **58-61** © Heraldic Heritage, Ltd. **64** GJP.

INTERNATIONAL STANDARD BOOK NUMBER 0-932575-23-4
LIBRARY OF CONGRESS CATALOG CARD NUMBER 86-081501
COPYRIGHT 1986 by Magna Carta in America
PUBLISHED JOINTLY by Magna Carta in America and
Graphic Arts Center Publishing Company
Portland, Oregon

★

CONTENTS

ACKNOWLEDGMENTS

★

Many people helped to produce this book. Among them, we wish to thank especially the Reverend Dedra Bell, James Clarke, Bruce Hamilton, Elizabeth Nurser, Canon John Nurser, Josee Overlie, and Thomas Stoel.

The book is part of a larger endeavor, which has required the belief and support of numerous people in England and the United States. "Magna Carta in America," the initiating sponsor of both the exhibition and this book, owes a great debt of gratitude to the following: the Very Reverend Oliver Fiennes, and Melvin "Pete" Mark, Jr.; also Terrence Pancoast, Senator Mark O. Hatfield, Dick Lewis, Gregory Stiverson, and Tom Mason.

The resulting exhibition, "Roads to Liberty: Magna Carta to the Constitution," is on tour in the United States from March to September 1987. Magna Carta will be seen by hundreds of thousands of Americans. It is accompanied by a superb display of original objects, assembled from collections throughout England and the United States, chronicling the evolution of liberty under the law from Magna Carta to the Constitution.

We hope that both this book and the exhibition will serve as an inspiration during the Bicentennial of the U.S. Constitution — an inspiration to extend and protect "the Blessings of Liberty to ourselves and our posterity."

We have received generous support from a variety of sources, in particular the Oregon Lottery Fund; Fred Meyer, Inc.; Trans World Airlines; Stoel, Rives, Boley, Fraser and Wyse; and Touche Ross and Co.

If success is the fruit of belief, hard work and support, this enterprise owes most to my colleague and wife, Gail, and to Brick, Charlotte and Elizabeth.

To all of these people and organizations, and the many not mentioned here, "Magna Carta in America" is most grateful.

P. St. J. P.

PREFACE

The Great Charter, or, to use the traditional Latin, Magna Carta, was negotiated at Runnymede on June 15th, 1215, when King John met with his bishops and barons. By the end of the month one of the several copies then made was at Lincoln.

If you visit Lincoln today, you may well wonder why anyone would have wanted to send Magna Carta to the city. It is a traditional county town, isolated from the mainstream of English life. It doesn't give the sense of being a place of any great importance in the world, apart from the astonishing domination of its vast and ancient cathedral, which is arguably the most beautiful of all Gothic buildings. But the city does have twenty-one centuries of history; it was a major Roman town, and in the year 1215 things were very different. It was the third-largest city of the

★

Opposite. Evening sunlight throws the colors of the stained glass windows onto an arch in Lincoln Cathedral.

★

A dog ambles across Castle Square. In the background is the castle, begun by order of William the Conqueror in 1086.

realm, the center of the wool industry, and thus enormously wealthy. The best quality regular cloth, the sort Robin Hood wore, was known as Lincoln Green. Lincoln was a famous place. It would still have been dominated by the great cathedral, standing high on its hill and visible for thirty miles and more, the center of a huge diocese stretching from the estuary of the Humber sixty miles north of the city to the mouth of the Thames a hundred and fifty miles south.

At the time of Magna Carta, the only way to let people know of the confrontation between the king and the barons, and of its successful conclusion, was by sending a copy of the Charter to the major centers of population. The Lincoln Magna Carta, therefore, arrived before the end of June. It came to a cathedral in a state of chaos, both from rebuilding and from the effects of the papal interdict of King John, which had disrupted and weakened the whole life and organization of the church.

★

The Cathedral Church of St. Mary the Virgin, Lincoln.

★

Stonemasons work to maintain and repair the cathedral, using materials and techniques similar to those used in the 13th century.

★

Opposite. The nave, built between 1200 and 1250.

After its arrival, we don't know what happened to Magna Carta for some six hundred years. But we must beware of any argument from silence; the cathedral probably possessed revised versions to which it referred, and the out-of-date copy would have had no particular contemporary significance. One can imagine some priest-vicar neatly filing it away.

We hear nothing of it again until 1800, when the charter clerk of the cathedral reported that he held Magna Carta in "The Common Chamber" (now the common room for the cathedral staff). Then there is no further reference until 1846, when the chapter clerk, Robert Swann, moved to Exchequergate opposite the great Norman West Front of the cathedral (beside what is now the Sabbatical Center, to which we welcome scholars from all over the world). In 1848 it was shown to a visiting group and was reported as hanging on the wall in an oak frame "in beautiful preservation."

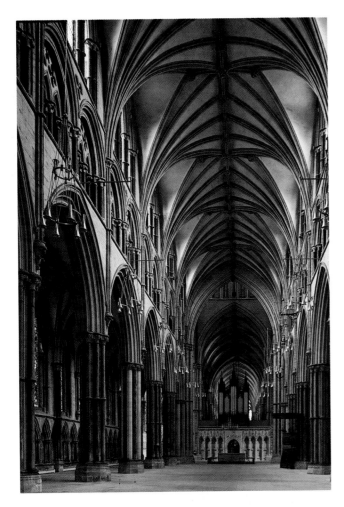

My colleagues and I, who are responsible for running the Cathedral, believe that Magna Carta should be seen by as many people as possible, and recognize that it is especially important in the United States. It is, after all, the forerunner of so many American documents relating to liberty, and it is exceptionally pertinent in the context of the Bicentennial of the American Constitution. We five priests, the Dean and Chapter of Lincoln, want Magna Carta to travel in the United States because we believe such willingness to share our inheritance greatly increases the friendship between our nations; we believe it is not only educational but inspirational. And we depend wholly on people's generosity. We are in charge of a medieval cathedral with more than five hundred windows and over two-and-a-half acres of lead roof; we have to raise half a million dollars a year just to keep it standing. The funds raised by Magna Carta as it travels are used to support a cathedral that was described by Ruskin as "the most precious piece of architecture in the British Isles."

We in Lincoln, England, hope that you will come and discover the beauties of our great cathedral, and the charms of our city. But, whichever side of the Atlantic Ocean we may be on, what really matters is that we should be persuaded by this extraordinary document to take more seriously in our own time the fundamental values of our common democratic heritage.

Oliver Fiennes, Dean of Lincoln

In 1939 the document came to the New York World's Fair, to be displayed in the British Pavilion. It received a triumphal welcome, but was caught by the war and, through the generosity of the American Government, was allowed to join the Constitution in the security of Fort Knox. It returned to the cathedral in 1947. In 1976 it was moved from the Cathedral Treasury to the Medieval Library, where it now is, a reorganization that was entirely due to the Bicentennial of American Independence. It was then, through the sponsorship of the Union Bank, that we were able to display Magna Carta for a month in San Francisco — a journey that demonstrated, in the modern world, the impact and excitement of the Charter as it traveled.

Magna Carta was written in 1215; the U.S. Constitution was not drafted until 1787. Whereas Magna Carta is a curious medley of demands and conditions, granted grudgingly by a king under duress, the Constitution is an elegant system of government, thoughtfully conceived to survive through many different political climates and eras.

Yet despite the span of 572 years, and the widely differing motives of the two groups involved, these great documents share a characteristic of profound significance to the democratic world. Both offer a written protection of individual rights and liberties under the law. Both establish that government shall be conducted according to the law of the land.

To commemorate the Bicentennial of our Constitution, in 1984 a small group of Oregonians incorporated "Magna Carta in America," a non-profit organization. Their purpose was simple: to bring to America the original King John Magna Carta, belonging to Lincoln Cathedral, England.

The resulting exhibition, "Magna Carta: Liberty Under the Law," is on tour in the United States from July 1986 to January 1988. Magna Carta will be seen by hundreds of thousands of Americans. It is accompanied by a superb display of original objects, asembled from collections throughout England and the United States, chronicling the evolution of liberty under the law from Magna Carta to the Constitution.

This book is intended both for those who see the exhibition and for those who do not; it tells in words and pictures the story told by the exhibition in paintings, artifacts and priceless documents.

"Magna Carta in America" wishes above all to thank the Dean and Chapter of Lincoln Cathedral, England, for their extraordinary generosity, goodwill and vision in lending Magna Carta to the American people. We also thank the innumerable people and organizations in Oregon, and throughout the United States, who have made this program possible.

We hope that "Magna Carta: Liberty Under the Law" will serve as an inspiration during the Bicentennial of the U.S. Constitution — an inspiration to protect and extend "the Blessings of Liberty to ourselves and our posterity."

Paul St. John Parker
Executive Director
Magna Carta in America
Portland, Oregon

★
_____
Steep Hill, aptly named, is the most picturesque route between uphill and downhill Lincoln.

INTRODUCTION

In 1987 the United States celebrates the bicentennial of its Constitution. The last two hundred years have witnessed a steady confirmation and expansion of those values and principles expressed in the Constitution, the Bill of Rights and the subsequent amendments.

The relationship between state and citizen contained in the Constitution derives from a tradition of liberty that can clearly be traced to Magna Carta of 1215. "The Charter of Liberty because it maketh freemen," the great English jurist Sir Edward Coke was to say of that document in 1621. Some one hundred and fifty years later, as the American colonists labored to ratify a federal constitution, they struggled to preserve and extend a legacy of rights, liberties and constraints set down in the Great Charter.

The American Constitution embodied the best of the old world in the beliefs of a new country. Now the oldest written national constitution in existence, it can claim its descent from the document drawn up at Runnymede by the English barons on the one hand and King John on the other.

The ensuing pages show briefly how the tradition of liberty inherent in Magna Carta has grown in widely different times and places: in England in the thirteenth and seventeenth centuries, and in America in the seventeenth and eighteenth. Several themes illustrate this development: the rule of law, the concept of due process of law, the principle of freedom of religion, and the idea that there can be no taxation without representation.

THE RULE OF LAW

A document hurriedly drawn up to settle a dispute between king and subjects, Magna Carta embodied the principle that both sovereign and people are beneath the law and subject to it. When, in the seventeenth century, the Stuart kings held once again that their word was law, the Great Charter, written into the statutes of the realm in 1297, forced them to acknowledge the law's supremacy. The Petition of Right, sometimes called a second Magna Carta, lent weight to the law's authority under Charles I at the expense of the royal prerogative. In 1689, as part of the Revolution Settlement, the English Bill of Rights drew on the principles of Magna Carta, settling for all time the superiority of Parliament and the law over the rights of sovereigns.

In America, colonists demanding their rights as Englishmen cited Magna Carta as a source of their freedoms, especially freedom from abuses of imperial authority. The concept of the rule of law has reached its fullest extension in the United States, where the courts not only have the power to circumscribe the authority of the executive, but also to determine the validity of acts of legislative bodies.

Closely connected with the rule of law is "due process of law." Perhaps the best-known clause of Magna Carta is Chapter 39, which provides that "No freeman shall be taken, imprisoned, disseised, outlawed, banished, or in any way destroyed ... except by the lawful judgment of his peers or by the law of the land." This language, in one form or another, has been repeated in the Petition of Right, the English Bill of Rights, the American Bill of Rights, and the Fourteenth Amendment to the U.S. Constitution, as well as in many colonial declarations and state constitutions.

The interpretation of the clause has changed over the centuries. In the thirteenth century "judgment by peers" did not mean "trial by jury," for the jury system as we know it did not exist. That meaning evolved during the fourteenth century, when "due process of law" and "law of the land" became interchangeable.

In America, where it was first relied on by colonists as a guarantee of trial by jury and of other lawful procedure, Chapter 39 later became the model for the due process clauses in the Constitution. The due process requirement, applicable to both federal and state governments, is recognized as one of the most significant mandates in American constitutional law. It has been interpreted not only to require lawful procedure in the courts and by the police, but also to give the courts the power to review legislation and to declare an act unconstitutional as depriving a citizen of life, liberty, or property.

FREEDOM OF RELIGION

During the medieval period, most people accepted the doctrines of the Roman Catholic Church much as they accepted the idea of royalty and kingship. The church was the mediator between man and God, and without the church's bless-

> No free man shall be taken, imprisoned, disseised, outlawed, banished, or in any way destroyed, nor will we proceed against or prosecute him, except by the lawful judgment of his equals or by the law of the land.

Chapter 39, Magna Carta, 1215

ing there was no certainty of salvation. Magna Carta's two clauses relating to freedom of the church, Chapters 1 and 63, were not grants of individual religious liberties, but safeguards of the integrity of the church as an institution.

Personal religious liberty became an issue after England's break with the Roman Church under Henry VIII in 1534, particularly with the rise of Protestantism. The persecution of religious nonconformists in seventeenth-century England became a chief reason for the settlement of the American colonies. Once established, however, some of those sects became as intolerant of other faiths as their persecutors had been, and in the debates on the American Bill of Rights it was urged that a guarantee of religious freedom be included. The First Amendment to the United States Constitution provides that "Congress shall make no law respecting an establishment of religion, or prohibiting the free exercise thereof." Under the due process provision of the Fourteenth Amendment, this has been held equally applicable to the states since the 1930s.

Throughout history people have defied the imposition of taxes they believe are unjustly imposed; to remedy the crushing demands of King John, Chapter 12 of Magna Carta provides that scutages and aids (taxes) shall be imposed only with the common counsel of the kingdom, and Chapter 14 sets out the procedure for summoning such a counsel. Although these terms are precise and narrow, they were interpreted as standing for the principle that there shall be no taxation without representation, and were incorporated into the Petition of Right as a prohibition against requests for "any gift, loan, benevolence, tax, or such-like charge, without common consent by act of parliament." Later, when taxation of the American colonies by Parliament became a rallying point for independence, the colonists relied on Magna Carta and the Petition of Right to support their position.

Thus it was that the practical agreement drawn up in 1215, a set of specific remedies for specific problems, came over the years to stand for a series of principles that aided our forefathers in founding a nation based on liberty and equality.

No person shall be held to answer for a capital, or otherwise infamous crime unless on a presentment or indictment by a Grand Jury . . . nor shall any person . . . be deprived of life, liberty, or property without due process of law.

Fifth Amendment, the Constitution, 1791

The contract agreed to at Runnymede in 1215 was the culmination of grievances long held by the English barons against their king. In the demands they made of King John, they had recourse to concepts of the rights and duties of freemen derived from ancient law, as well as to more recent precedent, particularly a charter drawn up by Henry I in 1100.

THE ANGLO-SAXONS

By the eleventh century, in late Anglo-Saxon times, England had been united into one kingdom ruled by a king and his council. The concept of kingship was one of limited powers. The king was bound by his coronation oath to defend the church, to punish crime and violence, and to rule with clemency and mercy. He was also bound by customary rules of law, and to some extent his power was restricted by his council. He was viewed as a religious and moral leader, a protector of the people in war and in peace. Later, Anglo-Saxon kingship was idealized to stand for the principle that the king rules not according to his will alone, but under God and the law.

The English king was not regarded as a source of law, although occasionally he might declare the law with the consent of his council or issue written laws called "dooms." The great body of Anglo-Saxon law was the unwritten folk law, handed down from one generation to the next, giving the common people certain rights and setting out procedures for determining fault or guilt and methods of punishing wrongdoers. While change was not impossible, arbitrary alteration of the rules bordered on impiety. The early courts were assemblies of the folk; cases were decided by ordeals of fire and water, and by "compurgation," in which the kin of the accused testified to his honesty and reliability. In each community it was the folk who were responsible for seeing that the judgments of the court were enforced.

In addition to duties in the courts, the freeman was responsible for military service, repairing strongholds, and building and repairing bridges — the *trinoda necessitas*. Certain rights accompanied his status as a freeman. His life was valued in monetary terms: if he were killed, his relatives received a fixed sum of money (a *wergild*); if he were injured, he was entitled to a payment commensurate with his injury (a *bot*). This principle of Anglo-Saxon law, that the common freeman is endowed with rights and duties of what we would today call citizenship, has been a basic concept in the development of Anglo-American constitutional principles.

A new era in government began after the conquest of England in 1066 by William, duke of Normandy. A ruthless conqueror and an able administrator, William preserved those Anglo-Saxon institutions that would strengthen his regime, grafting onto them the practices of Norman feudalism and monarchy.

England soon became the most feudal of the European states. As conqueror, William had dominion over all the English lands, and these he parceled out to the great barons who had supported him during the invasion, to the church, and to others in his favor. In return he received promises of loyalty, counsel, and services of

★

The sacred nature of kingship was especially important to the Anglo-Saxon King Edgar (959-975). The first king of all England to enjoy a largely tranquil reign, he revived the monasteries, advanced the bishops and abbots in his councils, and endowed the church with great wealth. This illumination from the Winchester New Minster foundation charter (966) shows Edgar reaching up to God, ruler of kings and princes.

13

varying kinds and significance, whether personal, religious, or purely honorary. The most important were military. Thus, a tenant-in-chief might agree to supply forty knights for the king's army. Since maintaining knights was costly, he might grant some of his lands to other men who would supply goods and services in exchange for protection. These men in turn would follow the same procedure, so that each man was both lord and tenant, both protector and protected, until the bottom rung of the feudal ladder was reached. Here were the peasants, who performed agricultural services in return for a small parcel of land and a dwelling.

The king and the lords had the right to certain feudal *incidents*, or forms of taxation. These included a son's payment of money (*relief*) to inherit his dead father's land; management (*wardship*) of a minor's estate until the heir came of age; arrangement of marriages for heiresses and widows; imposition of levies on the transfer of lands; forfeiture of lands when services were not rendered; and *escheat*, or appropriation of lands when a tenant died without heirs or was executed for a felony. Monetary levies (*aids*) could be imposed by the tenants-in-chief for special purposes; fines (*amercements*) were common to all for offenses or irregularities.

Land tenure was not only the basis of social distinctions and of taxation, but also of obligations and privileges. A tenant's duty to attend his lord's court and to take part in its judgments eventually became a right to participate in the judicial process. A son's payment of a relief became a right to inherit his father's land if the monetary fee were paid. A peasant's right to be a freeman or a serf depended on his right to cultivate part of the land for himself and on the nature of the services required of him. Little by little, duties and privileges connected with landholding became inviolable rights.

★

The last two kings of Anglo-Saxon England, Edward the Confessor and Harold, face one another upon Earl Harold's return from France. This dramatic scene from the Bayeux Tapestry depicts the moment when the old king learns of Harold's oath to Duke William of Normandy, promising him the English crown.

★

Hic Harold Rex Interfectus est. *"Here, King Harold is killed," reads the Latin inscription over this scene from the Bayeux Tapestry. The Battle of Hastings in 1066 changed the course of English history forever. Despite the brave resistance of Harold and his forces, the Normans' combination of cavalry and archery was too much for the exhausted Anglo-Saxons. Below the main scene, scavengers strip the armor from the stricken soldiers' bodies.*

Feudal kings in Europe were often weak, sharing power with the great magnates on whom they depended. William the Conqueror, however, established a government strong enough to withstand the threat posed by the nobles. He was able to do so in part because the nobles themselves were weakened by the scattered nature of their lands, because the king maintained some direct ties with the people, and because he was never wholly dependent on the barons for revenues. William raised money independently of the barons by retaining the Danegeld, a direct tax on land; partly to this end he commissioned the great Domesday Survey of 1086. He kept for the use of the Crown large amounts of land—the *royal demesne*—which produced substantial hereditary revenues; enormous forest preserves were also set aside for the sole use and pleasure of kings. Harsh laws protected the forests against hunting by others and became a major source of complaint by nobles and commoners alike.

Eager to reform the English church, and working with Lanfranc, the archbishop of Canterbury, William instituted policies that would more closely accord with church practice on the continent. However, he refused to pay homage to the pope or to permit his bishops to do so, and continued to nominate prelates and to reward secular services with church benefits. One of the changes he made was to establish separate church courts with jurisdiction primarily over spiritual and moral matters. Previously, both religious and secular cases had been heard in the shire courts, at which the bishop, the earl, and the shire reeve, or sheriff, had presided. By separating ecclesiastical matters from the lay courts, William prepared the way for a rival authority with its own system of laws, thus opening the door to future conflict.

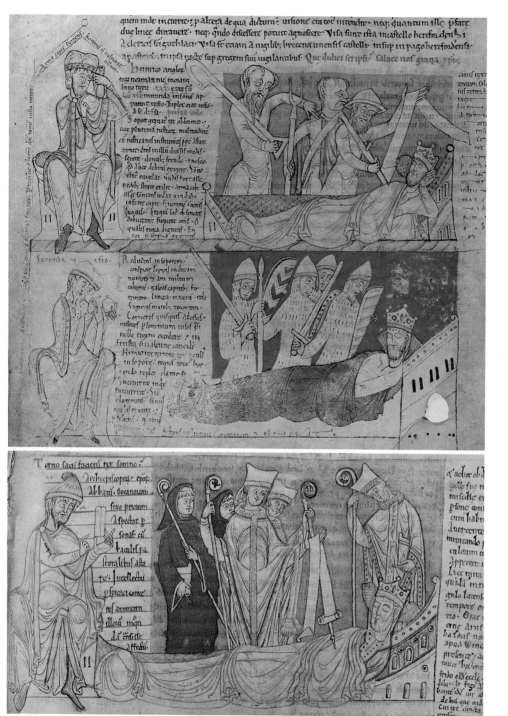

THE CHARTER OF LIBERTIES

During his brief rule William's son, William Rufus, enraged his subjects by enriching his coffers at their expense. His younger brother, Henry, who acceded to the throne in 1100, sought to assuage the barons' anger and to secure his claim to the throne more firmly. He therefore issued a coronation charter, known as the Charter of Liberties and regarded by many historians as a model for the Great Charter of King John's reign. In it, Henry promised to observe the feudal code and to correct the abuses of his predecessors against the barons and the church. He commanded the barons, his tenants-in-chief, to behave in like manner to their tenants. Most significantly, he made the Charter applicable to all his subjects: "I henceforth remove all bad customs through which the kingdom of England has been unjustly oppressed."

While the Charter was no more than a proclamation of intentions and promises, binding only insofar as Henry saw fit to observe them, its form — a written royal grant—gave it legality and lasting significance. Its chief importance was its admission by the king that even his powers were limited under the feudal contract.

Because he spent much of his time on the continent, Henry I had to develop a system of government that would function smoothly in his absence. This included the office of justiciar, with the power to govern when he was abroad, and an Exchequer, whose work greatly enhanced the collection of revenues. The broad authority granted to appointed officials diminished that of the barons, who became increasingly restless.

STEPHEN, HENRY II AND RICHARD I

The barons reasserted their independence during the reign of Henry I's nephew and successor, Stephen (1135-1154). Lawlessness and anarchy held sway, proving that even an oppressive king was less to be feared than an incompetent one. Under Henry II, count of Anjou (1154-1189), one of England's most able kings, order was restored and the machinery of government established by Henry I was reinforced.

The powers of the justiciar were enlarged, and a system of central courts and traveling judges who took the king's law to the shire courts laid the basis of English common law. Among Henry's innovations were the establishment of the accusing jury (ancestor of the modern grand jury), and the creation of assizes, juries composed of sworn witnesses to settle disputes about land (forerunner of the civil trial jury).

Carefully regulated as it was, Henry Plantagenet's administration greatly increased royal revenues and further strengthened the monarchy at the barons' expense. Disaffection was again growing. Henry's troubles were compounded by the refusal of his friend the archbishop of Canterbury, Thomas Becket, to support his policies; by Becket's subsequent murder and martyrdom; and by having to relinquish to the church courts the right to try many of the cases that, according to the king, belonged in the lay courts. Toward the end of Henry's reign, the plot by his own family to seize his French lands led to a ruinous struggle by the English Crown to retain its Angevin inheritance. The groundwork for the crisis of 1215 was already being laid.

The extravagant campaigns of the soldier and crusader Richard I (1189-1199) caused much suffering and bitterness, and in 1197 his tenants-in-chief refused to supply the knights he demanded to fight in France. However, because of his personal popularity and his ministers' ability, serious confrontation did not occur. With his brother, John, it was a different story.

Opposition to King John (1199-1216) solidified from 1209 to 1215, as magnates and lesser tenants alike suffered increasingly from taxation, appropriation of their possessions, and arbitrary justice. A cruel, greedy and ambitious man, the king pressed his rights as a feudal monarch to the limit, abusing the incidents of relief, wardship and marriage for political as well as financial ends and imposing heavy taxes on the kingdom to support his battles for his lands in France. The fires of resistance were fanned higher by John's quarrel with Pope Innocent III and his defeat in France by Philip Augustus.

★

John loved to hunt, and the royal forests gave him ample opportunity to indulge his taste for the chase. His arbitrary seizure of additional hunting land and ruthless enforcement of the forest laws were a major source of complaint at Runnymede. Magna Carta abolished "all forests that have been created in our reign" and "all evil customs relating to forests and warrens, foresters, warreners, sheriffs and their servants...."

JOHN AND THE CHURCH

With its wealth and its political privileges, the medieval Roman Catholic Church frequently rivaled secular rulers. Kings could not rule effectively without adequate control of the church, nor could they rule without its blessing and its favors. Its riches made it powerful, its lands held in knights' service provided military resources, and its clergy, as the only literate class, filled essential secular offices.

John's predecessors had sought to control papal authority in England by the appointment of prelates sympathetic to the crown. The death in 1205 of Hubert Walter, archbishop of Canterbury and former justiciar, left vacant the most influential office in the English church. By canon law the monks of the cathedral chapter had the right to fill the position, but the king was determined that a royally appointed official should have the post. Fearing a usurpation of their right, some of the monks secretly elected one of their number and sent him to Rome for official approval. John insisted that his own candidate also be endorsed and presented to the pope. Confronted with the rival candidates, Innocent refused to confirm either and appointed Stephen Langton, a learned English cardinal, as archbishop.

★

Architect of Magna Carta, Archbishop Stephen Langton acted as mediator between king and barons at Runnymede. He was born in the Lincolnshire village of Langton-by-Wragby; the tiny church there not only commemorates the fact in one of its stained-glass windows, but also boasts, by chance, a sturdy bell-tower built in 1215, the very year of Magna Carta.

The pope had chosen the best qualified man. Langton had spent his boyhood not far from the great Cathedral at Lincoln, from whose clergy he probably received some of his early education before studying and teaching in Paris for over twenty years with some of the leading theologians of the day. Notwithstanding these eminent qualifications, John categorically refused to accept Langton. To do so would have set a dangerous precedent, considerably diminishing his authority over the church. In turn, the pope placed England under an interdict: the churches were closed and the people denied the services of the clergy, with the exception of baptism and confession for the dying. In 1209 King John was excommunicated. He retaliated by seizing the lands and wealth of the churches and monasteries within his domain. Clergymen were abused and many fled the country.

In 1213 John capitulated, realizing that his ambition to regain his Norman kingdom through a European coalition could not be attained unless he ended his quarrel with the pope. He agreed to accept Stephen Langton as archbishop of Canterbury, to pay homage to the pope and submit England to him as overlord, and to make reparation to the church for the wealth and lands he had seized. Before absolving John from his sentence of excommunication, the archbishop required that he swear "to restore the good laws of his ancestors and invalidate all bad laws."

PRELUDE TO RUNNYMEDE

The defeat of England's allies at Bouvines in 1214 ended John's dreams of restoring his French empire. The unsuccessful war and the constant requests for money sparked the resentment that had smoldered for years. At a gathering at Bury St. Edmunds in November, the disaffected barons secretly agreed to petition the king to grant the liberties and laws of the Charter of Henry I, swearing that if he refused they would renounce their allegiance to him and go to war. In January 1215 they met him in London.

The king was not prepared to consider their demands seriously, and during Easter week the barons assembled at Stamford with their armed retainers. The chronicler Roger of Wendover lists forty-two nobles as "the chief promoters of this pestilence." The largest group of twenty came from the north; eight of these held lands in Lincolnshire. John sent his emissaries, Archbishop Langton and John Marshall, to find out what reforms were wanted. When he heard the barons' demands he exploded: "Why, among these unjust demands, did the barons not ask for my kingdom as well? Their demands are vain, foolish, and utterly unreasonable."

This was taken as a declaration of war. The barons renounced their fealty to the king and began attacking his castles. On May 17, when they marched on London, the city opened its gates to them, and they were joined by many others who had hitherto stayed out of the conflict. Seeing his situation as desperate, John again sent emissaries to the barons, this time with the message that he was willing to grant the charter of liberties they demanded. On June 15 he met the rebels in a meadow on the Thames, at a place called Runnymede.

RUNNYMEDE

In his *History of the English-Speaking Peoples*, Winston Churchill describes the meeting between John and the barons on June 15, 1215:

> On a Monday morning in June, between Staines and Windsor, the barons and Churchmen began to collect on the great meadow at Runnymede. An uneasy hush fell on them from time to time. Many failed to keep their tryst; and the bold few who had come knew that the King would never forgive this humiliation. He would hunt them down when he could, and the laymen at least were staking their lives in the cause they served. They had arranged a little throne for the King and a tent. The handful of resolute men had drawn up, it seems, a short document on parchment. Their retainers and the groups and squadrons of horsemen in sullen steel kept at some distance and well in the background. For was not armed rebellion against the Crown the supreme feudal crime?
>
> Then events followed rapidly. A small cavalcade appeared from the direction of Windsor. Gradually men made out the faces of the King, the Papal Legate, the Archbishop of Canterbury, and several bishops. They dismounted without ceremony. Someone, probably the Archbishop, stated briefly the terms that were suggested. The King declared at once that he agreed. He said the details should be arranged immediately in his chancery. The original Articles of the Barons on which Magna Carta is based...were sealed in a quiet, short scene, which has become one of the most famous in our history....

Churchill's colorful description may be fanciful, but his outline of events is probably accurate. The documents were most likely the work of the barons themselves with the assistance of clergy sympathetic to their cause; some historians have given Stephen Langton much of the credit for the ideas embodied in the Charter.

★

Seated in royal majesty, the king grants Magna Carta to his rebellious barons. This nineteenth-century engraving gives full rein to the Victorians' image of kingship, endowing John with an apparent ascendancy he surely could not have felt at Runnymede.

★

The central tower of Lincoln Cathedral, home of the Lincoln Magna Carta. Completed in 1311, it originally had a spire of wood and lead, and at 525 feet was the tallest building in the world. In 1548, the spire was blown off by a gale. The tower alone is 271 feet high.

★

"I desire that my body be buried in the church of the Blessed Virgin and St. Wulfstan at Worcester"— King John's wishes were fulfilled more willingly in death than in life. Flanked by bishops, his effigy covers his tomb, before the high altar of Worcester Cathedral.

Although the Charter marked the end of the baronial war against the king, it was not in essence a peace treaty, but, rather, a contract or royal grant, whereby the king made concessions to the people in return for the renewal of homage by his vassals. The settlement became effective upon the exchange of oaths; the written, sealed charter was simply a record of the agreement. However, the document was of immense importance, reminding the king of his promises and informing those who had not been present at Runnymede of the terms of the settlement. That it took the form of a charter was to prove invaluable in later times, as a reference and as a model for constitutional documents.

King John probably could not write, and his seal was affixed to the Charter in the chancery. A number of copies were made and distributed throughout the kingdom — the habitual method of publicizing important decrees of the king. Of these copies, four are still in existence: two in the British Museum, one in Salisbury Cathedral, and one — considered the most perfect of the four — in Lincoln Cathedral.

PROVISIONS OF THE CHARTER

The barons confronting the king at Runnymede wanted a declaration from him on what the law was, and a promise from him to observe it. Magna Carta therefore sets out the king's undertakings in specific terms; there are no broad statements of individual rights or monarchical responsibility.

The Charter has frequently been described as a feudal document, and much in it is concerned with the inner workings of the feudal system, spelling out its rules in an effort to make the king conform to earlier custom, and to bind him against future infringements. Typical provisions — now known as chapters — relate to reliefs, wardships, marriages of heiresses and widows, services due on knights' fees, and escheats. Several clauses have to do with the royal forests, a source of complaint and contention since the time of William the Conqueror.

The feudal aristocracy was not the only beneficiary of the Charter. Both church and freemen benefited. Thus Chapter 1 provides that

...the English church shall be free, and enjoy her rights in their integrity and her liberties untouched.... We have also granted to all free men of our kingdom, for us and our heirs forever, all the liberties underwritten, to have and to hold them and their heirs of us and our heirs.

This language is repeated in Chapter 63, and Chapter 60 makes it clear that all nobles are expected to observe the same "customs and liberties" toward their tenants. Chapter 13 provides that the City of London and "all other cities, boroughs, towns, and ports" shall have their ancient liberties and free customs. This was a boon to townsmen and traders who sought freedom from excessive regulation of trade and commerce.

A number of clauses are worded in general terms and are applicable to all except the villeins, or serfs, who were denied access to the king's courts. The most famous is Chapter 39, which provides that

No freeman shall be taken or imprisoned or disseised or exiled or in any way destroyed, nor will we go upon him nor send upon him, except by the lawful judgment of his peers or by the law of the land.

Thus, in its medieval context, a man could not be tried by his inferiors, but only by his peers, and judgment should precede execution of his sentence. Over the years the loose wording of the clause has made possible a much broader interpretation, a guarantee of trial by jury and of due process of law.

★

"Being overtaken by a grievous sickness...." Thus begins King John's will, dictated during a howling October storm, as he lay dying at Newark Castle.

★

The coat of arms of King John, at Worcester Cathedral.

Other clauses of Magna Carta are still pertinent because their content was adaptable to changing times. Chapter 12, which states, "No scutage nor aid shall be imposed on our kingdom, unless by common counsel of our kingdom ...," and Chapter 14, which sets out the procedure for summoning a common counsel, have come to stand for the principle that there can be no taxation without representation.

Chapter 20 provides that a freeman shall be amerced, or fined, in accordance with the gravity of his offense, that a merchant or a villein shall not be deprived of his livelihood by heavy fines, and that fines shall be imposed only "by the oath of honest men of the neighborhood," language regarded as meaning that the punishment must fit the crime.

The statement in Chapter 40, "To no one will We sell, to none will We deny or delay, right or justice," declares that justice should be available to all on an impartial basis, although it does not mean that civil suits could be brought without cost. In the thirteenth century a litigant instituted his suit in the king's court with the purchase of a writ; Chapter 40 was aimed at excessive charges that might prohibit the suit's being brought at all.

An enforcement clause was inserted in the Charter to ensure that the king observed its provisions. Chapter 61 states that, if John breaks his promises, twenty-five elected barons are charged with enforcing his compliance. Specific procedures for the barons are set out, including the power to seize the king's lands and possessions. In Chapter 61, later generations have found principles of majority rule and of representation, essential components of democratic government.

King John failed to comply with the Charter's provisions, although whether he had ever intended to do so is a matter of dispute. He appealed to the pope to absolve him of his oath of observation; the pope responded by annulling the Charter as a "shameful and iniquitous agreement, granted under duress." In the meantime civil war had already begun. Only John's death in 1216 brought the conflict to a halt.

The ministers acting on behalf of John's young son, Henry III, accepted the reforms of Magna Carta willingly and sincerely and granted three reissues of the Charter during Henry's minority. Henry himself confirmed the Charter a number of times. All the revisions differed from the original in several important aspects. The clauses forbidding levies of scutage and aids "without the common counsel of our kingdom" were dropped, as were those relating to the royal forests. None of the reissues contained the controversial enforcement provision, and all received papal approval.

The final revision of 1225 emphasized the Charter's contractual nature. The barons' promise to pay the king a substantial tax and the king's declaration that the grant of liberties was made by his own free will were incorporated in the document. The Charter also contained a clause stating that the king would not attempt to infringe on or weaken it, "and if any thing shall be procured by any person contrary to these premises, it shall be held of no validity or effect," a phrase that suggests the idea of the Charter as fundamental law, not to be contravened by other laws.

Despite Henry's repeated confirmation of Magna Carta, his reign was marked by continued friction between king and barons, and by enormous anti-papal feeling as the king pursued the pope's ends. In 1264 civil war broke out. In the absence of an enforcement clause in the Charter, there was no peaceful alternative. The brief victor of the war — until his defeat the following year by the king's son Edward—was Simon de Montfort, earl of Leicester, to whose support many knights, members of the gentry and clerics had rallied.

After Edward's accession in 1272, the law became more closely defined as the king passed statutes that marked a new phase in England's statute law. Royal jurisdiction increased as private courts came to an end. Recognizing that a great source of conflict between king and subject was taxation, Edward broadened the taxation base, in turn broadening the basis of Parliament—a trend that continued de Montfort's policy of drawing on the growing middle classes for support. The king confirmed Magna Carta in 1297, declaring that its clauses should be incorporated in the common law. In 1301 he reconfirmed it, together with the Charter of the Forest, agreeing to annul statutes contrary to both documents. Thus, "The ultimate triumph of the principles underlying Magna Carta was assured not through any executive committee of rebellious barons, but through the constitutional machinery devised by Edward Plantagenet."*

★

In 1301, Edward I (1272-1307) held a Parliament in the Chapter House of Lincoln Cathedral. Ten years earlier, his Queen, Eleanor, had died nearby; her viscera—or intestines—are buried within the cathedral. Both king and queen are shown here, still watching over the people of Lincoln from high on the cathedral's outer walls.

THE CREATION OF THE MYTH

At Runnymede, the barons sought remedies for the wrongs and abuses of an unreasonable king. They did not seek to abolish the monarchy or change the basic structure of government. They did not regard the Charter as a declaration of new freedoms, but as a means of compelling the king to fulfill his obligations. Nonetheless, reissue and confirmation of Magna Carta encouraged the belief that it had significance far greater than its specific language. The myth thus begun was to grow increasingly as the years went by. As G. M. Trevelyan puts it,

It was the abstract and general character of the event at Runnymede that made it a great influence in history....A process had begun which was to end in putting the power of the Crown into the hands of the community at large. It is for this reason that a document so technical as the Charter, so deficient in the generalizations with which the Declaration of Independence abounds, so totally ignorant of the "rights of man", has had so profound and lasting an influence on the imagination of succeeding ages.

*McKechnie

THE CHARTER REVIVED: SEVENTEENTH-CENTURY ENGLAND

The story of Magna Carta and fundamental liberties is not one of continuous development. After its initial impact, the Charter lapsed into relative obscurity until the seventeenth century. However, without Parliament's occasional reaffirmations during the fourteenth and fifteenth centuries, it might not have survived at all. Its sporadic appearance in such Parliamentary records as the Year Books and Statute Books shows that it was occasionally invoked to protect individuals in cases of private law. These actions kept Magna Carta alive as a statute and created a legal resource for seventeenth-century judges and lawyers as they sought to settle disputes between Parliament and the Stuart kings.

In the early seventeenth century, Englishmen were again confronted by kings whose policies infringed on what had become the accepted rights of all men. Most threatening was abuse of the royal prerogative — arbitrary authority attached to the Crown. English monarchs had traditionally counted on the fruits of justice and feudal dues as sources of revenue, but the Stuart kings James I and Charles I pressed their subjects further by exacting loans and imprisoning those who refused to pay. In the opinion of Parliament, these acts infringed on basic liberties. Magna Carta became an important element in the constitutional struggle between king and Parliament over money and the prerogative, culminating in civil war and execution of Charles I in 1649.

JAMES I (1603-1625)

Before he came to the throne of England in 1603, James I had been king of Scotland for thirty-six years. There, asserting his divine right to rule, which placed the king above the church and the law, he had learned to manage the nobility and tame the church. During his first years as king of England, he was a popular ruler. He avoided the stigma of claiming to rule absolutely by assuming only the right to override and set aside laws; he did not claim to make them. Consequently, early cases affecting the prerogative were decided in his favor. However, he underestimated the English Parliament, which regarded itself as a representative body with rights and privileges protected by the common law — views that conflicted with Stuart claims to rule by divine right. Eventually James's policies, actions and attitudes so offended his English subjects that he forced the crystallization of adverse opinion that Elizabeth I had avoided.

James I called his first Parliament in 1603; it was not dissolved until 1611. From the outset, there was controversy over application of the royal prerogative. *Bate's Case* (1610) concerned the legality of new customs duties imposed by the Crown without the consent of Parliament, and led to heated dispute. When Thomas Bate refused to pay a duty on currants, the Crown sued him. His defense argued that the tax imposed on him was void, since Magna Carta Chapter 41 assured free trade to foreign merchants traveling in and out of England during peacetime. The judgment went for the Crown, but the case is significant in being the first time a chapter of Magna Carta was used as a major precedent.

★

After the glorious reign of Elizabeth, the throne of England passed to James I (1603-25). His strident assertion of the divine right of kings, coupled with a weak personality and an outrageous personal style, steadily eroded the credibility of the monarchy.

★

Sir Edward Coke did more than anyone to revive Magna Carta and elevate it to a pinnacle of constitutional importance in seventeenth-century England: "If my sovereign will not allow me my inheritance, I must fly to Magna Charta and entreat explanation of his Majesty." James I, far from explaining, promptly had "Captain Coke" locked away in the Tower of London for seven months.

Magna Carta also appears in Parliamentary debates over purveyance, orders for the involuntary provision of goods or services to the Crown. James believed this to lie within the royal prerogative, but learned counsel, including Sir Francis Bacon, referred to the Charter in arguing against the practice. In discussions concerning the proposed union of England and Scotland, Magna Carta was cited as a broad guarantee of liberties that made a man "not limited, not to be restrained." The Charter was thus being interpreted as including rights that extended to all subjects, a concept far from the minds of the barons calling their king to order in 1215.

28

The reign of James I is punctuated with similar references to Magna Carta as his subjects retaliated against royal incursions on their rights. Much of the credit for the extended implications of the Charter in the seventeenth century belongs to Sir Edward Coke.

SIR EDWARD COKE

Without Coke, there might have been no Petition of Right, and no Bill of Rights in England or America. For it was Coke who gave new and continued life to Magna Carta in his judicial decisions, declarations in Parliament and written commentaries on English law.

Coke became attorney general in 1594 and retained this Elizabethan appointment until 1606, when James made him chief justice of Common Pleas and, later, chief justice of King's Bench, a post he kept until his dismissal in 1616. Before beginning a new career as a member of the House of Commons in 1620, he devoted himself to writing, and spent his final years revising his *Reports* and *Institutes*, which became the basis of legal education in England and America through the eighteenth century.

As a student, Coke began to trace the medieval origins of common law, collecting ancient precedents that later filled the volumes of his *Institutes* and *Reports*, known formally as *The Institutes of the Laws of England and the Reports of Sir Edward Coke Kt. in English in Thirteen Parts Compleat.* Thus preserving the law's continuity, he reinterpreted it in his own way, defending it against all encroachments, arming Parliamentarians with examples in debate. In his opinion in *Dr. Bonham's Case* (1610), he declared, "...when an act of Parliament is against common right and reason, or repugnant, or impossible to be performed, the common law will control it, and adjudge such an act to be void." The decision was soon discredited in England, but was later to fire the imagination of Englishmen in America, who quoted Coke in their arguments against the Stamp Act of 1765.

As a member of the House of Commons, Coke became a champion of the common law. In the Parliament of 1621, he and his colleagues resumed consideration of the royal prerogative, basing broad claims on Magna Carta and thereby adding to its myth. They also addressed such problems as impositions (involuntary tariffs) and Parliament's right to free debate.

James's intransigence over these issues led to the first formal statement of complaint against the Crown in his reign. The Great Protestation of 18 December 1621 incorporated the language and spirit of Magna Carta:

> *That the liberties, franchises, privileges, and jurisdictions of Parliament are the ancient and undoubted birthright of the subjects of England.*

In the final tense moments before the Great Protestation was adopted, Coke spoke on the issue of freedom of

★

England has been ruled by sovereigns for over a thousand years. Only once, from 1649 to 1660, was the monarchy abandoned in favor of a Commonwealth, when Charles I lost his throne—and his head—after the Civil War. During the war, Charles desperately sought help from the king of France. Here, Van Dyck portrays him calmly controlling his charger. Later events proved this symbol of regal power to be woefully inaccurate.

speech, the very essence of Parliament's existence:

> *The privileges of this House is the nurse and life of all our laws, the subject's best inheritance. If my sovereign will not allow me my inheritance, I must fly to Magna Charta and entreat explanation of his Majesty. Magna Charta is called "Charta libertatis quia liberos facit."... The Charter of Liberty because it maketh freemen. When the King says he cannot allow our liberties of right, this strikes at the root. We serve here thousands and ten thousands.*

James dissolved Parliament and sent Coke to the Tower, charged with treason, where he remained for seven months.

In 1624, in order to fund a war with Spain, James called a Parliament that brought the return of Coke and other members who had been active in 1621. After granting the king his subsidies, the Commons turned its attention to the prerogative. Again Magna Carta was a source of argument for Parliamentarians in their successful attempt to end royal monopolies. During the 1620s, the need to protect individual liberties from encroachment by the Crown honed the skills of members of Parliament, particularly Coke, who manipulated old principles into modern doctrine that brought continuity and change to Magna Carta and the English constitution.

CHARLES I (1625-1649)

Like his father, James, Charles I believed devoutly in his divine right to rule and his duty to preserve the royal prerogative. Yet he had neither the character to rule absolutely nor the inclination to compromise, and relations between Crown and Parliament deteriorated rapidly. When the House of Commons responded coolly to his requests for money, he warned its members: "Remember that Parliaments are altogether in my power for their calling, sitting, and dissolution; therefore as I find the fruits of them good or evil, they are to continue or not to be." In 1629, after four years of intermittent confrontations, he dissolved Parliament and ruled alone until 1640, when financial exigency moved him to call the Short Parliament (13 April to 5 May 1640), and then the Long Parliament, which sat throughout the campaigns of the Civil War and found Charles guilty of treason in January 1649.

THE PETITION OF RIGHT

The Parliament of 1628, called because Charles was desperate for funds, included John Selden, John Pym, John Hampden, Sir John Eliot, Oliver Cromwell, and Sir Edward Coke. The gathering constituted what a contemporary newspaper described as "the most famous, magnanimous assembly ever those walls contained." Charles recognized the challenge. In an effort to woo Parliamentary support, he freed men imprisoned for failure to pay forced loans and granted favors to influential members.

His tactics were unsuccessful. The opposition returned to the issue of personal liberties and problems that had led to the Great Protestation: royal absolutism, powers of the prerogative courts and the Crown's control over the judiciary and Parliament. Leaders of the House of Commons met at the home of Sir Robert Cotton (whose library held the two copies of Magna Carta now in the British Museum) to devise a strategy for presenting their protests to the king. They decided on a Petition of Right, which would require a personal response from the king.

Magna Carta became the central feature of their argument in the ensuing Parliamentary debates. Coke, Eliot and Selden led the House of Commons, supported in the House of Lords by William Fiennes, Lord Saye and Sele. Once again they addressed the principle of individual liberty as it centered on forced loans and arbitrary imprisonment. Points from Magna Carta were incorporated in the Petition. In return for a grant of subsidy, Charles assented to the following: no man could be compelled to pay a forced tax without consent of Parliament; no man would be imprisoned without cause shown — that is, without an arraignment; troops would not be billeted on private citizens; martial law would not be declared in peacetime, unless Parliament so decreed.

Like Magna Carta, the Petition of Right was a statement of liberties to be protected from the centralization of royal power. Although in 1628 Parliament had no means of enforcement (a petition is, after all, merely a request), the limitations it placed on the Crown became legally binding in the settlements of the Glorious Revolution in 1688-89.

Magna Carta thus began a new chapter in its history, as a seventeenth-century document useful in England and useful, too, in the new colonies in America. Coke's pronouncements upon the law, whether or not they were accurate, had become the received authority. Harking back to the Charter, Coke stated not only that "lex terrae is the common law of the land," but that the law of the land meant "due process of law."

Magna Carta's stature also grew through accident and error. It became the attributed source of the Writ of Habeas Corpus, the requirement to show cause for imprisonment. In 1625, Writ and Charter were linked in an argument against the imprisonment of Sir John Eliot:

The rule of law is now because the king did it therefore well done but we must inquire into the cause — Magna Charta. No man committed but "per legale Iudicium" and this the ground for the writt of Habeas Corpus: 34 Eliz. a Resolution of all the Iudges of England that the Queen nor Counsell can committ above 24 howres but the cause must be rendred.

That habeas corpus did not in fact originate in Magna Carta did not diminish the ardor with which seventeenth-century lawyers underscored the association of the two.

THE REVOLUTION SETTLEMENT

Between 1642 and 1688, England experienced civil war, the Protectorate of Oliver Cromwell, the restoration of the Stuarts under Charles II, and finally the Glorious Revolution, which brought William and Mary to the throne as constitutional monarchs. Magna Carta reenters the story in the legislation that accomplished the Revolution Settlement.

Political theorists have analyzed the Revolution in terms of constitutional principles and of concepts of natural law and social contract. Magna Carta was a feudal contract, based on mutual obligations within the hierarchy from king down through the tenantry. Sir Edwin Sandys first introduced the concept of social contract in parliamentary debates of 1624, arguing that a king owed his position originally to the consent of the governed. It followed that when a king ceased to rule within the conditions of the contract between sovereign and subject, he ceased legally to be king.

This was the case of James II, who fled the English throne in 1688. His Roman Catholic sympathies, his extension of the royal prerogative and his alienation of Parliament were seen as a breach of his duty to rule justly. His daughter Mary and her husband, William of Orange, were invited to rule England under the restrictions of the Declaration of Rights. The Declaration was revised in 1689 as the Bill of Rights, a fundamental statement of the relationship between sovereign and subjects. The Triennial Act and the Act of Settlement subsequently passed by Parliament completed the Revolution Settlement that forms the basis of the modern British constitution.

The Bill of Rights established a limited monarchy and the sovereignty of Parliament. It strengthened Parliament by ensuring free election of its members and free speech during its sessions, granting it control of taxation, and stating that Parliaments should be held frequently; and it prohibited excessive bail and unusual punishment. England's Bill of Rights incorporated the principles of Magna Carta by guaranteeing fundamental liberties. A century later it inspired Americans to amend the United States Constitution in 1789 with a Bill of Rights assuring liberty under the law to all who came within its jurisdiction.

THE HABEAS CORPUS ACT

Although it was passed by Parliament in 1679, the Act is considered part of the reform legislation of the Glorious Revolution. It gave the force of law to the prohibition of arbitrary imprisonment included in the Petition of Right, and its accepted, if incorrect, connection with Magna Carta lent it added weight in cases involving imprisonment without trial.

The seventeenth century was thus the pivotal period in the history of both Magna Carta and the English constitution as lawyers looked to the past to solve current problems. Interpreted to meet the needs of Stuart England, the Charter had a flexibility that ensured its continuity from the medieval world to the modern era.

★

Opposite. The Lord Protector of England from 1653 to 1659, Oliver Cromwell presided over his country's one and only brush with Republican government. A sincere believer in "liberty of conscience," especially in religion, he nevertheless had little time for Magna Carta, which he found incompatible with his own dynastic ambitions.

★

Before 1688, England had never been ruled jointly by a queen and king. But the Glorious Revolution brought William and Mary to the throne together; their accession marked a turning point in English history. For William and Mary came to the throne by the will of the propertied classes, expressed through Parliament. England had become a constitutional monarchy.

Unlike that of the United States, the British constitution is not a specific, written document articulating a government and its relationship to the people. Rather, it consists of numerous Parliamentary statutes, including Magna Carta, as well as principles of common law and judicial decisions. It represents rights and liberties accumulated over a long time, and the emergence of a government from the struggle for supremacy between monarch and people.

During the reign of James I, men crossed the Atlantic to found settlements in America. They came to the New World for different reasons, but they shared a common inheritance. They were Englishmen, and continued so to think of themselves for several generations. They cherished certain traditional rights and liberties, and looked to principles of English law when they needed models for their own charters and rules of government. Central to that law, in the minds of many of them, was Magna Carta, known to them through Coke's interpretations. They continued to rely on English law throughout the colonial period and the revolutionary years, and turned to it in drawing up a Constitution in 1787.

The first settlement of Virginia was the result of commercial speculation. In 1606, lured by gold and gain, a hundred and twenty settlers set out from London in three small ships to establish a colony in Virginia to grow tobacco and promote trade with the Indians. Their authority for this was the first Virginia Charter, issued in London that year. A contract between the sponsoring Virginia Company and James I, it spelled out the rights and responsibilities of the Crown and the settlers, explained why the plantation was being established, provided for a governing council, and specified the financial obligations between the planters and their investors in England.

The charter is the first colonial document based in part on Magna Carta. It extended the king's law to Englishmen abroad (unlike the colonists of France and Spain, who were considered beyond the protection of their domestic laws). The guarantees spelled out in the first Virginia Charter were inherent in Magna Carta:

And we do…Declare that all and every of the Persons, being our Subject, which shall dwell and inhabit within every or any of the said several Colonies and Plantations, and every of their children which shall happen to be born within any of the Limits and Precincts of the said several Colonies and Plantations, shall Have and enjoy all Liberties, Franchises, and Immunities, within any of our other Dominions, to all Intents and Purposes, as if they had been abiding and born, within this our Realm of England, or any other of our said Dominions.

★

"He who doth not work, shall not eat." Captain John Smith's rugged philosophy at Jamestown in 1607 was born of necessity. Although James I's First Virginia Charter declared that the colonists should "have and enjoy all Liberties, Franchises, and Immunities" accorded to Englishmen, it is unlikely that they found his royal generosity of much comfort as they struggled to survive.

By 1609 the company needed fresh capital, and the Crown issued a second Virginia Charter designed to attract new investors. In an effort to improve both governance and profit, it shifted control of the colony from the Crown to the company by creating a joint-stock company charged with administering the colony through a treasurer and council. It was a step toward local, representative control.

These early charters drew on English land law, specifically the feudal restrictions by which land was held of the Crown in return for some service. With the ancient land law came the ancient language of Magna Carta, protecting and perpetuating the rights of Englishmen wherever they were.

PLYMOUTH

Persecution of religious nonconformists in Stuart England violated the principles of individual liberty implicit in Magna Carta and led to the second settlement in America. Jamestown had been founded for economic gain; the Plymouth Plantation was established for religious freedom.

Several years of negotiations were necessary before the Pilgrims were able to set sail for America in 1620. One of their tasks was to convince prospective financiers that, despite the fact that they were religious dissidents—Separatists—they were loyal subjects of King James. They therefore presented to the Virginia Company a statement of loyalty to the Crown, the Leyden Agreement of 1618. It employs the language of Magna Carta, calling upon the king to govern "according to ye Lawes of ye Land, unto whom ye ar in all things to fine an account & by them to bee ordered according to Godlynes."

★

Boston Stump, or St. Botolph's church, towers more than two hundred and seventy feet above the docks of this historic town in South Lincolnshire. In 1607, the Pilgrim Fathers made their first attempt to escape from Boston to Holland, but were caught and imprisoned in the Guildhall cells. Some twenty years later, Boston had its own band of dissenters, inspired by the spiritual guidance of the Reverend John Cotton, vicar of St. Botolph's. These men and women formed the nucleus of the Massachusetts Bay Company.

★

Forty-one men (and no women) signed the Mayflower Compact on November 16, 1620, as their ship stood off Cape Cod. The document was initially intended by the Pilgrims' leaders to act as a constraint on the more unruly followers they had recruited in London. However, because no official charter was ever granted, the Compact became in effect a form of constitution for the colony.

While the first Charter of Virginia had outlined rules for governing the Jamestown colony, no such structure existed for the *Mayflower* Pilgrims. Faced with forming a government for their new colony, they composed the document known as the Mayflower Compact, whereby they undertook, "solemnly and mutually in the Presence of God and one another," to "covenant and combine our selves togeather into a civill body politick, for our better ordering and preservation and furtherance of ye ends aforesaid: and by virtue hearof to enact, constitute and frame such just and equall lawes, ordinances, acts, constitutions and offices from time to time, as shall be thought most meete and convenient for ye generall good of ye Colonie, unto which we promise all due submission and obedience."

In their desire to conform to the laws of England, they drew on concepts of fundamental law, combining Separatist principles with provisions that safeguarded the civil liberties of Englishmen. Bound together by religious persuasion, professing allegiance to King James and an assumption that their compact was valid under English law, they formulated a covenant that was political and secular. It became the operating instrument of government for the colony.

MASSACHUSETTS BAY COLONY

The survival of the fledgling settlements in Jamestown and Plymouth encouraged others to emigrate for religious freedom, for earthly treasure, or for both. Massachusetts Bay Colony differed from the two newly formed colonies, yet combined characteristics of each. On the one hand, the company charter received from Charles I in 1629 made it a trading company organized for profit; on the other, its participants were Puritans, predominantly university educated men, determined to found a community free from interference. Their charter placed the seat of government in Massachusetts, rather than in England; there they set up a colony that was to be ruled by the will of God as they interpreted it, restricted in matters of free speech, suffrage and religious toleration.

Since Massachusetts Bay Colony had been founded to promote the interests of the Puritan oligarchy, rather than the protection of individual rights, it was not long before strictures of the colony's rulers and laws made by judges rather than parliaments caused resentment among the settlers. Public demands that laws be made in a General Court forced Governor John Winthrop to form a representative assembly. In 1635, Winthrop

ANNE BRADSTREET

In 1630, Ann Bradstreet boarded the Arbella with her husband, Simon, bound for the New World. She was the first American woman to have a book printed. This window in Boston parish church, England, shows her holding a clutch of chicks, representing the eight children she bore in Andover, Massachusetts.

"...offend not the poor nations, but as you are partakers of their land, so to make them partakers of your precious faith." The Reverend John Cotton bids farewell to the Arbella, in which members of the Massachusetts Bay Company sailed from England to New England on April 7, 1630, under the leadership of John Winthrop. Cotton, whose sermons had so inspired the Puritan adventurers, followed soon after. In 1635, Governor Winthrop ordered the Massachusetts General Court to draw up a set of laws "in resemblance to a Magna Carta, which... should be received for fundamental laws."

reported that the General Court had decided "that some men should be appointed to frame a body of grounds of laws in resemblance to a Magna Carta which ... should be received as fundamental laws." As voting remained restricted, in 1641 dissidents drafted a written statement of constitutional principles, the Body of Liberties.

The document addressed such matters as due process of law, judicial procedures and the relationship of church and state. It was a peculiar blend of common law, tenets of Magna Carta, and the Old Testament (on which the criminal code was based). It anticipated eighteenth-century constitutional concepts by protecting life, liberty and property from seizure "unless it be by virtue or equitie of some expresse law of the Country warranting the same, established by a generall Court and sufficiently published."

Links with the concepts, language and form of Magna Carta exist in other colonial documents, all based on the "Rights of Englishmen." Just as in the Body of Liberties and the Virginia charters, Magna Carta echoes in the charters of Massachusetts, Maryland, Maine, Connecticut, Rhode Island, Carolina, and Georgia.

Bequeathed by Annie Clarke 1944

1630. John Cotton bids farewell to his parishioners on the Arbella.

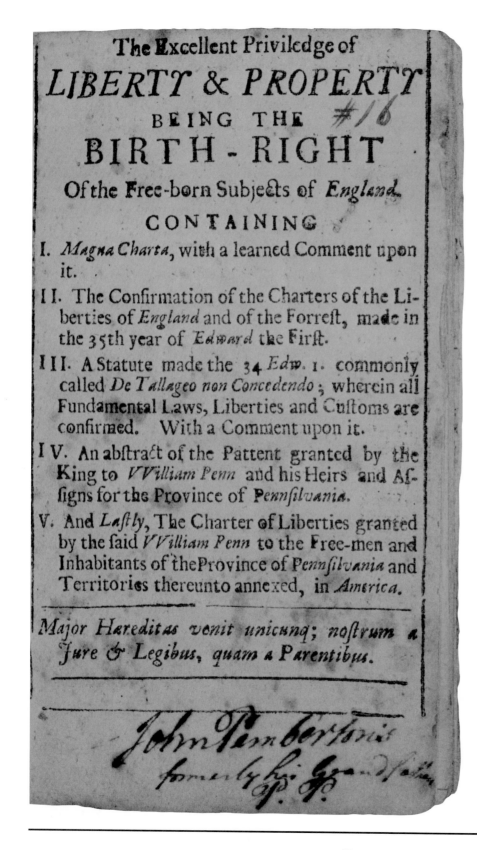

The Excellent Priviledge of
LIBERTY & PROPERTY
BEING THE
#16
BIRTH - RIGHT
Of the Free-born Subjects of *England.*
CONTAINING

I. *Magna Charta*, with a learned Comment upon it.

II. The Confirmation of the Charters of the Liberties of *England* and of the Forreſt, made in the 35th year of *Edward* the Firſt.

III. A Statute made the 34 *Edw.* 1. commonly called *De Tallageo non Concedendo*; wherein all Fundamental Laws, Liberties and Cuſtoms are confirmed. With a Comment upon it.

IV. An abſtract of the Pattent granted by the King to *VVilliam Penn* and his Heirs and Aſſigns for the Province of *Pennſilvania.*

V. And *Laſtly*, The Charter of Liberties granted by the ſaid *VVilliam Penn* to the Free-men and Inhabitants of the Province of *Pennſilvania* and Territories thereunto annexed, in *America.*

Major Hæreditas venit unicunq; noſtrum a Jure & Legibus, quam a Parentibus.

John Pemberton's
formerly his Grandfather

The link between Magna Carta and the American colonies is clearly stated on this frontispiece to William Penn's publication The Excellent Priviledge of Liberty and Property.... Penn begins with the Great Charter of 1215, and ends with "The Charter of Liberties granted by the said William Penn" in 1682.

William Penn, devout Quaker and founder of Pennsylvania, firmly believed that liberty was a fundamental right of all men. Unlike the Puritans, he did not exclude native Americans from this definition. Here, Penn is seen presenting a treaty to some Indians. Note the peace pipe in the foreground.

In 1670, William Penn, a student at Oxford University, was tried in London at the Old Bailey for preaching Quaker beliefs, thereby causing "tumultuous assembly." The trial was a significant step toward assuring the right to trial by jury. In his successful defense Penn evoked Magna Carta, drawing on Coke's *Second Institute* in claiming that his treatment was "directly opposite to, and destructive of the undoubted right of every English prisoner." Stating that rights guaranteed by the Charter had been denied him, he cited his arbitrary imprisonment, the prosecution's refusal to cite cause, the charging of the jury in the absence of prisoners, and the fining of prisoners for contempt. (Members of the jury, including Edward Bushell, were sent to Newgate prison as punishment for their vindication of Penn, despite a 1667 resolution that such practice was illegal and contrary to Magna Carta. In 1670, in *Bushell's Case,* the court ruled that such imprisonment was illegal, a principle thereafter respected in English courts of law.)

Penn's use and analysis of Magna Carta demonstrated his understanding of its concepts and their practical application; his knowledge was to have a direct effect on the laws of the new colonies. In 1676 he assisted in writing the *Fundamental Laws of West New Jersey,* protecting them in an introductory clause from contradictory legislation, just as Coke held Magna Carta as unassailable. In 1682 he arrived in America to establish a colony for Quakers. With him he carried the "Frame of Government of Pennsylvania," a draft of his constitutional ideas based on the Great Charter and on Coke. No doubt with his own trial in mind, it emulated Magna Carta Chapter 40 in guaranteeing speedy trials and equal justice, and Chapter 20, in assuring fines commensurate with the crime. In 1687 in Philadelphia he published an extensive commentary on Magna Carta, *The Excellent Priviledge of Liberty and Property Being the Birth-Right of A Free-Born Subject of England.* It was the first time a commentary on the Charter had been printed in America. Following Penn's lead, the Assembly of Pennsylvania passed laws guaranteeing due process, trial by jury, and taxation by consent. Incorporating the principles of Magna Carta as well as its language, the statements appeared in printed form for use in schools so that "every person may have knowledge therefore."

From the founding of Jamestown in 1607 to the decade before the Declaration of Independence in 1776, the American colonists looked to British constitutional principles for their fundamental rights. Only when imperial policies appeared to threaten those rights did they begin to think in terms of union and independence. Their claims of violation of liberty rested on concepts of law that included those embodied in Magna Carta, and on theories of natural rights, particularly those of John Locke.

At the time, knowledge of Magna Carta was based on Henry III's revised version of 1225. The original Charter was not published until 1759, when William Blackstone's edition of *The Great Charter and the Charter of the Forest* made the 1215 document available. In his *Commentaries on the Laws and Customs of England* (first published in America in 1771-72), Blackstone clearly traced the relationship between Magna Carta and English liberties, and in eighteenth-century America his works replaced Coke's as a source of information about the Charter. Influential on political thinkers (an influence that Thomas Jefferson deplored as making tories of young Americans), the *Commentaries* was widely read and used as a law-school text until the early twentieth century.

John Locke was developing his theories at the time of the Glorious Revolution. In the second of his *Two Treatises on Government,* written in 1689, he had

The BLOODY MASSACRE perpetrated in King—-—Street BOSTON on March 5th 1770, by a party of the 29th REGT.

BUTCHER'S HALL

CUSTOM HOUSE

Engrav'd Printed & Sold by PAUL REVERE BOSTON

Unhappy BOSTON! see thy Sons deplore,
Thy hallow'd Walks besmear'd with guiltless Gore:
While faithless P—n and his savage Bands,
With murd'rous Rancour stretch their bloody Hands;
Like fierce Barbarians grinning o'er their Prey,
Approve the Carnage, and enjoy the Day.

If scalding drops from Rage from Anguish Wrung,
If speechless Sorrows lab'ring for a Tongue,
Or if a weeping World can ought appease
The plaintive Ghosts of Victims such as these;
The Patriot's copious Tears for each are shed,
A glorious Tribute which embalms the Dead.

But know, FATE summons to that awful Goal,
Where JUSTICE strips the Murd'rer of his Soul:
Should venal C—ts the scandal of the Land,
Snatch the relentless Villain from her Hand,
Keen Execrations on this Plate inscrib'd,
Shall reach a JUDGE who never can be brib'd.

The unhappy Sufferers were Messrs SAML GRAY, SAML MAVERICK, JAMS CALDWELL, CRISPUS ATTUCKS & PATK CARR
Killed. Six wounded, two of them (CHRISTR MONK & JOHN CLARK) Mortally

asserted that by nature man was "free, equal and independent." Governments, he wrote, were rightly formed by "agreeing with other men to join and unite into a community, for their comfortable, safe and peaceable living one amongst another, in a secure enjoyment of their properties, and a greater security against any, that are not of it." One of the limits on those governments, according to Locke, was that "the supreme power cannot take away from any man any part of this property without his own consent."

After George III's accession to the throne in 1760, the colonists became increasingly reluctant to support England in its wars and its concomitant taxation. They saw themselves as subjected to policies over which they had little influence, pawns in the larger game of preserving the interests of the British Empire. One of their many complaints was about enforcement of England's Trade and Navigation acts, under which general search warrants permitted customs officers to enter and search private property on suspicion of smuggling. In a case in the Massachusetts Court in 1761, James Otis contended that such writs violated fundamental principles of law, quoting as precedent Coke's decision in *Dr. Bonham's Case*. His language went beyond Coke's in advocating judicial review of legislation:

> *An Act against the Constitution is void: an Act against natural Equity is void; and if an Act of Parliament should be made, in the very Words of this Petition, it would be void.*

★

Overleaf. Without representation in Parliament, the American colonists reacted angrily to the imposition of taxes by a government 3,000 miles away. In Boston, the English troops sent to keep order were provoked to open fire on March 5, 1770, killing five of the crowd. Known as the Boston Massacre, it became a symbol of British tyranny to the colonists.

★

The Death of General Warren at the Battle of Bunker's Hill, June 17, 1775. "This painting represents the moment when...the British troops became completely successful..." wrote the painter John Trumbull. It was, however, the beginning of the end for Britain in America. At the far left, brandishing his sword, is Israel Putnam: "Don't fire, boys, until you see the whites of their eyes," he is said to have cried.

In letters published in the *Boston Gazette* in 1766, John Adams repeated the colonists' arguments against the tax, and held further that it was contrary to Chapter 40 of the Charter, which forbade any sale, delay or denial of justice.

The tax was repealed in March that year, but Parliament made it clear in a Declaratory Act that the constitutional arguments advanced by the colonists were unacceptable. A permanent solution to the question of taxation of the colonies had not been found.

★

John Dickinson of Philadelphia was one of America's leading moderates, from the Stamp Act crisis of 1765 to the Constitutional Convention of 1787. The title page of his popular book shows Dickinson, his elbow resting on Magna Carta. At his shoulder is one of Coke's legal commentaries.

★

The Commander in Chief, General George Washington.

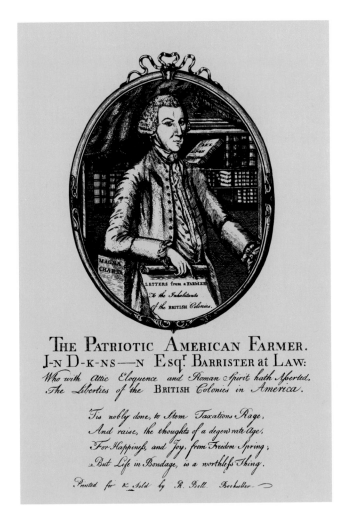

THE PATRIOTIC AMERICAN FARMER.
J-N D-K-NS——N Esq.ʳ BARRISTER at LAW:
*Who with Attic Eloquence and Roman Spirit hath Asserted,
The Liberties of the* BRITISH *Colonies in America.*

*Tis nobly done, to Stem Taxations Rage,
And raise, the thoughts of a degen'rate Age,
For Happiness, and Joy, from Freedom Spring;
But Life in Bondage, is a worthless Thing.*

Printed for & Sold by R. Bell. Bookseller

In a pamphlet in 1764 in response to the Sugar Act, Otis challenged the right of Parliament to tax the colonies, claiming that the right not to be taxed without consent was a part of every Englishman's birthright. Parliamentary rights versus the rights of the colonial assemblies had become a crucial issue.

When the colonists found that the Stamp Act of 1765 could be contested only in the courts of admiralty, where traditionally there was no jury, they were quick to declare that the Act violated Magna Carta by authorizing taxation without consent and trial without a jury. At the ensuing Stamp Tax Congress in New York, the resolutions adopted by Congress affirmed the colonists' rights as Englishmen, particularly "The invaluable Rights of Taxing ourselves, and Trial by our Peers" which are "confirmed by the *GREAT CHARTER* of *English* liberty."

In 1768 the Massachusetts House of Representatives sent the other colonial assemblies a circular letter, written by Samuel Adams, denouncing the new customs duties imposed by the Townshend Acts of the previous year as a usurpation of fundamental rights protected by the British constitution. Later, when resentment against the last remaining tax — the tea tax — surfaced in 1773, most of the colonies again relied on constitutional rights in defending their position, insisting that Magna Carta and other precepts of English law forbade taxation without representation. Some used theories of natural rights to bolster their arguments; others looked to their colonial charters for support.

INDEPENDENCE

The Declaration of Rights and Resolves adopted at the First Continental Congress in Philadelphia in 1774 embodied the principles of common law and natural rights affirmed by the colonists. Considered a forerunner of the Declaration of Independence, it stated that "there should be no taxation of the colonists without adequate representation in Parliament, that the right of trial by jury should be preserved intact, and that the colonists should be allowed freely to petition the king and Parliament for redress of grievances."

"THE RIGHTS OF MAN; — or TOMMY PAINE, the little American Taylor, taking the Measure of the CROWN, for a new Pair of Revolution-Breeches.

Giving force to the Declaration of Rights and Resolves was a boycott of trade with Britain until colonial grievances were remedied. In the absence of substantial concessions from the prime minister, Lord North, the delegates reconvened in May 1775. With the near certainty of war, they voted to raise an army and appointed George Washington of Virginia as its commander.

Among the moderates urging a final attempt at reconciliation was John Dickinson, whose *Letters From a Pennsylvania Farmer* had spearheaded opposition to the Townshend Acts. Although the group's views prevailed and the "Olive Branch Petition" was drawn up for presentation to the king, no redress was forthcoming from the Crown, and the colonists faced a critical choice: submission or independence.

The choice for independence was spurred on by the publication in January 1776 of Thomas Paine's *Common Sense,* in which Paine argued for direct representation of the people in government and against kingship as contrary to common sense and natural right. "In America," he wrote, "the king is law." It was Paine who questioned whether the British constitution was suited to colonial needs; his writings had widespread appeal and solidified public sentiment in favor of independence.

The final draft of the Declaration of Independence, largely the work of Thomas Jefferson, was adopted on July 4, 1776. The statement of a political theory justifying the break with Great Britain, it reflects Locke's doctrines, which were popular with the less conservative members of the Congress: men are created equal and have inalienable rights, among which are life, liberty and the pursuit of happiness (this last phrase a substitution by Jefferson for Locke's concept of "property"); governments are instituted to secure those rights with the consent of the governed; if a government is tyrannical, if it abuses or usurps the rights of the people, it is their right and duty to "alter or abolish it and to institute a new government." Such, charged the Declaration, was the government of George III, and the colonists chose to reject it.

Resolving to declare their country's independence from the British Crown, the representatives at the second Continental Congress had to fill the void created by the dissolution of their political bonds with Great Britain. On June 7, 1776, even before the Declaration of Independence, Congress resolved that "a plan of confederation be prepared, and transmitted to the respective Colonies for their consideration and approbation."

THE ARTICLES OF CONFEDERATION AND THE STATE CONSTITUTIONS

The resulting Articles of Confederation, presented to the states on November 17, 1777, demonstrated above all the profound distrust of centralized government that had developed in America over the previous two decades. Article II sets the tone of the proposed confederation: "Each state retains its sovereignty, freedom and independence, and every Power, Jurisdiction and right, which is not by this confederation expressly delegated to the United States, in Congress assembled." In the event, the Articles proved inadequate to the real needs of the new nation.

Some of the Articles appear to imply substantial authority for the federal Congress to conduct the affairs of the United States, especially in the vital matters of common defense and the making of foreign treaties. But there were no teeth to the new system of government: no effective national executive, no national system of law courts, no power to raise taxes or enlist troops, and no authority to compel the states to obey its international treaties. This failing reflects the determination of the representatives to preserve real power and control within the states themselves.

While the ratification of the Articles of Confederation dragged on until March 1, 1781, between 1776 and 1780 all the states except Rhode Island and Connecticut had adopted new written constitutions. The ideas they contained came from several sources, among them natural law, natural rights, provisions in colonial charters, and principles of British constitutionalism. In drafting them, conservative delegates preferred to use constitutional principles, while the more radical wanted to incorporate the newer doctrines of natural rights. In most of the states debate centered on the Bill of Rights.

★
_____

George Washington the statesman, at the Constitutional Convention in Philadelphia. As President of the Convention, Washington naturally stood apart from the other delegates. However, as this picture suggests, his presence lent great authority to the proceedings through the long summer of 1787.

The Virginia Declaration of Rights, written by George Mason, combined theories of both natural and fundamental law. Adopted on June 2, 1776, it became a model for bills of rights of other state constitutions, and, in 1791, of the United States Bill of Rights. The Constitution of Massachusetts, drafted by John Adams, reflected both the Lockean idea that government is based on a social contract and precepts of English law. The influence of English precedents is particularly evident in the Constitution of Maryland, in which a number of the provisions are specifically comparable to those of Magna Carta, the English Petition of Right, and the English Bill of Rights. Almost all the state constitutions included provisions directly traceable to Chapter 39 of Magna Carta, guaranteeing trial by jury and by the law of the land, and to Chapter 40, forbidding the "sale, denial, or delay of justice."

The contrasting significance of the Articles of Confederation and the state constitutions soon emerged. While the war of independence lasted, the Continental Congress and its implied powers carried some weight among the thirteen states. However, with the end of the war in September 1783, Congress became increasingly ineffectual. Its lack of control over the economy undermined any authority it may have had. Individual states began to ignore the obligations they had to the confederation, disregarding the terms of foreign treaties made on their behalf, arming themselves independently, sometime failing to send representatives to Congress, and frequently refusing Congress's requests for money to pursue its business.

The period from 1781 to 1787 not only demonstrated the inadequacy of the Articles of Confederation, but indicated that the states, despite the internal strength and energy of their fledgling governments, were not necessarily in a "league of friendship." Interstate trade disputes began to sever the bonds that had held the states together against their common enemy. Paradoxically, the weakness of the Articles of Confederation, which failed to address the regulation of trade, gave the United States another opportunity to form a government that would sustain and advance those causes and aspirations expressed in the Declaration of Independence.

★

Eighty years old in 1787, Benjamin Franklin brought to the Convention a lifetime of experience in the affairs of his country.

★

Thirty-nine men signed the Constitution of the United States. Only three who attended — George Mason, Edmund Randolph and Elbridge Gerry—withheld their names. Rhode Island was not represented, by its own choice.

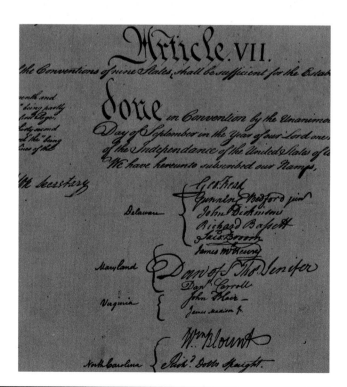

The distinguished group of delegates who assembled in Philadelphia in May 1787 included many who would be important in the conduct of the new nation's affairs. Among them were George Washington, James Madison, Edmond Randolph, and George Mason of Virginia; Benjamin Franklin, James Wilson and Gouverneur Morris of Pennsylvania; Alexander Hamilton of New York; John Dickinson of Delaware; and Charles Pinckney of South Carolina.

The convention had been called for the purpose of revising the Articles of Confederation, but the delegates quickly decided to go beyond their mandate and construct an entirely new constitution. A new government had to be formed that could deal successfully with the critical issues of finance, commerce and security—a government that, in the words of James Madison, would achieve a balance between power and liberty. Despite the wide differences between those with nationalist leanings and those who supported states' rights, a spirit of compromise ruled, and at length a constitution was hammered out. It was adopted by the convention on September 17, 1787.

After the many debates and writings on individual liberties preceding the Revolution, it is surprising that the original Constitution did not contain a bill of rights. The only provisions reminiscent of the earlier demands for guarantees of rights and liberties are those of Article I, section 9, denying Congress the power to suspend the writ of habeas corpus or to pass bills of attainder or ex post facto laws; those of Article III, section 2, providing for jury trial in the federal courts, and section 3, placing limitations on trials for treason; and that of Article VI, section 3, prohibiting religious tests for officers.

The question of including a bill of rights was considered during the convention. Charles Pinckney submitted a list of thirteen propositions on the liberties of the citizen for consideration, but no action was taken on his proposal. As the final vote on the Constitution approached, George Mason urged that it be prefaced by a bill of rights to "give great quiet to the people." This plea was brushed aside. Many members of the convention, particularly 'the Federalists, believed that such a bill was unnecessary. Its purpose, they contended, was to protect the subject from tyrannical rulers, and such provisions had no place in a constitution in which the ultimate power was in the people; moreover, to specify particular rights was to limit constitutional protection to those rights only. This was the prevailing view; nevertheless, the omission of a bill of rights became a rallying point for the Anti-Federalists in the state ratifying conventions.

The Constitution of 1787 was a practical document aimed at creating a machinery of government. Inherent in that machinery was protection against arbitrary authority in the division of power among the executive, legislative and judicial branches. The Constitution represented an experiment in government, and was written with little basis in experience. Still, in the minds of many of the delegates were principles of the British constitution, which Pinckney declared to be "the best constitution in existence." Those principles would be evidenced more clearly in the subsequently enacted Bill of Rights.

★

George Mason was the author of the Virginia Declaration of Rights (1776). This great document was quickly imitated by many of the other states of the Union, and profoundly influenced the federal Bill of Rights proposed in 1789.

THE STRUGGLE FOR RATIFICATION

The Constitution had been approved by thirty-nine of the fifty-five delegates regularly attending the Philadelphia convention. Now it faced the crucial test of ratification by the states. Approval came with unexpected speed. Within nine months of the adjournment of the convention, eleven of the thirteen states had ratified. However, the victory was not easily won; nor was it attained without concessions. In the first five states to ratify, the document was approved by sizable majorities (in Delaware, New Jersey and Georgia the vote was unanimous). In other states the battle for approval was much closer. In

Massachusetts, Virginia and New York, the specter of rejection loomed large. The loss of even one of these populous states would have destroyed any chance of success of the new government.

The debates again centered on the question of a bill of rights and the nature of individual liberties in a nation where there was no king and where the danger of repression could come only from a government chosen by the people themselves. British constitutionalism was praised, but distinguished from constitutional government in America. Magna Carta was cited as precedent by proponents as well as opponents of ratification.

In Massachusetts ratification was accompanied by a list of proposed amendments, including provisions that all powers not delegated to the federal government be reserved to the states; that Congress be prohibited from levying direct taxes; that there be grand jury indictment in criminal cases and jury trials in civil cases between parties of different states. The way was now clear for other states to take similar action.

In the debate in the Virginia convention, George Mason, Richard Henry Lee and Patrick Henry led the fight against the Constitution, while James Madison, John Marshall and Governor Randolph spoke for it. The arguments chiefly concerned the absence of a bill of rights. After lengthy debate the Constitution was approved by a vote of 89-79. Immediately afterward a committee headed by Henry and Mason set to work to draft proposals for constitutional amendments. Among the forty proposed were a declaration of rights, and several provisions drawn almost directly from Magna Carta, including the procedural guarantees of Chapter 39, and the injunction against the denial and delay of justice in Chapter 40.

In New York the Constitution won approval by only three votes. The strong Anti-Federalist group was led by the governor, George Clinton, who argued against the Constitution in a series of published letters signed "Cato," attacking the centralization of power in the federal government and raising fears about the dangers such centralization posed to the liberties of the people. In counter-attack, another series of letters, signed "Publius," written by Alexander Hamilton, James Madison and John Jay and later published as *The Federalist*, was a clear statement of political thought predominant in America at the time. In attempting to hew to the line between power and liberty,

★

Begun in 1787 as a newspaper series in defense of the proposed Constitution, The Federalist *emerged as one of the great works of American political theory. Written by Alexander Hamilton, James Madison and John Jay, it remains a primary interpretive source for the Constitution to this day.*

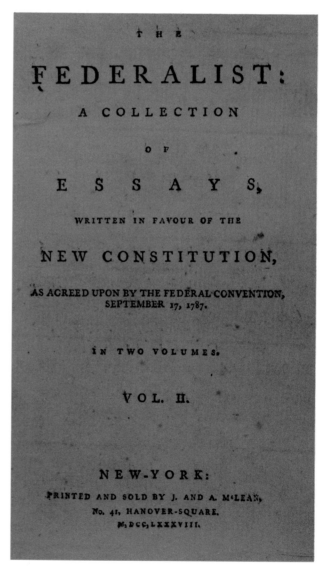

THE

FEDERALIST:

A COLLECTION

OF

ESSAYS,

WRITTEN IN FAVOUR OF THE

NEW CONSTITUTION,

AS AGREED UPON BY THE FEDERAL CONVENTION, SEPTEMBER 17, 1787.

IN TWO VOLUMES.

VOL. II.

NEW-YORK:

PRINTED AND SOLD BY J. AND A. M'LEAN, No. 41, HANOVER-SQUARE. M,DCC,LXXXVIII.

the Federalists believed that the checks and balances embodied in the Constitution would adequately safeguard individual liberties. Thus Hamilton asserts that Magna Carta, the Petition of Right, and the English Bill of Rights are "stipulations between kings and their subjects, abridgments of prerogative in favor of privilege, reservations of rights not surrendered to the prince," and for this reason have "no applications to constitutions, professedly founded upon the power of the people...." The Anti-Federalists, on the other hand, fearful of the uncurbed power of governments and of popular majorities, insisted on guarantees of civil liberties.

★

Energy, ability and education combined to make James Madison the single most active figure in the formulation and ratification of the U.S. Constitution. He was its principal author, and kept comprehensive notes of the Convention's proceedings. He worked furiously—and successfully—to get the Constitution ratified in Virginia, and in 1789 he initiated the federal Bill of Rights.

THE BILL OF RIGHTS

Although its final passage must be credited to the Anti-Federalists, leading the fight for the Bill of Rights in Congress was that staunch Federalist, James Madison. During his election campaign he had written:

> *It is my sincere opinion that the Constitution ought to be revised, and that the first Congress meeting under it, ought to prepare and recommend to the States for ratification, the most satisfactory provisions for all essential rights, particularly the rights of Conscience in the fullest latitude, the freedom of the press, trials by jury, security against general warrants etc....*

He was supported by Thomas Jefferson, at the time minister to France. The inclusion of a declaration of liberties in the Constitution would, in Jefferson's opinion, offer protection against abuses by both the executive and legislative branches of the government, and would put a "legal check ... into the hands of the judiciary." He saw the Bill of Rights as a tool that would enable the Supreme Court to protect citizens' basic liberties.

The debate over the bill was long and arduous. Madison's amendments were revised in both houses of Congress and in committee, and his proposal prohibiting state violation of individual rights failed. (His belief that there was greater danger of abuse of power from state government than from the government of the United States was not widely endorsed.) Nevertheless, the Bill of Rights that was finally adopted in September 1789 was essentially his work.

In drafting the bill, Madison relied heavily on the Declaration of Rights of Virginia. In tone and in substance, the provisions of the two are similar; both emphasize individual liberty and specify the same rights. However, while the Virginia document is a statement of standards by which to judge government, the Bill of Rights is a list of specific protections of traditional civil rights; consequently it is judicially enforceable.

Most of the ten short articles of the Bill are prohibitions against government action that infringes on individual rights. The Bill protects the traditional liberties cherished by free men: of religion, of speech, of the press, of assembly, of petition to the government for the redress of grievances (Article I); of the right to bear arms (Article II). It prohibits the quartering of soldiers in private homes in peace time (Article III), and forbids unreasonable searches and seizures (Article IV). Procedural guarantees enumerated in Articles V, VI and VII include indictment by grand jury, trial by jury in both civil and criminal cases, and the mandate that no one shall "be deprived of life, liberty, or property, without due process of law." Article VIII forbids excessive bail, excessive fines, and cruel and unusual punishments. Article IX specifies that the enumeration of rights in the bill does not mean that other rights are not retained by the people. Article X provides that powers not delegated to the federal government, or prohibited to the state governments, are reserved to the states or to the people.

Magna Carta is the distinguished ancestor of the Bill of Rights, and its influence is obvious. Some of the provisions of Articles V, VI, VII, and VIII draw heavily on guarantees and language found in Chapters 20, 28, 39, and 40 of the Great Charter. The Petition of Rights and the English Bill of Rights furnish material for the guarantees of Articles I, II and III.

As A. E. Dick Howard writes in his definitive work *The Road from Runnymede,* "Nearly two centuries of jurisprudence have added considerable breadth to the meaning and uses of the provisions of the Bill of Rights. The ever-dynamic patterns of American constitutional law have evolved dimensions for one or another of the first eight amendments which simply did not exist in the English law. But the origin in, and debt to, Magna Carta remains."

EPILOGUE

From 1215, when King John first assented to Magna Carta, to the enactment of the American Bill of Rights in 1791, the progress of liberty was never continuous. Even with our rights apparently secure, the preservation of freedom has required constant struggle. There have been dark periods in the nation's history when the true meaning of the word "liberty" seemed utterly lost.

After the civil war, many people believed that the Thirteenth, Fourteenth and Fifteenth amendments to the U.S. Constitution assured blacks equal treatment under the law. However, it was soon evident that practices circumventing the obvious intent of the amendments were widespread. In 1896 the U.S. Supreme Court, in *Plessy* v. *Ferguson*, upheld those practices, saying that the Constitution required no more than "separate but equal" public facilities for blacks. The case concerned segregation in trains but was subsequently used to sustain segregation in public schools, and the doctrine remained valid until in 1954 the Court held that it had no place in public education. Notwithstanding this decision,

★

The Supreme Court Building, Washington, D.C. The inscription above the entrance says: "Equal Justice Under Law."

many schools and other public places remained segregated until the 1970s, when protestations, civil disobedience and federal court action finally succeeded in bringing about meaningful change.

When we view the record of the past two hundred years, however, setbacks and uneven progress do not obscure the evidence that the principles of Magna Carta and of the Bill of Rights are enshrined in our laws and affect our everyday lives. The right to vote and to have fair representation in legislative bodies has at last been secured. The Fifteenth Amendment gave the suffrage to blacks in 1869, and the Nineteenth Amendment, fifty years later, gave women equal status. Freedom of the press and of religion are liberties we take for granted. The traditional rights of the accused—trial by jury, assistance of counsel and other procedural safeguards — have been extended to include protection from police harassment and notification of the right to remain silent. The controversial question of a woman's right to choose whether to bear a child has been protected as a right of privacy, guaranteed by the Fourteenth Amendment.

The expansion of individual freedom has not been regarded as an unmixed blessing, especially when it interferes with what the majority sees as its best interests. Thus requirements designed to protect the accused have at times made law enforcement more difficult, arousing protests from the victims of crime and from the law-abiding public. Many believe that the courts have erred in holding that the First Amendment permits the dissemination of obscene and pornographic materials, particularly in places frequented by young people. Extending the protective mantle of the First Amendment to ultra-conservative or radical organizations has brought strong protests from those who see such groups as a threat to government and society. Religious freedom, some contend, should not include the right to an allocation of any public funds for sectarian schools. A woman's "right to choose" has been violently opposed as a denial of rights to the possible life she might bear.

On the other hand, it is argued that even today liberty and equality are only ideals, that law and justice are never even-handed, that many people are denied basic freedoms, and that some are inevitably the victims of discrimination and inequality. Nevertheless, while justice in the sense of equal treatment for all may not be possible when other things remain unequal,

society can seek to achieve a measure of justice for all that guarantees basic rights and offers fair redress for grievances. Despite our significant accomplishments toward this goal, much still remains to be done.

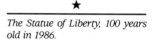

The Statue of Liberty, 100 years old in 1986.

We, the people of the United States, share with the people of Great Britain a common heritage of liberty under the law that goes back to Magna Carta. We are fortunate that our heritage includes such fundamental rights as freedom of speech, freedom of religion, and trial by jury, privileges that are denied the inhabitants of many parts of the world. Such fortune carries with it a heavy responsibility. Governing bodies and courts reflect the traditions, beliefs and morals of the society they serve, and the law is changed and shaped by those institutions in response to the expectations and demands of the populace. Only as vigilant citizens in the true sense of the word will we be able to preserve our liberties and remain free.

THE BILL OF RIGHTS

ARTICLE

Congress shall make no law respecting an establishment of religion, or prohibiting the free exercise thereof; or abridging the freedom of speech, or of the press; or the right of the people peaceably to assemble, and to petition the government for a redress of grievances.

ARTICLE

A well regulated Militia, being necessary to the security of a free State, the right of the people to keep and bear Arms, shall not be infringed.

ARTICLE

No Soldier shall, in time of peace be quartered in any house, without the consent of the Owner, nor in time of war, but in a manner to be prescribed by law.

ARTICLE

The right of the people to be secure in their persons, houses, papers, and effects, against unreasonable searches and seizures, shall not be violated, and no Warrants shall issue, but upon probable cause, supported by Oath or affirmation, and particularly describing the place to be searched, and the persons or things to be seized.

ARTICLE

No person shall be held to answer for a capital, or otherwise infamous crime, unless on a presentment or indictment of a Grand Jury, except in cases arising in the land or naval forces, or in the Militia, when in actual service in time of War or public danger; nor shall any person be subject for the same offense to be twice put in jeopardy of life or limb; nor shall be compelled in any criminal case to be a witness against himself, nor be deprived of life, liberty, or property, without due process of law; nor shall private property be taken for public use, without just compensation.

ARTICLE

In all criminal prosecutions, the accused shall enjoy the right to a speedy and public trial, by an impartial jury of the State and district wherein the crime shall have been committed, which districts shall have been previously ascertained by law, and to be informed of the nature and cause of the accusation; to be confronted with the witnesses against him; to have compulsory process for obtaining witnesses in his favor, and to have the Assistance of Counsel for his defence.

ARTICLE

In Suits at common law, where the value in controversy shall exceed twenty dollars, the right of trial by jury shall be preserved, and no fact tried by a jury, shall be otherwise re-examined in any Court of the United States, than according to the rules of common law.

ARTICLE

Excessive bail shall not be required, nor excessive fines imposed, nor cruel and unusual punishments inflicted.

ARTICLE

The enumeration in the Constitution, of certain rights, shall not be construed to deny or disparage others retained by the people.

ARTICLE

The powers not delegated to the United States by the Constitution, nor prohibited by it to the States, are reserved to the States respectively, or to the people.

Also known as the First Ten Amendments to the Constitution

adopted on December 15, 1791

MAGNA CARTA of KING JOHN A.D. 1215

It was on the 15th of June 1215 that King John accepted the forty-eight Articles of the Barons at Runnymede, a meadow of about one hundred acres between Windsor and Staines in the county of Berkshire. These articles were then embodied in a charter, which provided the basic fundamental principle of human rights, since known as Magna Carta. On the 19th June 12 copies were sealed and sent to lords of the manors throughout England. Of these only 4 remain. This translation was taken from the original now lying in Lincoln Cathedral.

John, by the grace of God, King of England, Lord of Ireland, Duke of Normandy and Aquitaine, and Count of Anjou: To his Archbishops, Bishops, Abbots, Earls, Barons, Justiciaries, Foresters, Sheriffs, Reeves, Ministers and to all Bailiffs and faithful subjects, Greetings. Know that in the presence of God, and for the health of Our soul, and the souls of Our ancestors and heirs, to the honour of God, and the exaltation of the Holy Church, and amendment of Our kingdom, by the advice of Our reverend fathers, Stephen, Archbishop of Canterbury, Primate of all England, and Cardinal of the Holy Roman Church; Henry, Archbishop of Dublin; William of London, Peter of Winchester, Jocelin of Bath and Glastonbury, Hugh of Lincoln, Walter of Worcester, William of Coventry, and Benedict of Rochester, Master Pandulf, the Pope's subdeacon; Brother Aymeric, Master of the Knights Templar in England; and the noble persons, William Marshall, Earl of Pembroke; William, Earl of Salisbury; William, Earl of Warren; William, Earl of Arundel; Alan de Galloway, Constable of Scotland; Warin Fitz-Gerald, Peter Fitz-Herbert, Hubert de Burgh, Seneschal of Poitou, Hugh de Neville, Matthew Fitz-Herbert, Thomas Basset, Alan Basset, Philip Daubeny, Robert de Roppeley, John Marshal, John Fitz-Hugh, and others Our loyal subjects.

We have, in the first place, granted to God, and by this Our present Charter confirmed for Us and Our heirs forever—that the English Church shall be free, its rights undiminished, its liberties unimpaired. And that We wish this to be observed appears from the fact that We of Our own free will, before the outbreak of the disputes between Us and Our barons, granted and confirmed by Charter the freedom of elections, which is considered most important and necessary to the English Church. We have also granted to all the free men of Our kingdom, for Us and Our heirs forever, all the liberties underwritten, to have and to hold to them and their heirs of Us and Our heirs. If any of Our earls, barons or others who hold lands of Us by knights service shall die, and at the time of his heir shall be of full age and owe a relief, he shall have his inheritance, on payment of ancient relief. If any such heir shall be under age and a ward, he shall, when he comes of age, have his inheritance without relief or fine.

The guardian of the land of any such heir shall take therefrom only reasonable revenues, customs, and services, without destruction and waste of men or property; and if We shall have committed the wardship of any such to a sheriff, and he commits destruction, We will take amends from him, and the land shall be committed to two lawful and discreet men of that fee, who shall be answerable for the issues to Us.

The guardian, so long as he shall have the wardship of the land, shall keep up and maintain the houses, parks, fishponds, pools, mills, everything pertaining thereto, out of the issues of the same, and shall restore the whole to the heir when he comes of age, stocked with ploughs and grain as the season requires and the issues of the land can reasonably bear. Heirs shall be married without loss of station, and the marriage shall be made known to the heirs next of kin before it be contracted. A widow, on the death of her husband, shall immediately and without difficulty have her marriage portion and inheritance. She may remain in her husband's house for forty days after her husband's death, within which time her dower shall be assigned to her.

No widow shall be compelled to marry so long as she wishes to live without a husband, provided, however, that she give security that she will not marry without Our assent. Neither We nor Our bailiffs shall seize any land or rent for payment of debt so long as the debtor's chattels are sufficient to discharge the same: nor shall the debtor's sureties be distrained so long as the debtor is able to pay the debt. If the debtor fails to pay, then his sureties shall answer the debt. If anyone who has borrowed from the Jews any sum, great or small, dies before the debt has been paid, the heir shall pay no interest on the debt so long as he is under age. If the debt shall fall into Our hands, We will only take the principal sum named in the bond. If any man dies indebted to the Jews, his wife shall have her dower and pay nothing of that debt; if the deceased leaves children under age, they shall have necessities provided for them in keeping with the estate of the deceased, and the debt shall be paid out of the residue, reserving the service due to the deceased's feudal lords. So shall it be done with regard to debts owed persons other than Jews. No scutage or aid shall be imposed on Our kingdom unless by common counsel except to ransom Our person, make Our eldest son a knight, and once to marry Our eldest daughter, and for these only a reasonable aid shall be levied. So shall it be with regard to aids from the City of London:

The City of London shall have all her ancient liberties and free customs, both by land and water. Moreover, We decree and grant that all other cities, boroughs, towns, and ports shall have all their ancient liberties and free customs. For obtaining the common counsel of the realm for the assessment of aids (other than in the three cases aforesaid) or of scutage. We will cause to be summoned, severally, by Our letters, the archbishops, bishops, abbots, earls, and great barons; We will also cause to be summoned, generally, by Our sheriffs and bailiffs, and all others who hold lands directly of Us, to meet on a fixed day, but with at least forty days' notice, and at a fixed place. In all letters of such We will explain the cause thereof. The summons being thus made, the business shall proceed on the day appointed, according to the counsel of those who shall be present, although not all the persons summoned have come. We will not in the future allow any man to levy an aid upon his free men, except to ransom his person, make his eldest son a knight, and once to marry his eldest daughter, and on each of these occasions only a reasonable aid shall be levied. No man shall be compelled to perform more service for a knight's fee than is due therefrom.

Common Pleas shall not follow Our Court, but shall be held in some fixed place. Recognizances of "novel disseisin," "mort d'ancestor," and "darrein presentment" shall be taken only in their proper counties, We or, if We be absent from the realm, Our Chief Justiciary shall send two justiciaries through each county four times a year, who with four knights elected out of each county by the people thereof, shall hold the said assizes in the county court, on the day and in the place where that court meets. If the said assizes cannot be held on the day appointed, so many of the knights and freeholders as shall have been present on that day shall remain as will suffice for the administration of justice. A free man shall not be fined for a small offence only according to the measure thereof, and for a grave crime according to its magnitude, saving his means of livelihood, and in like manner a merchant saving his merchandise and a husbandman saving his village. None of these fines shall be imposed except by the oath of honest men of the neighbourhood. Earls and barons shall be fined only by their equals, and only in proportion to the measure of the offence. No fines shall be imposed upon a clerk's lay property, except after the manner of the other persons aforesaid, and without considering his ecclesiastical benefice. No village or individual shall be compelled to build bridges over rivers except those bound by ancient custom and law to do so. No sheriff, constable, coroners, or other of Our bailiffs shall hold pleas of Our Crown. All counties, hundreds, wapentakes, and tithings (except Our demesne manors) shall remain at the old rents, without any increase. If anyone holding a lay fee of Us shall die, and the sheriff or Our bailiff exhibit Our letters patent of summons for the debt due to Us from the deceased, it shall be lawful for such sheriff or bailiff to seize and catalogue the chattels of the deceased to the value of that debt as assessed by worthy men. If any free man shall die intestate, his chattels are to be distributed by his nearest kinsfolk and friends, under supervision of the church, saving to each creditor the debts owed him by the deceased. No constable or other of Our bailiffs shall take corn or other provisions from any man without immediate payment, unless the seller voluntarily consents to postponement of this. No constable shall compel any knight to pay money in lieu of castle-guard when the knight is willing to perform it in person or has some other free man to do it. No sheriff or officer of Our bailiffs, or any other man, shall take the horses or carts of any free man for transport without the owner's consent. Neither We nor Our bailiffs will take another man's wood for Our castles or for any other work without the owner's consent. We will retain the lands of persons convicted of felony for only a year and a day, after which they shall be returned to the lords of the fees. All fish-weirs shall be entirely removed from the Thames and Medway, and throughout England, except upon the seashore. The writ called 'precipe' shall not in the future be issued to anyone regarding any tenement if thereby a free man may not be tried in his lord's court. There shall be one measure of wine throughout Our realm, and one of ale, and one measure of corn, namely the London quarter, and one width of dyed cloth, russets, and haberjects, namely two ells within the selvedges. As with measures so shall it also be with weights. In future nothing shall be given or taken for a writ of inquisition upon life or limbs, but it shall be granted free and not be refused. If anyone holds of Us by fee-farm, socage, or burgage, and holds land of another by knight's service, we will not have the wardship of his heir, or of the land which belongs to another man's fee, on account of that fee-farm, socage, or burgage. In the future no bailiff shall upon his own unsupported accusation place any man upon trial without producing credible witnesses to the truth of the accusation. No free man shall be taken, imprisoned, outlawed, banished, or in any way destroyed, nor will We proceed against or prosecute him, except by the lawful judgment of his equals and by the law of the land. To no one will We sell, to no one will We deny or delay, right or justice. All merchants shall have safe conduct to go and come out of and into England, and to stay in and travel through England by land and water, for purposes of buying and selling, free of illegal tolls, in accordance with ancient and lawful customs, except in time of war. In the future it shall be lawful for anyone to leave and return to Our kingdom safely and securely by land and water, except those who have been imprisoned or outlawed according to the law of the land, people of a country at war with Us, and merchants, who shall be dealt with as aforesaid. If anyone die holding of some escheat such as the honour of Wallingford, Nottingham, Boulogne, Lancaster, or other escheats which are in Our hands and are baronies, his heir shall not give any relief or perform any service to Us other than he would owe to the baron. We will appoint as justiciaries, constables, sheriffs, or bailiffs only such men as know the law of the realm and will observe it well. All barons who have founded abbeys, evidenced by charters of English kings or ancient tenure, shall have the wardship of them when vacant. All forests which have been made in Our time shall forthwith be disafforested. So shall it be done with regard to river banks which have been enclosed in Our time. All evil customs connected with forests and warrens, foresters and warreners, sheriffs and their officers, or river banks and their wardens shall be immediately investigated in each county by twelve sworn knights of such county, chosen by honest men of that county, and shall within forty days after the inquest be completely and irrevocably abolished. We will immediately restore all hostages and charters delivered to Us by Englishmen as security for the peace or for the performance of loyal service. We will entirely remove from their bailiwicks the kinsmen of Gerard de Athyes, so that henceforth they shall hold no offices in England. As soon as peace is restored, We will banish from Our kingdom all foreign knights, crossbowmen, attendants, and mercenaries who have come with horses and arms to the harm of the kingdom

If anyone has been dispossessed or deprived by Us, without the legal judgment of his peers, of lands, castles, liberties, or rights, We will immediately restore them to him. And if any dispute shall arise thereupon, the matter shall be decided by judgment of the twenty-five barons.

Likewise, We shall have similar respite in rendering justice with respect to the disafforestation or retention of those forests which Henry Our Father or Richard Our Brother afforested, and concerning wardships of lands belonging to another's fee, and to abbeys founded in another's fee than Our own, whereto the lord of that fee asserts his rights. When We return from Our crusades, or if We remain behind from it, We will immediately grant full justice to the complainants in these matters.

No one shall be arrested or imprisoned upon a woman's appeal for the death of any other person than her husband.

All fines unjustly and unlawfully given to Us, and all fines levied unjustly and against the law of the land, shall be entirely remitted or the matter settled by judgment of the aforesaid Stephen, Archbishop of Canterbury, if he himself can be present.

If We have dispossessed or deprived the Welsh of lands, liberties, or other things, without legal judgment of their peers, in England or Wales, they shall immediately be restored to them. The same shall the Welsh do to Us and Ours. But with regard to all those things of which any Welshman was dispossessed or deprived, without Our legal judgment of his peers, by King Henry Our Father or Our Brother King Richard, and which We hold in Our hands or others hold under Our warranty, We should remain behind from it. We will Do full justice according to the laws of the Welsh and the aforesaid regions.

We will immediately restore the son of Llywelyn, all the Welsh hostages, and the charters which were delivered to Us as security for peace.

With regard to the return of the sisters and hostages of Alexander, King of the Scots, and of his liberties and rights, We will do the same as We would with regard to Our other barons of England.

All the customs and liberties aforesaid, which We have granted to be enjoyed, by Our people throughout Our kingdom, for all Our subjects, whether clerks or laymen, observe, toward their dependents.

Whereas We, for the honour of God and the amendment of Our kingdom, and in order the better to allay the discord arisen between Us and Our barons, have granted all these concessions aforesaid, We, willing that they be forever enjoyed wholly and in lasting strength, do give and grant to Our subjects the following security, to wit, that the barons shall elect any twenty-five barons of the realm, who shall, with their utmost power, observe, hold, and must to be observed the peace and liberties which We have granted unto them and by this Our present Charter have confirmed, so that if We, Our Justiciar, bailiffs, or any of Our ministers offend in any respect against any man, or shall transgress any of these articles of peace or security, and the offence be brought before four of the said twenty-five barons, those four barons shall come before Us, or Our Chief Justiciar if We are out of the kingdom, declaring the offence, and shall demand speedy amends for the same.

We have also wholly remitted and pardoned all ill-will, wrath, and malice which has arisen between Us and Our subjects, both clergy and laity. Moreover, We have fully remitted and, as far as in Us lies, wholly pardoned to and with all, clergy and laity, all trespasses made in consequence of the said disputes from Easter in the sixteenth year of Our reign till the restoration of peace. Over and above this, We have caused to be made in their behalf Letters patent by testimony of Stephen, Archbishop of Canterbury, Henry, Archbishop of Dublin, the Bishops above-mentioned, and Master Pandulf, for the security and concessions aforesaid.

Wherefore We will and firmly command that the English Church shall be free, and that all men in Our kingdom shall have and keep all the aforesaid liberties, rights, and concessions, well and peaceably, freely, quietly, fully, and wholly, to them and their heirs, of Us and Our heirs, in all things and places forever. Given by Our hand in the meadow which is called Runnymede, between Windsor and Staines, on the fifteenth day of June in the seventeenth year of Our reign.

1042

Edward the Confessor becomes King of England.

1066

William the Conqueror invades England from Normandy, defeating King Harold at the Battle of Hastings.

1086

The Domesday survey is carried out.

1100

King Henry I grants his Charter of Liberties.

1170

Thomas Becket, Archbishop of Canterbury, is murdered by King Henry II's knights in the Cathedral at Canterbury.

1199

King John comes to the throne.

1207

Pope Innocent III consecrates Stephen Langton as Archbishop of Canterbury.

1209

King John is excommunicated by Pope Innocent III.

1212

King John's forces are defeated by King Philip II of France at the Battle of Bouvines, in France.

1215

Archbishop Langton and the barons force King John to accept Magna Carta at Runnymede, June 15-19.

1216

King John dies at Newark Castle and is buried in Worcester Cathedral.

1225

Magna Carta is revised for the fourth and final time, and reissued by King Henry III.

1297

King Edward I confirms Magna Carta. This confirmation declares that the king's courts shall incorporate its provisions into the common law.

1301

King Edward I again confirms Magna Carta at the Lincoln Parliament, agreeing to annul all contrary statutes. The Charter is elevated to the position of a fundamental statute.

1492

Columbus sails to America.

1531

King Henry VIII is acknowledged by Convocation to be the Supreme Head of the Church of England, thus severing England's ties with the Roman Catholic Church.

1594

Sir Edward Coke, who revived the importance of Magna Carta, is appointed Attorney General to Queen Elizabeth I.

1603

James Stuart becomes King James I of England.

1606

The first Virginia Charter is drawn up — in part by Sir Edward Coke — granting the colonists in Virginia "all Liberties, Franchises, and Immunities" due to Englishmen.

1607

Captain John Smith and his fellow settlers sail to Jamestown, Virginia.

1610

Magna Carta (Chapter 41) is used in Bate's Case as a major precedent in a Court of Law.

1620

The Pilgrim Fathers sail to Plymouth Plantation, Massachusetts, signing the Mayflower Compact before they disembark onto American soil.

1625

The English Parliament presents the Petition of Right to King Charles I.

1630

The Massachusetts Bay Colony is settled under the leadership of Governor John Winthrop.

1633

The first settlement is begun in Connecticut.

1639

The freemen of Hartford, Windsor and Wethersfield draw up the Fundamental Orders of Connecticut — the first written constitution that created a government.

1641

The General Court of Massachusetts declares the Body of Liberties.

1642

Outbreak of the Civil War in England.

1649

King Charles I is beheaded, and England is declared a Commonwealth under Oliver Cromwell's Protectorate.

1679

Parliament passes the Habeas Corpus Act.

1682

Pennsylvania and the Delaware colonies are settled.

1687

William Penn publishes The Excellent Priviledge of Liberty and Property, with its translation and commentary on Magna Carta, the first such publication in America.

1688

The Glorious Revolution drives James II into exile.

1689

William and Mary are called to the throne. The English Bill of Rights is passed. John Locke's Two Treatises on Government are published.

1760

King George III comes to the throne.

1765

Parliament passes the Stamp Act, March 22. The Stamp Act Congress meets at New York, October 7-24.

1766

The Stamp Act is repealed, March 18.

1770

The Boston Massacre, March 5.

1773

The Boston Tea Party, December 16. The colonists protest against the East India Company's monopoly of tea exports to America.

1774

The first Continental Congress meets, September 5 - October 27.

1775

The beginning of the War of Independence; the Battles of Lexington and Concord, April 19; the Second Continental Congress assembles, May 10; the Battle of Bunker Hill, June 17.

1776

Common Sense, by Thomas Paine, is published in January. Virginia adopts the Virginia Bill of Rights, framed by George Mason, June 12. Declaration of Independence adopted, July 4.

1777

The Articles of Confederation are presented for ratification by the States, November 17.

1781

The Articles of Confederation are proclaimed, March 1.

1783

The United States and Great Britain sign a peace treaty at Versailles, September 3.

1786

The Annapolis Convention meets, September 11-14, and proposes that a special convention be called to revise the Articles of Confederation.

1787

The Constitutional Convention is held at Philadelphia, May 25-September 17. Delaware becomes the first state to ratify the Constitution, December 7.

1788

New Hampshire becomes the ninth, decisive state to ratify the Constitution, June 21.

1789

The First Congress of the United States accepts a joint resolution proposing twelve amendments to the Constitution, September 25.

1791

The State of Virginia becomes the eleventh state to ratify the proposed Articles 3-12, December 15. The First Ten Amendments, known as the Bill of Rights, are therefore adopted.

SOURCES

★

Adams, John, *Legal Papers*, Vol. II, eds. L. Kinvin Wroth & Hiller B. Zobel, Cambridge, Mass., Belknap Press, 1965.

American Bar Foundation, eds. Richard L. Perry & John C. Cooper, *Sources of Our Liberties*, Rahway, N.J., Quinn & Boden Co., 1959.

Appleby, John T., *John King of England*, New York, Alfred A. Knopf, 1959.

Bowen, Catherine Drinker, *The Lion and the Throne*, Boston, Little, Brown & Co., 1956.

Bowle, John, *Charles the First*, Boston, Little, Brown & Co., 1975.

Chrimes, S. B., *English Constitutional History*, London, Oxford University Press, 1967.

Commager, Henry S., *Documents of American History*, New York, Appleton-Century-Crofts, Inc., 1948.

Cook, A. M., *Lincolnshire Links with the U.S.A.*, Lincoln, The Sub-deanery, 1956.

Corwin, Samuel, *The Foundation of American Constitutional Thought*, Vol. 1, ed. Richard Loss, Ithaca and London, Cornell University Press, 1981.

Churchill, Winston S., *A History of the English-Speaking Peoples*, Vol. II, New York, Dodd, Mead & Co., 1956.

Friedman, Lawrence M., *Law and Society,* , Edgecliff, N. J., Prentice Hall, 1977.

Gregg, Pauline, *King Charles I*, London, J. M. Dent & Sons, Ltd., 1981.

Hamilton, Alexander, James Madison, & John Jay, *The Federalist Papers*, New York, The New American Library, 1961.

Holt, James C., *Magna Carta*, Cambridge, Cambridge University Press, 1965.

Howard, A. E. Dick, *The Road from Runnymede*, Charlottesville, University of Virginia Press, 1968.

Jensen, Merrill, ed., *Tracts of the American Revolution, 1763-1766*, Indianapolis, The Bobbs, Merrill Co., 1967.

Jolliffe, J. E. A., *The Constitutional History of Medieval England*, New York, W. W. Norton & Co., 1961.

Kenyon, J. P., *Stuart England*, Harmondsworth, Penguin Books, Ltd., 1978.

Locke, John, *Two Treatises of Government*, ed. Peter Laslett, Cambridge, Cambridge University Press, 1960.

Macaulay, Thomas Babington, *The History of England from the Accession of James II*, Vol. I, Philadelphia, Porter & Coates, N. D.

Maitland, Frederic W., *The Constitutional History of England*, ed. H. A. L. Fisher, Cambridge, Cambridge University Press, 1965.

McIllwain, Charles H., *The Political Works of James I*, Cambridge, Harvard University Press, 1918.

McKechnie, William S., *Magna Carta*, New York, Burt Franklin, 1914.

Painter, Sidney, *The Reign of King John*, Baltimore, Johns Hopkins Press, 1949.

Powicke, F. M., *Stephen Langton*, New York, Barnes & Noble, 1965.

Rutland, Robert A., *The Birth of the Bill of Rights*, Chapel Hill, University of North Carolina Press, 1983.

Stephenson, Carl & Frederick G. Marcham, eds., *Sources of English Constitutional History*, New York, Harper & Brothers, 1937.

Thompson, Faith, *The First Century of Magna Carta*, Minneapolis, University of Minnesota Press, 1925.

Thompson, Faith, *Magna Carta: its role in the making of the English Constitution, 1300-1629*, Minneapolis, University of Minnesota Press, 1925.

Trevelyan, George, M., *History of England*, London, Longmans, Green & Co., 1926.

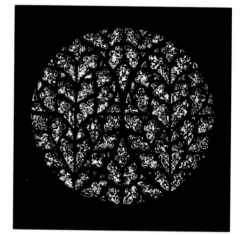

★

The "Bishop's Eye" rose window, in the south transept of Lincoln Cathedral.

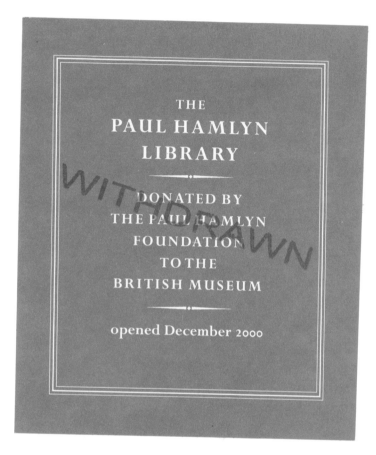

Museum Education

at The Art Institute of Chicago

THE ART INSTITUTE OF CHICAGO *Museum Studies*

THE ART INSTITUTE OF CHICAGO *Museum Studies*

Volume 29, no. 1

© 2003 by The Art Institute of Chicago

ISSN 0069–3235

ISBN 0–86559–202–0

Published semiannually by The Art Institute of Chicago, 111 South Michigan Avenue, Chicago, Illinois 60603–6110. Regular subscription rates: $20 for members of the Art Institute, $25 for other individuals, and $40 for institutions. Subscribers outside the U.S.A. should add $8 per year for postage. For more information, call (312) 443–3786 or consult our Web site at www.artic.edu/aic/books.

For individuals, single copies are $15 each. For institutions, all single copies are $19 each. For orders of single copies outside the U.S.A., please add $5 per copy. Back issues are available from The Art Institute of Chicago Museum Shop or from the Publications Department of the Art Institute at the address above.

Executive Director of Publications: Susan F. Rossen; Editor of *Museum Studies*: Gregory Nosan; Designer: Jeffrey D. Wonderland; Production: Sarah E. Guernsey; Subscription and Circulation Manager: Bryan D. Miller.

Volume 29, no. 1, was printed by Meridian Printing, East Greenwich, Rhode Island, and bound by Midwest Editions, Minneapolis, Minnesota.

Opposite: detail of Rice fig. 10.

Front cover: (top) detail of Nosan fig. 21; (bottom, from left) details of Rhor fig. 7, Eskridge fig. 12, and Rhor p. 29.

Back cover: (from left) details of Rhor p. 25, Eskridge fig. 11.

This issue of Museum Studies was made possible through a generous gift from the Woman's Board of The Art Institute of Chicago in celebration of its fiftieth anniversary. Ongoing support for Museum Studies has been provided by a grant for scholarly catalogues and publications from The Andrew W. Mellon Foundation.

Contents

Museum Studies, Volume 29, No. 1

Museum Education at The Art Institute of Chicago

Preface

One of the Art Institute's many strengths is its long tradition of reaching out to the wider community through education. Through its outreach efforts, the museum defines itself not simply as a repository of precious objects, for the edification of a select few, but rather as a teaching institution, open to all. For the last five decades, a major force driving this inclusive vision has been a cadre of volunteers, most of them women, many of whom have been drawn to the museum through the efforts of the Woman's Board of The Art Institute of Chicago. This year, as one way of celebrating its golden anniversary of service to the Art Institute, the Woman's Board underwrote the publication of this innovative history of museum education. While this issue of *The Art Institute of Chicago Museum Studies* includes a history of the board and its commitment to art education and volunteerism, I would like to preface the discussion by considering, in a broad way, how women volunteers have driven the museum's mission in the past, and how they may—or may not—continue to shape it in the future.

In an attempt to explain why people volunteer in the first place, the management expert Peter Drucker suggested that "working as unpaid staff for a nonprofit institution…gives people a sense of community, gives purpose, gives direction."[1] I, however, would argue that the reverse is also true—that at the Art Institute it is the volunteers who have brought to this institution a sense of responsibility to the greater community. Beginning in the 1950s, women volunteers have been instrumental in defining the museum's role as one of active service to a wide and varied audience. For example, when these early volunteers recognized the need for a special children's space and guidance service, they responded to it directly through programs that they established, nurtured, and ultimately entrusted to professional staff to continue.

Understanding the critical role that such women have played in the history of nonprofit organizations such as the Art Institute, though, only heightens the concern that they may become an endangered species. *In Bowling Alone: The Collapse and Revival of American Community*, sociologist Robert D. Putnam offered the reassuring fact that "philanthropy and volunteering are roughly twice as common among Americans as among the citizens of other countries."[2] But he also reminded his readers that "the movement of women into the paid workforce" was "among the most far-reaching upheavals in American society during the twentieth century."[3] In addition to changing the nature of work and home life from the 1970s onward, this development has also meant that, unlike their forebears in the 1950s, fewer women choose to engage in nonpaid work now that other options are open to them. In fact, Putnam reported that, all other things being equal, women who work full time presently volunteer half as often as those who do not.[4]

While there is fierce competition for the limited discretionary time of potential volunteers, the real challenge facing nearly all cultural institutions is to attract and retain their volunteer corps by recognizing the vitality and creativity they bring to their work, and by respecting and supporting their efforts. Without the longtime commitment of volunteers—and of women volunteers in particular—the character of The Art Institute of Chicago would be not only less vital, but far less inclusive. To acknowledge this fifty-year tradition and keep it alive are key, and it is my hope that this publication will help make that possible.

Cleopatra B. Alexander

President
The Woman's Board of The Art Institute of Chicago, 2000–03

Introduction and Acknowledgments

A museum comes alive when it is filled with the public for which it was built. It is altogether appropriate, then, that an issue of *Museum Studies* should at long last be devoted to the history of how the museum has interpreted its holdings and exhibitions to its audiences.

The four essays in this special publication investigate how the Art Institute, founded in 1879 at the center of one of the nation's most dynamic cities, has understood and responded to the particular needs and interests of a community that has developed in as complex and diverse a way as the museum's collection itself. Authors have immersed themselves in archival documents and images, oral accounts, and American museum history in the widest sense, working to chart the many ways in which the Art Institute has sought to help viewers more fully experience the objects within its walls. In her introductory essay, Danielle Rice, Director of Program at the Philadelphia Museum of Art, sets the stage by reminding us that education exists not at the periphery, but at the very center of museum work, and that it dramatizes the sometimes uneasy combination of responsibilities that lies at the heart of the institutions we serve. In the articles that follow, art historian and educator Sylvia Rhor; *Museum Studies* editor Gregory Nosan; and Robert Eskridge, the Woman's Board Endowed Executive Director of Museum Education at the Art Institute delve into the ways in which the Art Institute has approached its educational mission for the past 124 years. While each essay tells its own story, each also shows how the museum has reshaped its role as a center of public education in response to both the character of its audiences and larger shifts in American culture. These contributors' combined efforts have resulted in a publication that we hope will serve as a model of its kind for years to come. The more we understand our institutional and professional past, the closer we come to achieving that considered self-awareness which can inform our current work for the better.

Many staff in the museum's departments of Archives, Graphic Design and Communication Services, Imaging, Museum Education, and Publications worked hard to bring this ambitious project to completion, and we owe them a great debt of thanks. We offer our deepest gratitude, however, to the Woman's Board of The Art Institute of Chicago, which demonstrated its ongoing support of museum education by funding this publication, which also celebrates the organization's fiftieth anniversary. While the Woman's Board's singular dedication to developing and sustaining educational programs over the past half century is written about here, it is also exemplified by the efforts of the many longtime board members who graciously dedicated their time and labor to this project.

As this issue of *Museum Studies* goes to press, the Art Institute is set to take another defining step in its history, in the shape of a bold, new wing designed by the renowned architect Renzo Piano. One of the primary purposes of this structure is to improve and expand our educational facilities, and to make the Art Institute an increasingly accessible and attractive center of learning for audiences of all ages. As plans move forward, this issue of *Museum Studies* will both remind us of our significant accomplishments in carrying out our educational mission in the past, and help us sustain our clarity of purpose in the future.

James N. Wood

Director and President
The Art Institute of Chicago

Balancing Act:

Education and the Competing Impulses of Museum Work

Danielle Rice

Art is not destined for a small and privileged class. Art is democratic, it is of the people, and for the people and from the people have come some of its greatest creators. . . . Everyone to whom is entrusted the conduct of an Art Museum asks himself often and seriously, "What is the proper function of an Art Museum?" In former years this was usually answered by saying that it should preserve and care for the permanent collections entrusted to its keeping, to publish the catalogues of the same, and keep the galleries open under more or less severe restrictions to the public. But this answer no longer suffices. The Art Museum of today, if it properly fulfills its function, is no longer a mere storehouse. It must offer to the public changing exhibitions of contemporaneous Art. It should be the center of the artistic activities of the community in which it exists. The most successful Art Museum of today is at once a storehouse, a college, and a general exchange for the Art of the whole community.

Charles L. Hutchinson, c. 1915[1]

In this address to the Chicago Literary Club, the prominent businessman and Art Institute patron Charles L. Hutchinson (see fig. 2) voiced his ambitious vision of the public art museum's social potential by drawing upon an unexpected, iconic precedent: Abraham Lincoln's 1863 Gettysburg Address. Hutchinson echoed Lincoln's speech in a clever stroke of rhetorical borrowing, describing art—rather than government—as being "of the people, and for the people and from the people." Art, he seemed to imply, springs from the same impulses as American democracy, and in so doing takes on some of its patriotic, public power.

Hutchinson's choice of words reveals the central place that aesthetic experience, and museums as purveyors of that experience, played in his vision of community life. For Hutchinson and many of his moment, public museums such as The Art Institute of Chicago were a native, egalitarian alternative to "aristocratic" European galleries, and did their jobs best by turning outward and gearing their efforts squarely toward enriching the daily lives of a broad public in the most innovative ways possible. As American art museums have evolved since Hutchinson's time, their mission to be public, thoroughly accessible institutions has been interpreted and reinterpreted in a vari-

Figure 1 While originating the museum's program of gallery lectures, Art Institute director William M. R. French (1841–1914) was also an educator in his own right, offering popular slide presentations and "chalk talks" such as the one shown here.

ety of ways. With changing definitions of what it means to be "democratic" have come a variety of approaches to exhibition and public education. At different periods, for example, art museums have focused more intently on appealing to certain members of their core audiences, at times privileging artists and craftspeople, and at other times shifting their attention to so-called ordinary citizens. Educators have changed their programs both in form and content, adapting to shifting currents within art history and educational theory, and reaching out to new constituencies by taking advantage of innovations in information technology.

While wrestling side by side with the recurring issues of audience and accessibility, however, museum educators and curators have also been engaged in a long-standing debate about what art is and why it matters, and, by extension, how it should be presented to the general public. For professional museum educators—who have most often regarded art

objects as multivalent windows onto the history of human culture and creative endeavor—exhibition labels, public presentations, and general-audience publications have proven to be crucial means of making that history accessible. Their curatorial colleagues typically have taken an adversarial position by arguing that art, through its appeal to imagination and the senses, suffers from being overinterpreted; to this way of thinking, education need only, as Henry James put it, "be exclusively that of the sense of beauty."[2] To proponents of this second, aesthetic approach, any educator's attempt to stand between viewers and their intuitive, private communion with art objects registers as not only counterproductive, but downright misleading. Also often at odds with the accessibility issue so dear to public educators are traditional practices of connoisseurship, in which specialists, through years of focused study, aim to be as precise as possible about such issues as authenticity, dating, style, the artist's sources, subtleties of meaning, and so forth. As important as all of these considerations (which for brevity I categorize here as "aesthetic") are for a small audience of like-minded scholars and students, they can be difficult to communicate to a broad audience and equally difficult for that audience to understand.

The long history of this struggle, and of the relationship between museum education and wider practices of collecting and exhibiting art, is of course more complicated than this simple, binary model of educator vs. curator, didactic vs. aesthetic, suggests. At many moments and in various museums, educators have worked to attune their audiences to art's formal or aesthetic qualities, and curators have attempted to place works within historical contexts. What I hope to show here, however, is that this opposition between didacticism and aestheticism is a persistent and powerful one, and that while the attitudes and objectives of museum educators and curators have actually flip-flopped in recent years, the basic polarity remains in place. Indeed, these approaches—not to mention the work of the museum professionals who practice them daily—actually express and balance the conflicting impulses that lie at the heart of museum work. Is it better, for example, to envision looking at art as a private, aesthetic sort of experience or a social, didactic one? To see museums as inward-focused institutions devoted to collecting and preserving art, or as major forces for public education and social transformation?

Rather than offering a comprehensive history of museum education, about which much has been written, I would like to begin by briefly suggesting the changing ways in which American art museums have defined their audiences—and viewed their educative responsibilities to those audiences—over time.[3] The nation's first museum, established by Charles Willson Peale in Philadelphia in 1784, was not, strictly speaking, an art museum. A true product of the Enlightenment's emphasis on broad intellectual inquiry, Peale aimed to provide his audiences with "rational amusement" by guiding them from familiar objects toward novel ones, thus encouraging their inquisitiveness.[4] His displays featured a wide variety of "learned curiosities," including stuffed fish and mammals, mastodon bones, Native American artifacts, a zoo, and his own paintings (see fig. 3). It was the latter, and in particular his portraits of leaders of the newly formed United States, that received pride of place in his museum and in the natural and national hierarchies it worked to establish.[5] These grand, heroic images were intended to instruct the citizens of the new republic, inspiring feelings of patriotism and civic responsibility while also reminding them of humanity's superior place in the great chain of being.

Peale's institution typified most early-nineteenth-century American museums, blending spectacle and entertainment with art and natural history, striving for and often receiving widespread public interest. Since education and amusement were not considered mutually exclusive enterprises at that time, learning in these museums was seen as naturally pleasurable. As the cultural historian Lawrence W. Levine pointed out, before the 1870s Americans made little distinction between popular diversions and what we now call high culture. In institutions such as P. T. Barnum's American Museum in New York (see fig. 4), painting and sculpture were not elevated above other forms of art, but were placed alongside waxworks and singing dwarfs in displays that appealed to audiences of all social stations.[6] This cultural climate began to change in

Figure 3 Charles Willson Peale (American; 1741–1827). *The Artist in His Museum*, 1822. Oil on canvas; 263.5 x 202.9 cm (103 3/4 x 79 7/8 in.). Pennsylvania Academy of Fine Arts, Gift of Mrs. Sarah Harrison (The Joseph Harrison Jr. Collection).

Figure 4 William England (English; 1830–1896). Barnum's American Museum, at the corner of Broadway and Park Row, New York, 1858. Taken for the London Stereoscopic Company. Courtesy Picture History.

Figure 5 John Watkins (English; died 1908). *The South Court of the South Kensington Museum*, London, c. 1876. Ink on paper; 33.8 x 48.1 cm (13 1/4 x 18 5/8 in.). © The Board of Trustees of the Victoria & Albert Museum, London.

the last third of the century, due in large part to what Levine referred to as the "sacralization of culture," an impulse to elevate certain elements of artistic endeavor above others.[7] People began to see art, in particular, as possessing divine qualities capable of lifting humanity above its baser instincts and toward a more virtuous existence. In Henry James's 1875 novel *Roderick Hudson*, for instance, a Midwestern philanthropist remarks that "the office of art is second only to that of religion," and many of the practicing artists of the period would have agreed.[8] Not surprisingly, then, the post–Civil War economic boom gave rise to a number of museums devoted to promoting art's new, spiritualized power to inspire, refine, and elevate both taste and morality. These new cathedrals to art included the Metropolitan Museum of Art, New York (1870); the Museum of Fine Arts, Boston (1870); the Cincinnati Art Museum (1873); the Philadelphia Museum of Art (1876); and the Art Institute of Chicago (1879; see fig. 6).

Many of these institutions were inspired by and modeled on London's South Kensing-

ton Museum (now the Victoria and Albert Museum; see fig. 5), which opened in 1857. Devoted to the decorative arts, it was a product of the 1851 "Great Exhibition of the Works of Industry of All Nations," held in the splendid Crystal Palace in Hyde Park. Like that exposition, the museum was created to educate manufacturers of useful goods whose taste and standards of quality had declined, its founders argued, due to increased dependence on cheap materials and on methods of mass production. The South Kensington experiment established its international reputation for effectively uniting forward-thinking design with a social and commercial vision, and directing its efforts at the broadest possible public. The idealism of the enterprise embraced all segments of society in its belief that art could elevate taste, and in so doing inspire people to act for the greater good.[9]

In addition to showcasing decorative arts, the new American museums acquired plaster casts of famous classical sculptures and reproductions of Renaissance sculpture and paintings, continuing a collecting practice that had been popular since the early nineteenth century (see fig. 7).[10] Such works constituted the contemporary canon of taste, and were seen to exemplify the best that civilization has to offer. By the 1880s and 1890s, however, the pursuit of authenticity—what art historian Allan Wallach termed the "cult of the original"—meant that the casts which had formed the core of so many museum collections were supplanted by individual, original works of art.[11]

This transition represented a deep shift in the way that American museums defined, collected, and exhibited art, and conceived of their public mission. While replicas and handicrafts were primarily used to train the artists who studied and copied them, original paintings and sculptures were displayed for the express purpose of giving aesthetic pleasure. As one proponent of the original argued in the early 1900s, "The Museum is for... those who come, not to be educated, but to make its treasures their friends for life and their

Figure 7 View of the Art Institute's Michigan Avenue lobby, c. 1901/10. At center, in the space now occupied by the Museum Shop, was a gallery of plaster casts of antique sculpture, which included a prominent replica of the Nike of Samothrace (c. 190 B.C., Museé du Louvre, Paris).

standards of beauty. Joy, not knowledge, is the aim of contemplating a painting."[12] Art was seen to speak a universal, affective language accessible to all. From this notion sprang one of the great paradoxes underlying the practice of museum education: while aesthetes argued that anyone who could see could easily be stirred and inspired by the beauty of an object if its setting was appropriately resplendent, the fact was that many visitors remained unmoved, and even found the new museums' grand buildings strange and forbidding.[13]

Founders and trustees, who celebrated the role of their creations as temples of beauty and repositories of original masterpieces, soon discovered that they had to articulate, to an audience with little or no background in art, what it was that made these expensive, rare, and unique works so special. Museum educators—who did the explaining—thus came to play an essential role in achieving the goal of public accessibility that has remained at the core of these increasingly complex insti-

tutions. As early as 1895, William M. R. French, first director of The Art Institute of Chicago, appointed special lecturers "as a means of popularizing the galleries and making collections more useful to the public," and even served as one himself (see fig. 1).[14] Boston's Museum of Fine Arts, which is often regarded as the first American museum to embrace the aesthetic definition of art, initiated one of the most long-lived and influential education programs in the country. In 1907 the institution's chief executive officer, Benjamin Ives Gilman, coined the term "docent" (from the Latin *docere*, "to teach") to describe his volunteer guides, whom he charged with introducing visitors to the basics of art appreciation. Sermonizing and celebratory, these tours reflected the aestheticist approach to art that was predominant at the time, emphasizing the beauty and singularity of the works on display.

Throughout the 1910s and 1920s, museums began to devise many forms of educational programming that remain in place today, including tours for children, gallery talks for the general public, courses for teachers, and even offerings for the deaf and the blind. Indeed, by 1924 one researcher was able to characterize the art museum's service to the community as falling into five substantial categories: "For the Enjoyment of the Public," "For Advancement of Artists and Art Students," "To Aid the Expert," "To Serve Industry," and "For the Benefit of Children."[15] The 1930s, the decade of the New Deal and the Works Progress Administration (WPA), witnessed a remarkable expansion of educational activity in American museums. The economic strains of the Great Depression forced institutions to pursue government funding, which meant convincing public officials of their worth by increasing their services to the general population (see figs. 8–9).[16] In his 1930 annual report, for instance, Fiske Kimball, director of the Philadelphia Museum of Art, devoted five paragraphs to the newly founded Education Department. At the Art Institute, Daniel Catton Rich made education one of his top priorities in his first report as museum director to the board of trustees, in 1938. One year later, Rich reorganized the Children's Museum, which featured small exhibitions designed for young visitors, into the Gallery of Art Interpretation, which was to become the first interpretive space for adults established by an American museum (see Rohr, pp. 41–44).[17] It was also in the 1930s that researchers began to publish focused studies of museum audiences. Edward S. Robinson and Arthur W. Melton, for example, each applied the methods of behavioral psychology to examine how visitors responded to art exhibits. While the American Association of Museums, the professional body of museum employees, sponsored Robinson's research, the Carnegie Foundation, creator of libraries throughout the country, supported the work of Paul M. Rea, who analyzed demographic

data, attendance figures, and visitor services to determine how effectively museums fulfilled their public mandate.[18] These studies identified, among other things, a growing gap between the aesthetic approach to art, as emphasized in elegant but minimally interpreted gallery settings, and a public who clamored for specific information to help them make sense of the objects on view.

Many museum educators at this time felt as the director of the Brooklyn Museum of Art, Philip Youtz, did when he coined the term "museumitis" in 1934 to describe the fatigue that visitors often experienced in the pristine museum galleries of the time. Calling for a more historical and socially relevant approach to art, Youtz, a former museum educator, charged that art-appreciation courses had failed because they had neglected "the rich fabric" of a culture and made an "idol" of art.[19] Youtz's sentiments were mirrored by other museum directors and by leading educators of the period such as Theodore L. Low (Baltimore Museum of Art), Victor d'Amico (Museum of Modern Art, New York), and Francis Henry Taylor (Metropolitan Museum of Art, New York), who called for a con-

Figure 8 Charles Burkholder, Director of Finance and Operation for the Art Institute, signs a permit allowing unemployed visitors to enter the Century of Progress Exhibition free of charge, 1933. Burkholder (at center) was joined by Mrs. Lewis and Mr. Moss of the Illinois Department of Public Welfare (at left) and Walter J. Sherwood, the Art Institute's Manager of Printing and Publications.

Figure 9 This screen-
printed invitation was
created for the 1938
exhibition "Art For the
Public," which showcased
the work of Chicago
artists who were involved
in the Federal Arts Project
of the Works Progress
Administration.

Figure 9 This screen-printed invitation was created for the 1938 exhibition "Art For the Public," which showcased the work of Chicago artists who were involved in the Federal Arts Project of the Works Progress Administration.

textual approach to art even while they knew that they could not stem the tide of aestheticism in museum practice.

From the 1940s well into the 1970s, the gap between curatorial practice and museum education remained in place, as art museums continued to collect and exhibit the finest original masterpieces they could afford. Even as they instituted formal education programs to better serve their information-hungry audiences, many museum directors embraced an aesthetic definition of art. For example, Philadelphia's Fiske Kimball declared in 1942, "All the work of a museum—in acquiring and displaying its collections, quite as much as interpreting them—ministers to education, as well as to immediate enjoyment."[20] As late as 1978, Sherman E. Lee, director of the Cleveland Museum of Art, saw the museum's primary function as exhibiting beautiful objects in a beautiful setting. In that year, he wrote, "In the world of visual images…the museum is the primary source for education. Merely by existing—by preserving and exhibiting works of art—it is educational in the broadest and best sense, though it never utters a sound or prints a word."[21]

Art historian Andrew McClellan has recently argued that, while aestheticist thinking may appear elitist on the surface, it is actually rooted in a utopian belief in art's power to inspire. This line of argument holds that the encounter with a powerful art object in a perfectly conceived museum atmosphere can lead to a deeply transformative experience, one that is ultimately more lasting than

any educational endeavor.[22] Thus, paradoxically, some of the most conservative art museums in the country, such as Lee's Cleveland Museum, were often the most supportive of museum education. Educators, however, had to know their place. Museum instructors, often women working in basement offices, occupied a position of low status, and had to tread lightly in the hallowed halls where art supposedly spoke for itself (see fig. 10). Identified by curators and administrators with the non-specialist audiences they were committed to serving, and condemned for trying to trivialize sacred, intuitive encounters with art by explaining them away, museum educators often found themselves in conflict with the values of the very institutions they were hired to represent.[23]

It was not until the politically radical and socially conscious 1960s and 1970s that the debate about the nature of museum education began to shift. The operative word of this period was "relevance," as museums began to reach out to their audiences by meeting them at least half-way. In 1968 Thomas P. Hoving, the innovative director of the Metropolitan Museum of Art, urged his colleagues at the American Association of Museums to engage with their audiences' interests and needs on a far deeper level than formerly.[24] Taking his own advice, Hoving mounted "Harlem on My Mind: Cultural Capital of Black America, 1900–1968" (see fig. 11). While generating enormous controversy and criticism, this exhibition was also a watershed event in art-museum history: it inaugurated the era of the blockbuster, and can also be credited with bringing popular culture and multimedia technology into the world of high art.[25] Museum educators at this time developed new methods for making art relevant to their audiences, and embraced dance, music, poetry, and a variety of language-based approaches to help diverse populations discover the visual arts.[26] As one veteran museum educator recalls of this moment: "It seems to me that everywhere museums were trying hard to open their portals, let the stuffiness escape, and let the good times roll in the galleries."[27]

The traditional quarrel over whether art is better regarded as a source of aesthetic pleasure or as a focus of intellectual effort continues to shape the practice of museum education to this day. Over the last twenty years, however, both the terms of the debate and the positions of its contestants have shifted substantially.[28] In the 1970s, while museums continued to cele-

brate the power of the emotive encounter with original works, art history, the base discipline of most art-museum professionals, began to change. Scholars started to question the accepted artistic hierarchies—the favoring of Western over non-Western works and of painting over decorative art, for example—that had served museums as powerful organizing principles for so long. They also began to consider the social and cultural contexts in which art is made and understood.[29] This led them to challenge the often unreflective ways in which museums display their collections. For example, while often presented as neutral backdrops for art, museum spaces are in fact often carefully conceived for maximum theatricality, and inevitably privilege some objects over others. Likewise, the layout of a sequence of galleries can further inforce a particular narrative of "mainstream," canonical art, marginalizing or eliminating works that that do not

Figure 10 Art Institute staff lecturer Margaret Dangler looks at European paintings with a group of Chicago Public School students, c. 1960. Then, as now, women constituted the majority of the museum's education staff.

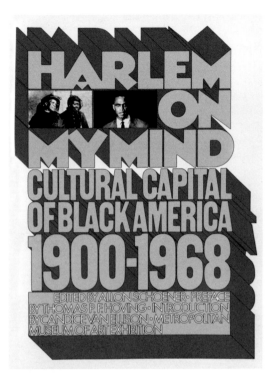

texts and objects on display.[31] Strangely enough, since the early 1990s, the increased art-historical emphasis on context, combined with new information about visitor learning preferences and styles, has led curators and educators to subtly reverse their traditional roles. Throughout most of the twentieth century, curators generally eschewed the use of didactic labels in favor of letting art speak for itself, while educators fought for verbal and written information of all kinds. Indeed, it was educators who argued for evaluations and visitor studies in order to help art museums communicate with their audiences more effectively. In the past decade, however, the pendulum has swung in the other direction. Many curators, influenced by contemporary academic approaches, are much more interested in using an exhibition, gallery talk, or publication to explore a work's cultural content and provide viewers with rich contextual and interpretive information.

No longer relegated to the margins, museum educators are now engaged in exhibiting art as well as making it accessible to visitors of all ages. Indeed, they work alongside curators to develop object labels, didactic panels, contextual displays, and interactive media that all serve to communicate carefully orchestrated "exhibition scripts" to their audiences. With their help, contextually rich, imaginatively interpreted installations and exhibitions have become the norm at art museums around the world. At the Victoria and Albert Museum, London, for instance, the planners behind the newly installed British Galleries succeeded in displaying objects beautifully, but also took pains to present them within a dazzling array of other features—family play areas, informational labels, digital videos, and interactive, computer-based information centers—that enable visitors with a range of experiences, interests, and learning styles to engage with

Figure 11 Designed by Herb Lubalin and Ernie Smith and edited by Allon Schoener, the catalogue for "Harlem on My Mind" gave visual expression to that 1968 exhibition's strong political and documentary goals, which included treating the audience itself as a "creative force."

neatly fit the story. Starting in the 1970s, moreover, academics began rejecting the notion of a "masterpiece" capable of educating and transforming viewers merely through its electrifying presence. Individual objects, instead of being seen as pleasing combinations of formal elements, came to be regarded as "elements of discourse" existing within a variety of belief systems, historical periods, and socioeconomic forces.[30]

While changes in art history have led to new ways of thinking about art, recent developments in art education and cognitive psychology have also altered the way in which museums understand and approach their audiences. Institutions no longer envision themselves as the creators of affective, aesthetic experiences for visitors who are content to passively receive them. Instead, museumgoers are now recognized as active agents who possess diverse backgrounds, assumptions, and learning styles, and who enter into a dialogue with one another and with the many art in their own ways. These professionals took audience research into account, adjusting their interpretive materials so that the exhibits would actually succeed in conveying the messages they intended them to.[32] In the galleries (see fig. 12), labels offer compelling, grabby headlines that capture viewer interest, and the presence of high-quality digital videos makes it virtually impossible to go through the exhibition looking only at the art. Rather than distracting audiences, however, this use of media aims to reinforce and enhance the act of seeing the original works on display.

Other contemporary museum educators, however, have sought less didactic, more aesthetically oriented ways to help visitors engage with art. They have emerged as proponents of an antididactic, "back to basics" movement that focuses on aesthetic experience. This effort places great store in the pleasure that can be gained by simply looking closely at an original

work of art and arriving at diverse, personal meanings from moments of intense perception. At the center of this movement is a program called Visual Thinking Strategies (VTS), developed in the late 1990s by cognitive psychologist Abigail Housen and Philip Yenawine, former Director of Education at the Museum of Modern Art, New York.[33] Together, Housen and Yenawine have invented a teaching technique for classroom use that relies on open-ended questions such as "What is going on here?" "What do you see that makes you say that?" and "What more do you see?" Such queries are used to guide students through the process of making their own meanings from art objects (see fig. 13). While educators facilitate these conversations, often repeating and rephrasing responses, they refrain from adding their own interpretive remarks into the mix.

Not surprisingly, the VTS program has gained a great degree of popularity in museum

Figure 12 The British Galleries at London's Victoria and Albert Museum, opened in late 2001, offer an influential model of how museum curators and educators are working together to display objects within an environment that includes cutting-edge audio, video, and interactive technologies. Photo: Deery Moore. © The Board of Trustees of the Victoria & Albert Museum, London.

Figure 13 Art educator Philip Yenawine shares the Visual Thinking Strategies teaching method with grade-school students in Bishkek, Ukraine.

settings. Whereas the many adherents of the traditional, Socratic approach to gallery instruction led visitors to see what they wanted them to see, this new method is open-ended, allowing viewers to identify visual evidence and create their own interpretations without introducing them to scholarly debates or expert opinions. Operating within a larger culture that is increasingly saturated by visual information, museum educators urgently seek ways to help authentic art objects make a deep, lasting impact on viewers. Moreover, the approach's emphasis on assisting individuals in looking more closely at art, and formulating their own opinions based on what they see, has offered educators a new way of balancing the traditionally opposed elements of intuitive, aesthetic response and didactic instruction. In this case, aesthetic experience receives the lion's share of attention, but is no longer treated as some inviolate, personal relationship between a viewer and an art object that is off-limits to educators, or one that only the most experienced and knowledgable can achieve. Indeed, the educator ideally helps shape the viewer's experience, stepping in not as an authority rendering judgment or spoon-feeding infor-

mation, but as an expert whose job is to help audiences articulate their own observations on and responses to art more clearly and powerfully.

Negotiating the polarities innate to the art-museum enterprise—between elitism and democracy, preservation and public access, for example—seems particularly important now that large American institutions have begun to recover the broad popularity they had in Peale's day, before the quasireligious aestheticism of the late nineteenth century chased out the popular casts, reproductions, and other nonart elements along with much of the public. As today's museum administrators respond to economic constraints and opportunities by marketing their institutions through crowd-pleasing blockbuster exhibitions and expanding attractions to include shops, restaurants, and catering services, they participate in blurring the very boundaries between high and popular culture that their predecessors, however inadvertently, helped construct. While some critics have complained that museums have abandoned serious educational efforts and remade themselves as theme parks, the fact is that education departments in art museums throughout the country have continued to flourish. Indeed, since 1992 museums have increased their investments in public education by an impressive ninety-six percent.[34]

Museum education has been called the "uncertain profession," in part because of its shifting disciplinary boundaries and the many intellectual and practical methods that have influenced its development.[35] Elsewhere, I have suggested that this uncertainty proceeds not from any deficiency within the field itself, but rather as a result of its practitioners' varied attempts to handle the frictions inherent in an environment that has tended to encourage object acquisition and preservation over education, scholarly innovation over intellectual accessibility, and esotericism over popularity.[36]

As we have seen, it is in the dynamism of these conflicts—in this case, between letting works speak for themselves and finding a way to help audiences interpret them—that the story lies, not in resolving the issues, but in engaging with them in innovative and increasingly subtle ways over time. As museum educators continue their balancing act, perhaps it is exactly this position, as dramatists of the very conceptual oppositions that at once vex and sustain their institutions, which helps make their work as rewarding and important as it is.

Every Walk of Life and Every Degree of Education:
Museum Instruction at The Art Institute of Chicago, 1879–1955

Sylvia Rhor

On our way to the Art Institute we went on the upper deck of the bus. We all sang merrily and talked about everything that came to our minds. When we arrived at the Art Institute we had to be very quiet. The first thing we did was hang up our wraps and get a camp stool. We started the tour by going to see things that existed in the fourteenth century. That was called the Gothic period. . . . Then we saw the Dutch paintings. . . . After seeing many paintings by Millet we went to see the Egyptian mummies. Some being thousands of years old! The bus ride home was different from that going. We had the lower deck and a few of us had to stand, but all and all we got along nicely. We ended a perfect trip with a song.

Constance Drinhaus, 1935[1]

Traditionally minded museum historians have often concentrated on their subjects' most obvious characteristics—the richness of a museum's collections, its architectural grandeur, and the efforts of the many collectors, patrons, and trustees who helped chart its path.[2] Recently other, more theoretically inclined scholars have attempted to dig beneath the surface of institutional histories, uncovering the ideological significance of particular museum spaces and curatorial practices.[3] Rarely have the voices of actual museum audiences been heard. In the letter quoted above, however, the impressions of Constance Drinhaus, a grade-school student recounting a class trip to the Art Institute, come through loud and clear. Through a mixture of detail, anecdote, and wonder, Drinhaus evoked a fledgling sense of the art-museum experience, where learning the conventions of spectatorship—keeping "very quiet" after a noisy bus ride, for instance—can take on as much weight as the artworks themselves. Her account also suggests how even a simple visit reflects a complex, changing set of ideas about how to act in a museum, how to look at art, and what kinds of art are worth looking at.

Whether geared to schoolchildren like Drinhaus or casual visitors who drop into the Art Institute for a quick gallery talk, museum education attempts to offer rich, meaningful encounters with art objects to visitors of all

Figure 1 A Children's Hour class meets in Blackstone Hall, c. 1919. This gallery, the Art Institute's chief repository for its collection of plaster casts, contained more than 150 replicas of works ranging from the classical era through the end of the eighteenth century.

Figure 2 On Monroe Street in Chicago's Loop business district, pedestrians throng the first streetcar to run after a 1916 streetcar strike. Such conflicts, often violent in nature, plagued Chicago and other major American cities during the Progressive Era, and represent just the sort of social and economic tensions museums aimed to help resolve. Photo: Chicago Daily News Collection, Chicago Historical Society.

ages, and often encourages them to shape these experiences on their own terms. The Art Institute stated its mission in a broad, ambitious way when it formally established a Department of Museum Education in 1934:

> The aims: To interpret the collections and current exhibitions to members and the general public; To develop an understanding of art in order to increase their appreciation and enjoyment of it; To foster a broader, more tolerant viewpoint towards the arts of all periods, including the experimental tendencies of contemporary art.
>
> The clientele: From every walk of life and every degree of education.[4]

This democratic rhetoric sprang from the same idealistic, egalitarian impulse that fueled the Art Institute's foundation a half-century before. "We have built this institution for the public…not for a few," proclaimed Art Institute president Charles L. Hutchinson in 1887. "We want the people to feel that this is their property."[5] Despite its strength and longevity, however, this almost utopian goal of accessibility and public identification was by no means static. As we shall see, the history of museum education at the Art Institute is a story of people who strove

to make the museum "open" and "democratic" in changing ways, ways that reveal the possibilities and limitations of particular historical moments, and allow us to chart shifting attitudes toward art, education, and audiences throughout the museum's history.

"A Community House for All": The Museum as Education

While it is true that the mainstays of the Art Institute's current education programs — gallery activities and tours, public lectures, and outreach projects — were initiated well before the 1934 creation of the Department of Museum Education, at the time of the Art Institute's founding there was actually no education department at all. Indeed, the very existence of the museum was seen as educational endeavor enough. Like America's other great museums, such as New York's Metropolitan Museum of Art and Boston's Museum of Fine Arts, the Art Institute was established during the museum-building boom of the 1870s. Unlike their European models, these institutions were not conceived as mere repositories for fine art, but as vehicles for public enlightenment and improvement — a mission that was driven home in many of their founding charters.[6]

The creation of public museums in the United States in the late nineteenth-century went hand-in-hand with the expansion of municipal culture and public education, and, like those developments, constituted a response to an increasingly complex urban environment. Between the years 1880 and 1920, many Northern cities were radically transformed through increased industrialization, rapid development, and heavy waves of immigrants. In Chicago alone, for example, the arrival during this period of over two million new Americans resulted in a more highly stratified society, and increased the already palpable tensions between the working and professional classes, between races, and between long-time residents and new settlers (see fig. 2). With a strong faith in the power of art to ameliorate societal ills and elevate viewers' sensibilities, civic leaders engaged in social and cultural reform on an unprecedented scale. Believing, too, that art was a vital mechanism in indoctrinating the legions of new immigrants into their narrowly defined vision of American culture and society, philanthropists geared many cultural reforms, at least in principle, to a broad public. Like libraries, parks, and schools, the museum was, in theory, open and accessible to everyone, and promoted itself as an ideal space in which people of all classes might peacefully mingle.[7] Influenced by the ideas of the English aesthetician and reformer John Ruskin, patrons championed the notion that by simply being exposed to fine art, viewers—and by extension society as a whole—would be transformed for the better. Thus by merely being built, housing a collection, and opening its doors to the people, a museum became synonymous with public education.

Despite the powerful idealism inherent in these populist goals, they were frequently compromised by actual institutional policies. Museums' often distant settings, restrictive dress codes, prohibitively high admission fees, and limited hours of operation could effectively discourage the "masses" that the institutions' founders had hoped to reach.[8] The attitudes of many cultural leaders, moreover, were often rooted in fanciful, abstract notions about the public, as well as in strict conceptions of fine art that bestowed highest ranking upon the classical world and European civilization, thereby excluding the art and craft of non-Western societies. Contemporary curatorial strategies, Carol Duncan has suggested, encouraged viewers to pay homage both to this

limited view of "civilization" and to the power and generosity of the civic patrons who built museums and donated "masterpieces" to fill them.[9] Although the Art Institute operated mainly within such restricted parameters in its own collecting, its wide-ranging activities and attractions, together with the philosophies of its founders, set it apart somewhat from other large urban museums.

One of the Art Institute's visionary leaders was Charles L. Hutchinson, who presided over its board of trustees from 1882 until his death in 1924. President of the Chicago Board of Trade and the city's Corn Exchange Bank, Hutchinson (see fig. 3) belonged to a group of wealthy, influential men who worked to construct a "new Chicago" through cultural reform after the Great Fire of 1871. From hanging paintings on the walls to defining institutional policy, Hutchinson—whom his wife called the "Eternal Improver"—was instrumental in shaping the Art Institute's physical and philosophical identity during its formative years.[10] Speaking in 1916, he pro-

Figure 3 Art Institute trustee Charles L. Hutchinson, photographed in Jaipur, India, with Mrs. Hutchinson, local guides, and the Martin A. Ryersons (at left), their close friends and frequent companions, c. 1892. Wide and passionate travelers, the couples brought an equally cosmopolitan spirit to their activities as art collectors and patrons of Chicago's cultural and educational institutions.

claimed the progressive function of a public museum in no uncertain terms:

> The value of an Art Institute should be measured by the services it renders to the community in which it stands. The principal function of the Art Museum is the cultivation and appreciation of the beautiful. The Trustees of our Art Museums are alive to the fact that in the advancement of the civilization of the present age, no agency save that of commerce can be more potent than that of Art. Art is a luxury for the rich, but a necessity for the poor. . . . The Art Museum of the past has been set aside. It has been transformed from a cemetery of bric-a-brac to a museum of living thought. The Museum of today is democratic in the best sense of the word.[11]

In accordance with such ambitious statements, Hutchinson and his colleagues set out to create a museum that would welcome and accommodate Chicago's diverse populations. "I want no cold mausoleum," Hutchinson insisted, "I want all Chicago here!"[12] Under

his leadership and that of the Art Institute's like-minded first director, William M. R. French (see Rice, fig. 1), and the sculptor Lorado Taft (see p. 25), the museum worked to reduce barriers between itself and the public. Situated in the center of the city's commercial district, the Art Institute was more readily accessible than other major American museums at that time. Not altogether against the idea of the museum as a "three-ring circus,"[13] Hutchinson promoted a variety of initiatives under its roof, ranging from free concerts and lectures to flower shows and spectacles such as large tanks filled with sixty

Lorado Taft

While the sculptor Lorado Taft (1860–1936) is perhaps best known today for his recently restored *Fountain of Time* (1922) in Chicago's Hyde Park neighborhood, and as the founder of Midway Studios at the nearby University of Chicago, his efforts as an artist and lecturer were also intimately tied to the The Art Institute of Chicago, and to the joint program of education in place during the museum and school's earliest decades.

An Illinois native, Taft studied for five years at the École des Beaux-Arts in Paris, where he developed a taste for the idealized, classically inspired sculptural forms that he would spend the remainder of his professional life creating and promoting. The ambitious young artist later settled in Chicago, hoping that the prosperous city's rough-and-tumble character would soon give way to a refining interest in culture, and in particular to a sustained project of beautifying the metropolis with works of grand public sculpture.[1]

Speaking at the 1913 ceremony dedicating his *Fountain of the Great Lakes*, presently installed in the Art Institute's south garden, Taft recalled realizing that while "our public needed sculpture, it did not know it and would never guess it unless someone showed it what it wanted!"[2] It was largely through his popular talks on sculpture that Taft worked to spread his gospel of art appreciation. While author of the seminal *History of American Sculpture* (1903) and head of the sculpture department at the rapidly growing School of the Art Institute, he gained much of his renown (and income) from an extensive series of entertaining presentations, many of them delivered on the traveling lecture circuit. By sculpting in clay to

Lorado Taft (middle row, right) posing with one of his classes at the School of the Art Institute, c. 1900. Courtesy University of Illinois Archives, Lorado Taft Papers, RS 26/20/16.

illustrate his points and avoiding technical jargon in favor of a witty, conversational speaking style, Taft made his reputation—and by extension the Art Institute's—in lyceum halls across the Midwest.

Taft was also a main attraction at the museum itself, which had since 1887 hosted Tuesday-afternoon talks by luminaries such as the architect Louis H. Sullivan, the expatriate Salon painter Hanry Bacon, and photographer Eadweard Muybridge.[3] Ten years later, these one-time offerings were supplemented by a comprehensive series of illustrated, ten-week lecture courses on European art (complete with syllabi), which were designed to translate the collections to a general audience of paying members, and at the same time supplement the technical studies of students in the school. For this series, which combined slide talks with work in the galleries, Taft launched his legendary "Lectures on Sculpture," in which he celebrated that medium's past history and explored its current state for the next thirty years.

thousand fish, in order to attract a wide cross-section of the city and bolster the Art Institute's reputation as "a Community House for all Chicago."[14]

The Art Institute also distinguished itself from other American museums by serving as a meeting place for many local organizations. By 1914 over eighty associations gathered weekly within its walls, among them several women's clubs and the Municipal Art League, an organization that promoted the purchase and display of local art in public spaces and encompassed a large number of smaller affiliated groups with similar aesthetic goals. These associations sponsored concerts, lectures, and exhibitions at the museum, supporting Chicago art and artists and creating a network of local patronage. Offering free admission three days a week, including Sundays, the museum catered to working people as well as to the leisure class. By the turn of the century, the Art Institute averaged nearly one-half million visitors per year, and three thousand on a typical Sunday—more than most of its American counterparts.[15] Chicago reporters comment-ed approvingly on the ethnic and social diversity of the crowd: "Workmen go stumping over the mosaic floor with their hob-nailed boots, and women, with no head covering but a shawl, stare respectfully at Old Masters."[16]

Just as importantly, the Art Institute's dual function—as both a school dedicated to the training of artists and a museum devoted to collecting and displaying fine art—also widened public access to its programs and determined its educational character to a great degree.[17] Founded concurrently, the museum and the School of the Art Institute developed along parallel lines and encouraged each other's aims. The museum sought to elevate public taste, develop a sound creative and consumer base for American art, and improve the quality of industrial products, all goals that traditional artistic training could help realize. The school, meanwhile, offered its students a classical course of instruction that included studying the very masterpieces the museum collected and exhibited. Staff members, moreover, often split their time between the two divisions. The design of the Art Institute's Beaux-Arts building on Michigan Avenue, opened in 1893, reinforced the intimate relationship between school and museum—classrooms and galleries existed side by side, allowing students to sketch live models posed in the galleries and copy plaster casts from the museum's collection (see fig. 4).

Figure 6 Ellen Gates Starr, cofounder of Hull-House and originator of the Chicago Public School Art Society, was also personally involved in Chicago's labor struggles. In this photograph, taken in March 1914, she is pictured while on trial for interfering with a waitress strike. Photo: Chicago Daily News Collection, Chicago Historical Society.

Figure 7 The fine-art reproductions supplied by the Chicago Public School Art Society were often useful as tools for teaching English as a second language. In this photograph, taken sometime between 1900 and 1915, grade-school students stand before a blackboard on which they have written out descriptions of the very images they display for the camera. Photo: Art Resources in Teaching Records (ART neg. 13), Jane Addams Memorial Collection, The University Library, University of Illinois at Chicago.

Public Schools and the Art Institute

Perhaps due to the fact that public museums and public schools were viewed as kindred educational institutions by their late nineteenth-century supporters, connections between the Art Institute and Chicago schools were forged early in the museum's history. Public-school teachers received free admission to the museum from the time of its inception (see fig. 5), and were encouraged to integrate its collections into their regular classroom curricula. Programs for teachers were so well developed that by 1907 the Art Institute could boast that one-third of all Chicago public-school teachers had attended courses at the school or registered for guided tours of the museum.[18] At first, most of the educational opportunities for teachers and students were offered through the School of the Art Institute. There, weekend classes accommodated student schedules, while teachers took specially designed certification courses in record numbers.

At this point, however, it was through the efforts of intermediary civic organizations that the Art Institute made its most significant contributions to public schools. Especially important was the Chicago Public School Art Society, which employed groundbreaking strategies to integrate the efforts of the museum and the city's school system.[19] The society, comprised of civic-minded women who promoted the role of art in public education, was established in 1894 by Ellen Gates Starr (see fig. 6), who with Jane Addams founded Hull-House, the influential settlement house on Chicago's near west side. The group began by distributing reproductions of works in the Art Institute's permanent collection to schools throughout the city, with the idea that they be used to decorate classrooms and supplement lesson plans (see fig. 7). It also organized school tours of the Art Institute, even assigning its own teacher to handle this gallery activity in 1914. It spearheaded a national campaign for the promotion of art in schools at the turn of the century, when the Chicago Board of Education began questioning the usefulness of fine-art programs in the curriculum.[20]

The society was also instrumental in placing original art, primarily murals painted by advanced students at the School of the Art Institute, in public schools (see fig. 8). Thomas Wood Stevens, an instructor in mural painting at the school from 1908 to 1913, called this effort a "knitting together of the influences of the museum, the art academy, and the public school unusual in character and amazing in scale."[21] In fact, this surge in mural painting for public schools resulted in the creation of numerous original works, and remains a legacy of the achievements of women's organizations at the turn of the century.[22] The elaborate art-education and art-donation programs they helped institute for Chicago's public schools made the women of the Public School Art Society and other similar clubs into patrons and cultural promoters in their own right. Embedded within schools that

were significant architectural achievements themselves,[23] the original murals and art-work, as well as the reproductions, transformed these buildings into informal neighborhood art galleries not only for students and teachers, but also for the community members who frequented them.[24] Inspired by historical events and literary classics, the murals sometimes complemented citizenship lessons and other classroom curricula; such themes were also popular for mural cycles commissioned for other types of public buildings such as city halls, court houses, and museums.

The achievements of the Public School Art Society in the early part of the century, together with the Art Institute's ongoing commitment to public education, laid a solid foundation for steady expansion. In 1922, for example, the Board of Education appointed Mary Hess Buehr the official instructor for Chicago public-school tours of the museum.[25] Three years later, the James Nelson Raymond Public School and Lecture Fund began sup-

Figure 8 Students in a mural-painting class at The School of the Art Institute of Chicago, 1918.

Dudley Crafts Watson

From the early 1920s through the mid-1950s, Dudley Crafts Watson embodied the role of museum lecturer at The Art Institute of Chicago. A talented artist in his own right, Watson attended the School of the Art Institute and studied with noted painters of the day, including Joaquin Sorolla and Sir Alfred East.[1] Early in his career he worked as an instructor at the school, and went on to serve as education director for the Minneapolis Institute of Arts and director of the Milwaukee Art Institute before returning to Chicago to take up the role of Extension Lecturer at the Art Institute. As Clarence J. Bulliet, longtime art critic for the *Chicago Daily News*, suggested in 1936, Watson's success resulted from a combination of professional know-how and personal magnetism:

> Dudley Crafts Watson began lecturing on art to preserve his integrity as an artist. Rather than paint potboilers, he decided early in his career he would talk about art for a living. . . . From the beginning he has developed into the most widely known lecturer in America. Perhaps more women have seen his smiling face than that of any other artist living.[2]

Watson gained nationwide celebrity status in large part through his work as a radio commentator, and through extensive "Art Pilgrimages" in Europe and Latin America, which he recorded on film and shared with paying audiences through movie, slide, and sound presentations that he delivered around the country.[3] His schedule at the Art Institute was equally impressive: while often speaking to clubs and organizations outside the museum, he also served as the official lecturer for the

"Century of Progress Exhibition of Painting and Sculpture" (1933–34). Just as popular were his regular sketch workshops for members, Raymond Fund classes for Chicago high-school students (see fig. 9), and his weekly members' series on home decoration (see Nosan, fig. 14) and art through travel, which remained the museum's most highly attended public programs for decades. Like many other lecturers of this time, Watson was both an educator and an entertainer: while instructing audiences on how to look at art, he also approached art appreciation more as a pleasing performance than a participatory endeavor. "As scholarly as a college professor, and as friendly as your next door neighbor," he crafted presentations that, as one appreciative listener told him, "cast upon your audience a spell from which we wished not to awaken."[4]

Dudley Crafts Watson and a group of Gold Star Mothers pause before James McNeill Whistler's Arrangement in Gray and Black: Portrait of the Painter's Mother (1872; Museé du Louvre, Paris) during the Art Institute's "Century of Progress Exhibition of Painting and Sculpture," 1933.

Figure 9 Chicago students sketch a model during a Raymond Fund class held in the Art Institute's Fullerton Hall, December 1941.

Figure 10 (below) Helen Parker, longtime head of the Art Institute's Department of Museum Education, and lecturer George Buehr collaborate on a gallery talk, 1945.

porting programs for talented Chicago students. Through the Raymond Fund, and in collaboration with the public schools, the Art Institute arranged visits for nearly one hundred thousand junior-high and high-school students annually.[26] Popular for decades, these classes (see fig. 9) encompassed both artistic training and art-history lectures: students could attend presentations or sketch sessions in the museum's Fullerton Hall on such topics as "Sketching for the Fun of It," "Lincoln and Washington in Art," "Stenciling," "The Easter Story in Art," and "First Step in Modeling." The program also enabled Art Institute lecturers such as Dudley Crafts Watson (see p. 29) to conduct sessions on similar topics at schools throughout the city.

Art and the Layperson: Lecturers, Docents, and the Department of Museum Instruction

By the second decade of the twentieth century, as museums throughout the country began to place a growing emphasis on acquiring original works of art rather than plaster casts and reproductions, their larger purpose became a popular topic of debate for curators and public alike. Critics such as Benjamin Ives Gilman, secretary of the Museum of Fine Arts, Boston, championed the museum as a showcase for high art, devoted above all to collecting, researching, and preserving masterpieces. Gilman would have understood the work of museum education as a purely scholarly enterprise, not a popular one.[27] But others, such as the Newark Museum's director John Cotton Dana, urged his colleagues to renew their commitment to educating the public at large. In 1917 Dana wrote, "A museum is an educational institution, set up and kept in motion

that it may help the members of the community to become happier, wiser, and more effective. It can help them only if they use it. They can use it only if they know of it. And only when they know much about it can they get much from it."[28]

Gilman and Dana represent the extreme poles of contemporary thinking; most major institutions sought a balance between acquiring art and serving the public.[29] For example, although the Art Institute was busy acquiring some of its most important works in the first decades of the century, it continued to affirm its public mission:

> The Art Institute is sometimes criticized, though more often praised, for what might be called its ultra popular management. . . . It is the avowed aim of the Art Institute to make itself useful to the community, and to this end, agreeable. . . . It is therefore highly desirable, from a popular point of view, that art museums be divested of their traditional char-

Figure 11 A crowd of adult visitors leaves one of Helen Parker's popular lectures in Fullerton Hall, December 1938.

A product of the same civic-minded decorating movement as the Art Institute's Better Homes Institute, this design for an efficient, modern kitchen was developed as part of the nationwide "Better Homes in America" effort, and was published in Blanche Halbert, ed., *The Better Homes Manual* (Chicago, 1931), p. 477.

The Better Homes Institute

In the spirit of audience expansion, the Art Institute launched the Better Homes Institute, "an organized project for community building and development" that aimed to extend the museum's influence directly into people's everyday living spaces.[1] Taking shape from 1920 onward, the effort constituted the museum's response to the Better Homes Movement, which was gaining popularity around the nation in the years following World War I. This wider experiment, according to the Art Institute's *Bulletin*, sought both to stimulate consumer demand for "beauty and quality in home furnishings" and to inspire the "community feeling" that undergirded "a constructive program for civic development."[2] Other initiatives of the period included the Own Your Own Home campaign, in which the federal government offered working- and middle-class families financial incentives to invest in a house, and

gave them instructions on how they might design and furnish their dwellings more carefully. The American Federation of Arts, meanwhile, sponsored the Art in Every Home program, which attempted to put reasonably priced reproductive prints of famous paintings and sculptures within reach of all consumers.

While held in various settings throughout the Chicago metropolitan area, the Better Homes Institute was actually geared largely toward the greater Mississippi Valley, and took place in locales as distant from Chicago (and each other) as Winnipeg, Alberta, and Muskogee, Oklahoma. Ross Crane, head of the Art Institute's Extension Division, originated the program, and often traveled to state fairs, colleges, and small towns to deliver five-day presentations meant to awaken a "desire for better and more artistic houses and better and more beautiful communities."[4] Paid for by local businesses and civic organizations, the training incorporated furnishings supplied by area merchants, in addition to over a ton of material shipped out from the Art Institute, including "twenty paintings, a three-wall collapsible room, a movable fireplace, windows, doors, house plans, drawings, and photographs."[5] Crane and his Art Institute colleagues used these props to illustrate their lectures on architecture, landscape design, interior decoration, and their connection to larger civic issues. Indeed, in its belief that good design might help produce a good society, the Better Homes Institute echoed the reformist ideals that spurred the Art Institute's foundation over four decades earlier. By attempting to connect the practical art of home furnishing with the fine-art world of the museum, moreover, the program exemplifies a strain of educational programming that found later expression in efforts such as the Clinic of Good Taste and the Art Rental and Sales Gallery (see Nosan, figs. 13–14).

acter as mere cold storage places for pictures and art objects, and should be given if possible a warm, living, human-hearted character which shall convey to both the critic and the ordinary visitor impressions of comfort and enjoyment.[30]

In its desire to create a welcoming environment, in 1913 the Art Institute established a Department of Museum Instruction, the first significant step in the evolution of a fully independent education division within the museum's administrative structure. The new department comprised a corps of lecturers, or docents, whose primary responsibility was to interpret the museum's collections to a wide range of audiences through lectures, tours, and classes.[31] Before this, staff members, including curators and the museum's director (see Rice, fig. 1), provided gallery tours upon request. Informally referred to as "museum guidance" and advertised in the Art Institute's *Bulletin*, these services were offered free to museum members and Chicago public-school teachers, but were not advertised to the general public nor made readily available to walk-in visitors.

Faced with filling the pivotal role of mediating between the museum's holdings and the public, lecturers concentrated on a target audience of interested nonprofessionals rather than on scholars or connoisseurs. Proceeding from the assumption that average viewers were unequipped to adequately guide themselves through the Art Institute's galleries, lecturers taught their audiences how to develop "discrimination between the fine and the commonplace in art."[32] They introduced visitors to the collection, pointing out works' formal aspects and historical significance, and providing guidelines for aesthetic judgments based on traditional art-historical approaches, which held that classical and European art were superior in idea and form to all else. Just as they led members and teachers through the

galleries, they became expert tour guides to a larger world as well. Department members Helen Mackenzie, Helen Parker, and Dudley Crafts Watson, among others, spoke on such subjects as "Art Centers of Italy, "Development of Painting in North Europe," and "History of Architecture." These choices indicate the continuing primacy of European civilization, and reflect the privileged viewpoint of some audience members, who may have attended such talks to prepare for future trips abroad. For many others, however, these popular programs offered a way to see the world without having to leave home. Lecturers also provided various services to nonmembers, including noontime programs for factory workers and, during World War I, guided

Figure 12 Helen Mackenzie, Curator of the Children's Museum, pauses before a doorway in the Art Institute's Gothic period room during a weekly gallery tour for members' children, c. 1937.

Figure 13 The north wall of the Children's Museum, c. 1924. Visible are a number of objects still in the Art Institute's collection, including (at center left) Edward Henry Potthast's painting *A Holiday*, c. 1915.

tours for servicemen.[33] Most of these offerings combined slide lectures with gallery visits, attracting some three thousand visitors per year by 1917.

Since specialized training for museum staff was virtually nonexistent at this time, instructors often came from diverse backgrounds. Director Helen Parker (see fig. 10), for instance, was a self-proclaimed "jack-of-all trades" who stumbled upon museum work after receiving a degree in English and French.[34] The majority of the Art Institute's educators, though, were artists working either at the School of the Art Institute or in the wider Chicago community; as such, they had practical experience that distinguished them from many of their counterparts in other museums. These artist-lecturers were able to discuss how objects were actually made, and often encouraged viewers to focus on such formal aspects as color, line, shape, and composition. By outlining "what to look for" in works of art, however, lecturers trained their audiences (see fig. 11) to discriminate by relying on well-estab-

lished canons of taste instead of their own individual experiences and perceptions.

The Children's Museum

Concern for the welfare of children was a mainstay of Progressive-Era reform, particularly for civic organizations and women's clubs, and manifested itself in ways that included laws on compulsory education and child labor, and expanded programs of public schooling and healthcare. Embodying both innocence and potential, children were seen as blank slates upon which civic virtues and cultural values could be imprinted. Thus, they were deemed most in need of—and receptive to—art's supposed power to uplift and transform. Following World War I, the Art Institute, like many other American museums, increased its educational offerings.[35] Before 1916, programs for children had been limited to the school's Saturday studio classes and school tours of the museum. In 1918, acknowledging its "tremendous responsibility" to help create a peace-loving society, the museum vowed to place the requirements of a juvenile audience squarely at the center of its educational agenda: "It is the children of today," explained an article in the Art Institute's *Bulletin*, "who will be carrying on the activities of those peace-filled days, which are certainly to come; and in those days art will be no mean factor. Obviously it is for us now to give the children a love for things beautiful."[36]

Inaugurated in 1916, Children's Hour, a storytelling program, marked the start of the Department of Museum Instruction's expanded response to the needs of children outside the classroom (see fig. 1). Young people were invited to attend talks every Saturday on a variety of subjects, ranging from "Lives of Great Artists" and "Animals in Art" to "Tales of Florence and the Florentines" and "Famous Stories and How Great Artists Have Told Them." Such programs were meant to stimulate an interest in art and provide the younger generation with an alternative form of recreation that parents might find more worthwhile than emerging forms of popular entertainment, such as comic strips, films, and magazines. These talks, the museum promised, would be "a plain diet, without moving pictures, with no dramatic presentations."[37]

While Children's Hour was highly successful, the Art Institute nonetheless lagged behind other major museums in its services for children. By the mid-teens, when Children's Hour was the only offering exclusively for a juvenile audience at the Art Institute, institutions such as Boston's Museum of Fine Arts and the Metropolitan Museum of Art, for example, had sponsored special children's rooms or children's museums related to their collections. These spaces were outfitted with art and objects intended to appeal to this special audience, and provided activities specially designed for it.[38] There had been talk about designating a section of the Art Institute's

Egyptian Room, where the Department of Museum Instruction was located, for the use of young visitors, but nothing materialized. "Chicago," Mrs. Leo Heller, a member of the Municipal Art League, lamented,"stands alone among American cities in its neglect of its children."[39] A 1918 article in the Art Institute's *Bulletin* outlined plans to rectify the situation: "The Art Institute is a labyrinth-like place to a child visitor. But some day there is to be a Children's Room with its setting specially designed for the use and enjoyment of children. It will then play its part in the forming of the men and women who are to carry on the spirit of freedom and joyousness."[40] Finally, in 1922 plans were developed for a children's center that would make the museum a more welcoming and useful environment in which to learn. An article that year in the *Bulletin* explained the initiative: " . . . a museum in little within the parent institution, especially equipped for children and with exhibits of a nature that will appeal to them."[41]

Figure 14 This process case, on display in the Children's Museum in 1932, offered young visitors a detailed, step-by-step explanation of cloisonné enameling, and included sections on media, tools, and firing techniques.

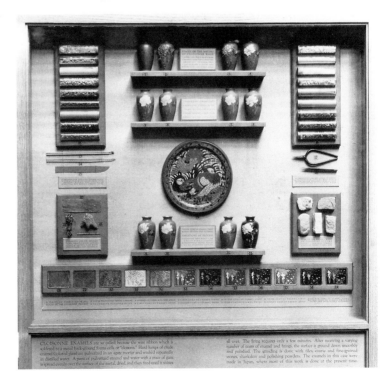

Local women's clubs and other civic associations began raising money for such a facility, and a $50,000 donation from Mr. and Mrs. Charles H. Worcester made the plan a reality.[42] In 1926 the Children's Museum was completed, and Helen Mackenzie (see fig. 12) was named its first curator. The underlying philosophy of the Children's Museum, like that of Children's Hour, was to cultivate "taste" and "the museum habit" in youngsters who would later be civic leaders and patrons of the arts. Conceived of as an Art Institute in miniature, the Children's Museum collected objects; mounted exhibitions; and offered tours, lectures, and classes. The shape and seriousness of its mission were reflected in its carefully designed space, which was divided into two smaller galleries with a latticework screen. The facility was located within Blackstone Hall, where the Art Institute's popular collection of plaster casts was displayed. Like many of the museum's "adult" galleries, the space was filled with plants and hanging vines to help create an air of rest and contemplation.

The first gallery was used for temporary exhibitions, which changed every few weeks. The list of shows held in the Children's Museum included illustrated books for children (1926), valentines (1927), and artwork done in the Art Institute's Saturday classes or at Hull-House and other settlement organizations. The second room (see figs. 13–14) housed large, wood-and-glass "process cases" that featured small displays explaining such techniques as fresco, woodblock printing, and ivory carving. This room also exhibited the Children's Museum's permanent collection, which included *Fighting Boys* (1912), a bronze fountain by the American Beaux-Arts sculptor Janet Scudder.[43] Influenced by a then-current belief that children's tastes were not fully developed, preventing them from being able to truly appreciate "finer masterpieces," the staff acquired, among

other examples of "primitive art of different lands," cameos, Japanese dolls, pottery, and embroidered Burmese scarves. In fact the Children's Museum purchased the very first African works to enter into the Art Institute's permanent collection.[44] Children, educators thought, were particularly drawn to such non-Western objects because of what was then perceived to be the straightforward process of their making and the simplicity, even naiveté, of their design. Drawing on contemporary biases about African art and culture, the staff of the Children's Museum considered teaching children to appreciate these works a key, if rudimentary, step in cultivating the aesthetic sensibilities of the young.

Those who ran the Children's Museum's employed a variety of display and teaching methods to capture and keep the interest of their audience. Because many educators believed that children preferred art's content over its formal elements, they used story hours and slide lectures to present objects as part of compelling narratives. Convinced that "the sense of touch, as well as the sense of sight, is a factor in education," the staff opted for installations that encouraged a multisensory experience.[45] They exhibited bronze jugs and pottery, for example, not under glass, but rather anchored to the center of low tables to encourage tactile exploration. They made pencil and paper available to children who wished to sketch, and sold color reproductions of popular objects so that young visitors could "collect" and "preserve" their favorites in their own homes. In order to further internalize the lessons learned in the museum, children who attended lectures or storytelling hours were also encouraged, like Constance Drinhaus, to create "memories" of their experiences by making drawings and fashioning stories about their Art Institute visits.

Museum Extension and the Garfield Park Art Galleries

While outreach to the wider community has been a important component of educational programming in recent decades, American museums' attempts to extend their services and collections beyond their walls have, in fact, been a part of their mission since the turn of the twentieth century. "Why Museum Extension?" Robert W. de Forest, of the Metropolitan Museum of Art, asked rhetorically in 1919. "For the same reasons," he answered, "which have led to university extension. Many could not come to the university to enjoy its educational opportunities, so the university has gone out to them."[46] The desire to extend the museum's sphere of influence was so strong that some early professionals even recommended abolishing large, centralized facilities in downtown areas, proposing instead that institutions disperse their collections to several small museums throughout the city in order to better meet the needs of the public.

Although the Art Institute never embraced this radical suggestion, it did engage in several endeavors that produced similar results. Beginning in 1909, for example, the museum exhibited works from its permanent collection in field houses of the Chicago Park District.[47] The Oak Park Extension was inaugurated one year later, bringing the museum's Saturday afternoon classes to children living in this progressive, small city west of Chicago. Through intermediary organizations such as the Chicago Public School Art Society, public schools came to serve as neighborhood ancillaries to the Art Institute. They displayed reproductions of pieces in the collections and housed original works that were often acquired through the museum's annual exhibitions of local art. In December 1916, concurrent with similar efforts by other museums, the Art Institute institutionalized these services by creating a new

Department of Extension, describing its rationale in these terms:

> The art development of the great environment of Chicago has reached a scale for which a wholly centralized activity on the part of the museums is inadequate. . . . The time has arrived at which the Art Institute of Chicago feels the necessity of taking upon itself responsibility for a part of this outside work. . . . Any educational effort, to be of definite and permanent value, should appeal to the interest of every class in the community.[48]

Geared toward schools and civic organizations, the division dedicated itself to "all who believe in the practical utility of the beautiful and in the development of the art of the community as a means to a richer, finer and more wholesome community life."[49] Extension programs included traveling exhibits for which the division also provided lectures, displays of local crafts, and "a permanent organization in each community to insure the continuance of the educational effort."[50] Lecturers included Charles Burkholder (see Rice, fig. 8), a curator at the Art Institute at that time; George Eggers, the Art Institute's director from 1916 until 1921; Lorado Taft (see p. 25); and architect Ross Crane, who also served as head of the department.

The Art Institute's extension efforts culminated in 1935 with the opening of the Garfield Park Art Galleries, which brought the museum more fully to the public by meeting it—literally—on its own turf. By developing an ancillary exhibition venue, the Art Institute drew on its mission to reach out to the community in a literal as well as metaphorical sense. Located on Chicago's west side, far removed from the Loop business district, the Garfield Art Gallery was the Art Institute's first (and only) attempt to establish branches of the main museum in outlying areas, an effort whose seeds had been sown in the initiatives of the Chicago Public School Art Society and the Department of Extension in earlier decades. *The Christian Science Monitor* reported: "The need for small branch museums in a metropolis the size of Chicago is apparent to all . . . small art centers, easily accessible to many who can't make frequent trips to the Art Institute will, it is hoped, do much toward stimulating the understanding and appreciation of the fine arts."[51]

Situated in Garfield Park's grand, gold-domed former administration building, the galleries (see fig. 15) were the first of several similar facilities planned for parks located in other middle-class, ethnically diverse neighborhoods.[52] The facility was meant to operate in much the same fashion as a branch library. The Art Institute provided insurance for the space; appointed its staff from the museum's education personnel; and loaned works from the permanent collection. Helen Mackenzie, head of the Department of Instruction, administered the gallery, curated its revolving exhibitions, and wrote guidebooks for shows. One reporter greeted the gallery's opening with unfettered acclaim: "No venture fraught with brighter, happier prospects for enriching the lives of the people has been launched in this community. In every respect—including admission, lectures, handsomely printed catalogs that are well worth saving, and cloakrooms—this new treasure house will always be free to the people."[53]

In their exhibitions, the gallery's staff members were committed to showing classical sculpture and American art from the late nineteenth and early twentieth centuries, with a special emphasis on the work of Chicago artists. In the inaugural show, for example, they included paintings such as Henry Ossawa Tanner's *Three Marys* (1910) and Elizabeth Sparhawk-Jones's *Shop Girls* (c. 1912), as well as reproductions of classical Greek sculpture.[54] The organizers expressed their commitment to tradition not just through their pedagogical choices, but also through the art they chose to display and the visual techniques they used to present it. The labels themselves were described in the local press as "little masterpieces of compactness and stimulation . . . literally eye-openers," and told viewers "what to look for and why." [55] The didactic text for Chauncy Foster Ryder's *Mount Lovewell* (c. 1920), for instance, described the work as "an unusual harmony of clear bright colors," and exhorted audiences to "notice the accents made by the pines against the repeated horizontals." [56] This sort of compositional analysis, along with the staff's penchant for showing academic American art and hanging paintings Salon style, one on top of the other, together constituted a strong statement in favor of traditional aesthetic ideals.

Such decisions must also be seen as a clear response to a heated local controversy regarding the value of emerging modernist art. One reporter described the political significance of the inaugural Garfield Park exhibition in no uncertain terms:

> It represents American art before American art went nuts. . . . Nowhere at Garfield is there a trace of what conservatives call "the didos in the chambers of horrors." In the new art palace on the west side all is alluring, all is significant and all represents painters of high distinction—no cranks, no daubers, no morons. [57]

The antipathy to modernism expressed so bluntly here was widespread in Chicago in the 1930s, and taken to extremes by the Sanity in Art Commission. Led by the wife of a leading patron of the Art Institute, Josephine (Mrs. Frank) Logan, the organization attracted Chicagoans who vehemently opposed modern art in all of its forms and denounced its public exhibition. Often employing guerilla tactics such as throwing bricks through the windows of galleries that showed works

deemed objectionable, Sanity in Art encouraged the academic choices and traditional methods of display used at the Garfield Park Art Galleries. In its capitulation to the conservative attitudes that the commission championed, the Garfield Art Gallery also represented a continuation of earlier educational strategies that sought to elevate particular schools of art above others, and prescribe certain modes of viewing to audiences.

The Garfield Park Art Galleries maintained its traditionalist agenda throughout its three-year existence, hosting shows that included "Etchings by American Artists," "Paintings from the Friends of American Art Collection," and several shows of Art Institute reproductions. Like the Better Homes Institute (see p. 32), the Garfield Park facility did not flourish for long, and plans for similar extension museums in other Chicago parks were soon abandoned. This was perhaps due to the many community art centers that sprang up in the city under the New Deal, rendering such satellite galleries redundant. Moreover, as we shall see, by the late 1930s and early 1940s, the conservative bent of projects such as the Garfield Park Art Galleries gave way to the Art Institute's growing interest in modern and contemporary art, and its use of more innovative exhibition techniques.

Figure 16 Art Institute lecturer Helen Barsaloux delivers a gallery talk during the 1933–34 "Century of Progress Exhibition of Painting and Sculpture," introducing visitors to Impressionist works including (from left) Édouard Manet's *The Railway* (1872–73; National Gallery of Art, Washington, D.C.); Pierre Auguste Renoir's *Luncheon of the Boating Party* (1880–81; Phillips Collection); and Manet's *Steamboat Leaving Boulogne* (1864; The Art Institute of Chicago).

The Century of Progress and a New Public

In the 1930s, even as it pursued the possibilities of extending its influence throughout the city, the museum was also rethinking its educational goals back in the main galleries. A watershed event in this process was the Art Institute's role in the "Century of Progress International Exposition." Centered along Chicago's lakefront, this world's fair marked the city's one-hundredth birthday with a display of streamlined products and futuristic buildings, and at the same time celebrated the potential of scientific ingenuity and corporate creativity, undimmed even in the midst of the Great Depression. During the fair's two-year run, over three million visitors flocked to the Art Institute, which hosted a special "Century of Progress Exhibition of Painting and Sculpture" that brought together more than two hundred works of art in order to meet the ambitious goal of offering "a

superb survey of painting and sculpture from the mid-thirteenth century to 1933."[58] Masterpieces arrived on loan from around the world, and were installed in a series of galleries organized along national and historical lines, and carefully designed to lead the public on a clear, step-by-step journey through the history of Western art. According to one prominent critic, the show's organizers succeeded at nothing less than assembling "the finest art exhibition ever held in America."[59]

If orchestrating an exhibition of this scale and complexity was a landmark accomplishment for the Art Institute's staff, so was the act of interpreting it to general audiences. Every day of the week, lecturers conducted general tours, focused gallery talks, and illustrated slide presentations, and succeeded at attracting what the museum's *Bulletin* characterized hopefully as a "new American public" bent on pursuing art education on a mass scale (see fig. 16). It was this public, eager to appreciate art and "trying consciously to understand" modernism, that the Art Institute hoped to serve when it inaugurated its first official Department of Museum Education in 1934.[60] While one would assume that all the educational activities of the museum were now centralized within this umbrella division, the Membership and Extension Departments and the Children's Museum continued to handle different aspects of education through the 1950s. Even as it recognized the emergence of more sophisticated, aesthetically adventurous audiences, the Art Institute remained effectively committed to the educational strategies and artistic preferences of previous decades. It was only after Daniel Catton Rich assumed the directorship of the Art Institute in 1938 that the museum succeeded in forging an innovative and forward-looking direction in education, as well as a clear dedication to helping the public understand and appreciate modern art.

The Gallery of Art Interpretation

Rich, who had risen to his new position from the curatorial ranks, declared the Department of Education one of his top priorities. Drawing on the three divisions primarily responsible for educational offerings, he initiated a series of lectures and symposia related to special exhibitions; promoted the integration of radio, film, and television into the museum's efforts; and in 1944 organized a national conference on "The Future of the Art Museum as an Educational Institution."[61] Perhaps his most important contribution, however, was to support the museum's Gallery of Art Interpretation, which revolutionized education at the Art Institute and served as a national model of progressive programming.

This pathbreaking effort began, in 1940, as a reinvention of the Children's Museum. That facility, which had been in operation for

sixteen years, was given a new mission and a new name—the Gallery of Art Interpretation. According to an article in the Art Institute's *Bulletin*, this decision was made "in order to have the title more fully indicate the activities of the department whose function is to give both children and adults a clearer understanding of different artists and their various means of artistic expression."[62] Under its curator, Helen Mackenzie, the gallery presented exhibitions—most of them organized by other museums—that were geared to a new, mixed audience of children and adults. With the exception of a show that introduced visitors to the work of the contemporary artist Pablo Picasso, the core of the gallery's offerings did not depart significantly from traditional approaches. Things changed when Mackenzie retired in 1943, and Rich appointed as her successor a Chicago-based art dealer and independent educator, Katharine Kuh (see p. 43), who welcomed the opportunity to inject new energy into what she considered the initiative's canned offerings.

The new curator believed that the public remained "confused" regarding the "why and how" of art, despite the fact that often-controversial modern works were being exhibited more frequently, and covered extensively in the press. Kuh wrote: "The secret language of art specialists is apt to antagonize the questioning layman. His ego is wounded and he retires armed with deadly and familiar clichés, 'My little boy Johnny can do better than that,' or 'why doesn't it look like what it is supposed to be.'"[63] Kuh launched an attack on what she considered to be the outmoded methods employed by the museum's Education Department, in particular the pedantic style of lecturers such as Dudley Crafts Watson, who, while extremely popular, pronounced aesthetic judgments based on what Kuh adamantly believed were false or

Figure 17 In a 1944–45 exhibition for the Gallery of Art Interpretation titled "From Nature to Art," Katharine Kuh juxtaposed two Dan masks from Liberia with Amadeo Modigliani's *Madame Pompadour* (1915; The Art Institute of Chicago).

rigid premises about art and audiences. She became determined to shift the emphasis of educational exhibitions and strategies away from the art specialist's point of view, and toward that of the average museum visitor.

Reinventing the gallery as a place devoted in large part to helping adult visitors explore modern art creatively, Kuh renovated the space on a shoestring with the help of the architect Ludwig Mies van der Rohe. The former director of the German Bauhaus, who had emigrated to Chicago in 1938 to teach at the School of Architecture at the Armour Institute of Technology (later the Illinois Institute of Technology), also designed Kuh's first show for the gallery.[64] Kuh arranged her exhibitions according to modernist design principles: they were sleek, minimal, and hung assymetrically. In them she employed a wide array of objects and media—three-dimensional designs, photography, and modern typography, for instance—to introduce variety and engage viewers' attention (see figs. 17–18).[65] She also replaced standard labels, which were often laden with the sort of technical jargon Kuh disparaged as "the curse of educational exhibitions," with simple texts and catchy phrases, all set in readable, modernist typography.[66] While traditional label copy told viewers what to look for, Kuh's prose encouraged people to think independently and come to their own conclusions.

Kuh challenged her audiences by posing questions and making comparisons, guiding them through a process of looking by using visual evidence to suggest how and why mod-

Katharine Kuh

For the general public, I feel that words [about art] are rather futile . . . such words as beautiful, or charming, or interesting. What do they mean? In the Gallery of Art Interpretation . . . my desire . . . was to explain to intelligent viewers how to see.

Katharine Kuh, 1982[1]

Between 1944 and 1952, Katharine Kuh (1904–1994) organized exhibitions for the Gallery of Art Interpretation that were predicated on basic principles of perception, and guided viewers through such varied and (at that time, unfamiliar) visual terrains as Cubism, Surrealism, African art, and art photography without becoming pedantic or intimidating. Thousands saw these exhibitions, which helped broaden public interest in the visual arts; enabled audiences to understand and value challenging trends in modern art; and brought Kuh and the Art Institute national and international acclaim.

In eleven exhibits over eight years, Kuh created interactive displays, each unique in its imaginative use of materials, installation techniques, and succinct, provocative commentary (see figs. 17–18). Subjects for shows varied; they could relate to special exhibitions, and sometimes to the museum's permanent collection. An installation might focus on one artist (the Mexican printmaker José Guadalupe Posada, for instance), or on a single work of art (such as a mythological painting attributed to Tintoretto). An exhibition might also highlight a particular medium (such as sculpture, which Kuh felt challenged viewers more than two-dimensional art), or explore formal problems shared by artists working in every era and medium (depicting still lifes, suggesting space and distance, considering how real realism is, or creating in an abstract style).

Katharine Kuh, 1953. In addition to her innovative experiments in the Gallery of Art Interpretation, Kuh served as the Art Institute's first curator of Modern Painting and sculpture, acquiring many of the museum's signal twentieth- century works.

In 1954 Kuh was named the first curator of modern painting and sculpture at the Art Institute. She then changed the function of the Gallery of Art Interpretation, using it to showcase the work of such contemporary artists as Jack Levine, Mark Rothko, and Mark Tobey. Nonetheless, by then Kuh had extended the influence of her approach to visual education even further, writing several books that were based on her experiments in the gallery, and that became standard references for teaching art appreciation in the later 1950s and 1960s.[2] Even after she left the Art Institute, in 1958, to become art critic for the national magazine *Saturday Review*, Kuh continued to think of herself as an educator: "I tried to be . . . a bridge between our readers and the works of art that I enjoyed and that I wanted them to look at and understand."[3]

Figure 18 Katharine Kuh's exhibition design for "Looking at Sculpture," on view in the Gallery of Art Interpretation from December 1, 1945 to June 1, 1946.

Figure 18 Katharine Kuh's exhibition design for "Looking at Sculpture," on view in the Gallery of Art Interpretation from December 1, 1945 to June 1, 1946.

ern artists arrived at their aesthetic choices. In 1947, for example, in anticipation of the Art Institute's pioneering show on American abstraction and Surrealism, she staged an exhibition in the Gallery of Art Interpretation that helped prepare audiences to better understand and appreciate these artistic trends. On view for an extended period, from July 1947 to January 1948, "Explaining Abstract Art" became perhaps the most popular and influential of Kuh's presentations there. She juxtaposed African masks, photographs of industrial sites, several reproductions of art works, a sculpture by Isamu Noguchi, seashells, and still lifes by art

students in order to explicate the principles underlying abstract art. By mixing media, Kuh challenged the traditional hierarchies that had informed most of the Art Institute's educational programs before that time. Indeed, by transcending narrow definitions of art, embracing modernism, and establishing a richer dialogue with ordinary museum visitors, she offered a powerful, alternative vision of what museum education could be and do.

Conclusion

In 1955 Daniel Catton Rich argued that the Art Institute's Department of Education "should be

made the core, rather than the fringe of a museum program."[67] In many ways, Rich's declaration echoes those of the museum's founders,
who conceived of education as the institution's
driving mission. As we have seen, however,
approaches to fulfilling this mission, and imag-
ining its scope and intention, changed dramat-
ically from the late nineteenth century to the
mid-twentieth. When the Art Institute first
opened its doors, the museum defined its educational goal by the mere fact that it existed as
a place which could expose a diverse audience
to art's "uplifting" effects. In developing a variety of classes, lectures, and exhibition spaces,
the museum expanded its educational agenda
to meet the needs of a broader range of audiences and neighborhoods. Finally, with Kuh's
Gallery of Art Interpretation, the narrow definitions of art and aesthetic experience that had
dominated the Art Institute's earlier educational
efforts gave way to more progressive approaches
to art, audience, display, and interpretation.

The history of museum education at the
Art Institute during the late-nineteenth and
early-twentieth centuries, however, is also a
tale of individual creativity and exploration
within a profession still in its infancy. When
Helen Parker reminisced about her early years
at the Art Institute, she recalled that it was
"like pioneering."[68] The department, as she
described it, was young, and role of the educator undefined. Kuh, for her part, admitted that
the exhibition strategies that she developed were
born not out of any single model, but out of simple "trial and error."[69] More than any of these
things, perhaps, the history of museum education
is the story of people like Constance Drinhaus,
who came in through the door, and, with some
help from the Art Institute, took away experiences and memories of their own.

Women in the Galleries:

Prestige, Education, and Volunteerism at Mid-century

Gregory Nosan

In its July 1952 issue, *Vogue* trained its sharp eye for fashion and culture on the Windy City. Introducing readers to many of Chicago's now-vanished attractions, from tours of the Union Stockyards to the swank Tip-Top Tap at the summit of the Allerton Hotel, the magazine paid special tribute to The Art Institute of Chicago, proclaiming that "Chicagoans love . . . and take much more than a civic interest in it."[1] The centerpiece and visual focus of this "Memo on Chicago" was a group of local women who had recently organized the glittering Masterpiece Ball to raise money for the Art Institute's Emergency Fund Drive, which was officially launched three months earlier to help shore up the museum's disintegrating physical plant. In a striking group of black-and-white photographs, prominent society figures were captured performing the living tableaus with which they entertained their fellow revelers (see fig. 5).

Perhaps the most intriguing image of these women, though, shows them not in costume at all, but posed confidently within the museum's galleries (fig. 1). This photograph, which features Mrs. C. Mathews Dick, Jr., and Mrs. Edward B. Smith standing in front of "the pride of the Institute,"[2] Georges Pierre Seurat's *Sunday on La Grande Jatte— 1884* (1884–86), seems almost to extend the Post-Impressionist's gallery of social types beyond the canvas and into the Art Institute itself. Echoing the position, posture, and dress of the painted couple behind them, the pair cuts an imposing figure, and appears—at first glance, at least—to announce to *Vogue*'s readers that the museum's female patrons and audiences had arrived as forces to be reckoned with. The presence of a uniformed, male security guard, however, complicates such an easy reading of the picture: while commanding much less visual and social attention than the two women, he seems at the same time to place himself between them and the work itself, a subtle reminder of the museum's watchful, proprietary eye.

The engineers of the Masterpiece Ball, who soon went on to help create the Woman's Board of The Art Institute of Chicago, were acutely aware of their unique position in respect to a curious public; the largely male philanthropic circles they moved within; and an increasingly professionalized museum staff that at once benefited from their patronage and sought to channel it in its own way. While the *Vogue* photograph only hints at this delicate

Figure 1 Horst P. Horst (American, born Germany, 1906). *Mrs. C. Matthews Dick, Jr., and Mrs. Edward B. Smith Standing in Front of Seurat's* La Grande Jatte *at The Art Institute of Chicago*, 1952 (detail). Published in *Vogue*, July 1, 1952, p. 69. © *Vogue*, The Condé Nast Publications Inc.

relationship to the powers that were, the Woman's Board's organizers acknowledged it far more explicitly. In their 1952 written proposal for the group, they promised the Art Institute's director, Daniel Catton Rich, that "the primary purpose of a Woman's Board would be to assist the Board of Trustees in raising needed annual funds," but took pains to assure him that it would also play a more traditionally "feminine" role:

> It would also assist in promotional, social, and housekeeping activities, in all instances avoiding any overlapping on the functions of trustees or staff. . . . The board could fill a gap in the present administration of the museum, studying and carrying out various details that may be too insignificant or too feminine for the trustees to be burdened with, too unprofessional or too time-consuming to add to the already heavy load of the staff.[3]

While choosing a stance of deference and accommodation, these women managed to claim for themselves an important sphere of influence which came, from the early 1950s onward, to include ambitious, related plans for audience relations and education in the broadest sense. Employing their own brand of publicity and spectacle, they worked to reassert the Art Institute's identity as a thoroughly open, accessible museum at a crucial

time of expansion, and moved on to extend its reach toward Chicago's burgeoning suburban population; the city's community of contemporary artists and amateur collectors; and record numbers of school children. In telling a tale of the Woman's Board and its efforts —among them the Community Associates (1953), the Art Rental and Sales Gallery (1954), the Staff Assistants program (1961), and the Junior Museum (1964)—this essay aims to bring to life a distinct yet largely forgotten moment in the history of the Art Institute and its relationship with the city it serves. It also attempts to suggest how, within that particular moment, this cadre of elite Chicago women came to collaborate with a team of talented, independent-minded museum educators and volunteers, shaping the Art Institute's public mission, and the real-life experiences of its visitors, through a shared focus of cultural, intellectual, and professional ambition.

I. From Morgue to Merry-Go-Round

In order to understand more clearly why the Woman's Board came to be, and how its emphasis on community relations and education captured a particular aspect of the Art Institute's spirit in the 1950s, there is no better place to start than the museum's unprecedented Emergency Fund Drive. First announced in late 1951, this was the Art Institute's first attempt to appeal directly to the people of Chicago for financial support.[4] Faced with rising operating costs, insufficient gallery space, and a crumbling building that had not been substantially altered since 1925, Rich and the museum's trustees launched a media-relations campaign that succeeded in sparking the imagination of the city's press and public in a profound way.[5] In interviews Rich (see fig. 2), who had for many years advocated a populist identity and agenda for the Art Institute, repeated almost word for word the progressive vision that the museum's patron Charles L. Hutchinson had voiced nearly four decades previously:

> The institute is a museum, a school, a theater, a library, and above all, a vital, stimulating place that reaches into the lives of countless persons. . . . The tradition of the institute since its beginning has been that art is something alive and going on, rather than finished and dead. If it comes to a choice, we would rather have an art merry-go-round than an art morgue.[6]

By reminding Chicagoans that the Art Institute belonged to them, and in fact existed for their own use, the museum's administrators were effectively able to transform financial vulnerability into an advantage. Turning to the public for help, they managed to rediscover a constituency that was flattered to be asked, and happy to contribute to the $1,600,000 campaign in whatever way it could. "Chicagoans Rally to Aid Art Institute," headlines blazed, as newspapers reported that "never before have so many who call Chicago home felt themselves so vital a part of that great institution's fame—and its future!"[7] While the museum's directors urged the populace to "tour the institute and see for themselves the magnificent things which must be preserved,"[8] culturally minded locals sent in contributions by the thousands, and dropped their spare change into a "treasure chest" placed prominently in the Michigan Avenue lobby (see fig. 7). One Mrs. John Grace of suburban Hinsdale, Illinois, even went so far as to compose a whimsical poetic appeal in which the Art Institute's prized paintings cry out for "succor": "Blakelocks and Sargents, Van Gogh and Gauguin, All beg you—together—Please Give All You Can!!"[9]

At the center of this whirl of civic excitement, and to a great degree responsible for generating it, was a group of influential Chicago women who possessed an acute sense of civic engagement and substantial experience as community leaders. Called the Women's Division of the Emergency Campaign, they worked in concert with Rich and the board of trustees to cultivate interest in the drive, creating a speaker's bureau to approach clubs and business organizations for contributions, and mobilizing teams of volunteers "to canvass the entire city and suburbs."[10] Perhaps most valuable, however, was the constant publicity that this band of friends was able to garner on the museum's behalf. Rich had created a formal Department of Public Relations at the Art Institute in 1938, in part to give the museum a more egalitarian image by generating "less coverage on the society pages of the newspapers and more as serious news."[11] The fact of the matter, however, was that society was serious business in its own right, and many prospective art-lovers were more interested in identifying themselves with the smart set

Figure 3 Margaret Day Blake (at left) and Mary Lasker Block test out the new gallery benches that the Woman's Board commissioned from the noted designer Florence Knoll, c. 1955.

than the proletariat. In the 1950s, the extensive social pages of daily newspapers commanded readers' attention in a way that is difficult to imagine today, and the personalities, activities, and amusements of prominent Chicagoans were a source of endless public fascination, particularly to women. Frequently pictured attending the gala opening of an art exhibit, lunching in one anothers' gracious homes, or lending their time and energy to a host of charitable causes, the members of the Women's Division were well-known figures before they ever turned their hands to the Art Institute's publicity campaign. As such, they were in a perfect position to bring it to fruition.

While creating fashionable public personae and benefiting from the wealth of the men who were their fathers, brothers, and husbands, these women also crafted their own brand of power and used it in individual and consistently creative ways. Often graduates of elite educational institutions such as Wellesley College in Massachusetts, which holds as its motto the phrase "Not to be ministered unto, but to minister," their lives were shaped by the still-current, late-nineteenth-

century ethos that women of means should direct their ambitions not toward professional careers outside the home, but to rearing children, managing a household, and maintaining a rigorous schedule of philanthropic work.[12] A 1959 column in the *Chicago Sun Times* captured the special possibilities and constraints of such an existence, commenting that "strong social pressures are put on these women to lend their apparent abundance of time—as well as their influential names—to charitable and civic affairs."[13]

It was through this tradition of service that such women as Margaret Day (Mrs. Tiffany) Blake (see figs. 3, 9), widow of the chief editorial writer at the *Chicago Tribune* and a prime mover in the city's social life, had become, among other things, the organizer of the first women's suffrage organization in Chicago; a trustee of the University of Illinois; and the chairperson of the state's branch of the Women's Land Army during World War I.[14] Blake's accomplishments, while exceptional, were by no means unusual in her wide circle of acquaintances. Her friend and colleague Florence Lowden (Mrs. C. Phillip) Miller, for instance, spent time running her family's Sinnissippi experimental forest in Oregon, Illinois, when she was not serving on the boards of such concerns as the Chicago Historical Society, the Welfare Council of Metropolitan Chicago, and the George M. Pullman Educational Foundation, named for her grandfather, the noted railroad-car magnate.[15]

Given their easy access to the press, public, and moneyed supporters, and their place at the center of an extensive, established network of civic organizations throughout the metropolitan area and beyond, the value of such allies would have been self-evident. Moreover, many of these women were already playing significant roles at the Art Institute. While the trustees had never yet elected a female

Figure 4 A crew of stonemasons works on much-needed repairs to the Art Institute's north wall, 1952.

member, many of the women who became active in the Emergency Fund Drive had firm ties to the Art Institute through longstanding, predominantly female organizations such as the Chicago Public School Art Society (see Rhor, pp. 27–28) and the Antiquarian Society, which had supported acquisitions of textiles and decorative arts since affiliating with the museum in 1891.[16] Others were members of departmental and trustees' committees. Blake, for instance, was a major force on the Prints and Drawings Committee, and since 1944 had been helping the museum build a collection of drawings that achieved international renown.[17] Still others were major purchasers of art in their own right. Mary Lasker (Mrs. Leigh B.) Block (see fig. 3), for example, both supported the Art Institute and worked with her husband, the president of Inland Steel, to build one of the city's finest private collections of modern art.[18]

Collectively, these women and others like them formed, in the words of early Woman's Board member Zoé Bakeeff (Mrs. Edward S.) Petersen, both a "nucleus of friends" and a battalion of "high-powered ladies" who "had a lot of sense of community, and of the city, and of themselves."[19] It was their talent at turning that sense into both positive publicity and real financial gain for the Art Institute, however, that made them crucial to the success both of the Emergency Fund Drive and the ambitious series of structural and institutional improvements it inaugurated. Throughout the 1950s and 1960s, the museum launched an ever more expansive (and expensive) course of renovations which included repairing the main Allerton Building (see fig. 4); remodeling the galleries; transforming the old, two-story Blackstone Hall (see Rhor, fig. 1) into two separate floors that contained a new auditorium and space for the display of Asian art; and constructing the Sterling Morton Wing (1962) to the south

Polly Clancy as Gainsborough's "Blue Boy."

Grand March at the Masterpiece Ball

THE MASTERPIECE BALL

It was a MASTERPIECE, all right!

CHICAGO DAILY NEWS
for and about WOMEN

Reg. U.S. Pat. Off.

SATURDAY, MAY 24, 1952. ★ PAGE 15

Mr. and Mrs. William Wood Prince as jockeys for Degas' "At the Races."

Hermon Dunlap Smith as Rembrandt's "Scholar with Gloves."

Mrs. J. Harris Ward as Gainsborough's "Lady Hamilton."

Mrs. Clymer Bowen as statue of Egyptian Queen Neferititi.

Dr. and Mrs. John Orndorff as Grant Wood's "American Gothic."

52

SOCIETY IN CHICAGO

Art Works Breathe As 600 in Costume Dance at the Hilton

Mrs. W. H. Mitchell Wins 1st Priz For Appearing as Institute Painti

BY ATHLYN DESHAIS

Try to recapture all the pictures you've seen in art gall in any part of the world. A good share of these came to life day night at the Art Institute's Masterpiece Ball.

Of the 800 guests, about 600 were in costume—so authentic and brilliant that it was a heavy responsibility for those who had to pass judgment.

In the Conrad Hilton ballroom, where the alabaster statues of Venus, Apollo, Juno, Pan and Caesar Augustus flanked the dance floor, the grand march paraded at midnight past the judges' stand.

*   *   *

TO DARK-EYED Mrs. William H. Mitchell went first honors for being the most authentic portrayal of a picture hanging in the Art Institute. She was the Matisse "Lady with White Plumes."

Award for the best individual costume went to Dr. and Mrs. John Orndorff as Grant Wood's "American Gothic."

Mrs. Orndorff commissioned an artist to paint the background scene and had it framed. She and her husband stood within the frame dressed authentically—"even to the underwear"—as the stern-faced farmer and his wife.

The Robert Hagey's takeoff on the Calder mobile won for them the most original award.

*   *   *

AMONG the classic paintings represented were Polly Clancy, in blue satin and plumed hat, as Gainsborough's "Blue Boy"; Mrs. J. Harris Ward, also in lavishly plumed hat, as the same artist's "Lady Hamilton"; Hermon Dunlap Smith as Rembrandt's "Scholar with Gloves"; Frederick Sweet as Frans Floris' 16th century work, "Portrait of a Gentleman"; Heaton Sykes as Du Plessis' "Louis XVI," with Cynthia Corning as Miltez' "Marie Antoinette."

The Laurence Cartons appeared as Botticelli's "Pellas and the Centaur."

In a more modern vein were Mrs. A. Watson Armour III and Mrs. Edward Byron Smith as "Majas on the Balcony" by Goya. Their husbands were Spanish

Weekend Calendar

SUNDAY

Musicale and tea at I Harold Simpson's Oak P home.

Annual musicale and tea musician members of Club, 3:30 p.m.

"Green-Back Open House" Art Institute fund drive at ert Lewis Fisher home in Park, 3-6 p.m.

Mixed 4-some tournam and informal supper in m locker room at Shoreacres

"A Foreign Af-fair," auc for Library of International lations at Saddle and Cy Cocktails and dinner be auction.

MONDAY

Meeting and luncheon lius Petersen home in K worth to map final plans opening of the Peacock C for Crippled Children at Villa, 10 a.m.

Election of officers by W en's auxiliary board of Wo hospital at Dixon Chapel of cago Temple, 10:30 a.m.

"Models of Yesteryear," ley hospital benefit lunche Field's Wedgewood Room

Key Club's final Cha Amateur Model Contest.

Highland Park-Ravinia fant Welfare's annual lunc at Country Fair, 1 p.m.

Luncheon for North S Auxiliary of the Chicago ternity Center at Mrs. Pau Cutler's Wilmette home.

representing "Jamila" by Alfredo Dominguez.

Mrs. Robert F. Spi trimmed a white pleated Chapman gown and cam one of the croquet player Winslow Homer's "Cro Scene."

Christopher Holabird and

of the Allerton Building. One of these projects, the B. F. Ferguson Memorial Building (1958), took on a particularly public and controversial nature, prompting an uproar from many civic leaders and artists, who accused the Art Institute of defacing Chicago's landscape by erecting another building in Grant Park, and misappropriating funds that were specifically intended to beautify the city with works of public sculpture. [20]

In the beginning, however, Blake, Block, Miller, and their compatriots capitalized on their public clout by staging a series of splendid spectacles that succeeded at the difficult—and by no means easily compatible—aims of raising money for the emergency drive and lending the Art Institute an extra touch of social spice, while at the same time giving concrete form to Rich's vision of the museum as an energized storehouse of knowledge and creativity for the widest possible range of visitors. Through the benefit Masterpiece Ball of May 1952, for instance, they managed to raise over $30,000 for the institute by luring hundreds of well-heeled citizens onto the dance floor of the Conrad Hilton Hotel, and convincing them to turn out in a wide array of Art-Institute-themed costumes that ranged from the extravagant to the outlandish (see figs. 5–6). Dancing the night away amid plaster statues affixed with masks and draped drolly with YMCA bath towels, more than a few party-goers competed for prizes while dressed as the dour farm couple from the Art Institute's iconic *American Gothic* (1930) by Grant Wood. More elegant personalities such as Mary Van Etten (Mrs. J. Harris) Ward modeled themselves on works by the eighteenth-century English portraitist Thomas Gainsborough, while others arrived wired together, ten-a-piece, impersonating a group of Claude Monet's famous *Haystacks*. "I went as Hecate," recalls Zoé Petersen, "because

we had a stuffed bird. . . . I thought this was great fun." [21]

The Masterpiece Ball is most compelling, however, not for its conviviality or lavishness (masked balls were long a staple of high life in Chicago, as elsewhere), but rather for the unexpected way in which its organizers were able to use such an exclusive social occasion as a tool for reaching out to a wide audience of potential museum-goers. [22] Through the medium of the press, people who might never actually attend the festivity were able to learn in great detail who was who and who wore what, and in the process establish their own, decidedly informal relationship to what might otherwise seem a stiff, imposing cultural institution. A month before the actual party, moreover, the Art Institute chose to promote both the ball and the fund drive by placing over $2,000,000 worth of its paintings and decorative art in the windows of retail stores along the main shopping thoroughfares of State Street and Michigan Avenue. Through this dramatic act of transforming everyday destinations into an extension of the Art Institute's galleries, the museum's planners can be seen to have blurred the boundaries between their institution and the city in the most literal of ways. Even more remarkable, perhaps, was how this presentation of rare artworks in shop windows—not in satellite museums such as the Garfield Park Art Galleries (see Rhor, pp. 38–39)—implied that these treasures could, like the consumer goods they replaced, somehow be "owned" by average Chicagoans. While ordinary citizens could not actually purchase these fine things for their homes, the Art Institute seemed to intimate that they might, as patrons of the museum, exercise a different proprietary relationship to these masterpieces that was no less alluring.

Figure 6 This full-page spread in the May 24, 1952 edition of the *Chicago Daily News* captures both the Masterpiece Ball's whimsical spirit and its real public-relations value to the Art Institute.

Figure 7 Visitors throng the Art Institute's Michigan Avenue lobby at the Merry-Go-Round, an open house sponsored by the Woman's Board in May 1953. At the lower right is the museum's "treasure chest," still open to receive contributions.

Billed as an "exhibition" that offered Chicagoans a chance to see on the street "objects that ordinarily are viewed only in museums," this venture was matched in spirit by later events such as the Merry-Go-Round of May 1953, in which the museum held an open house to celebrate the successful completion of the Emergency Fund Drive (see fig. 7).[23] "Welcome to your Art Institute," invitations proclaimed, as visitors were encouraged to tour the art-shipping room, carpentry shop, photography studios, school classrooms, and the backstage of the Goodman Theatre, all facilities normally off-limits to the general public (see fig. 8). In the museum's grand Fullerton Hall, members of the newly founded Woman's Board, many the same women who had earlier appeared in fancy dress in newspaper photographs of the Masterpiece Ball, performed living tableaux for appreciative crowds who had come to experience a behind-the-scenes look at the institute and, just as importantly, catch a glimpse of the people who had brought its needs and ambitions into their homes along with the latest edition of the *Chicago Tribune* or *Daily News*.[24] Named in order to recall

Rich's earlier paraphrase of Hutchinson, in which he presented a vision of the Art Institute as an "art merry-go-round" rather than an "art morgue," this was a performance designed to assure the public that when they opened their pockets to the museum, they actually got what they paid for.

This double gesture of transparency and accessibility—of making the museum's inner workings visible and at the same time including the public as active participants in the glamorous, eclectic social life it generated—was a prime characteristic of the many spectacles the Woman's Board staged during the 1950s and 1960s to continue the spirit of the Merry-Go-Round.[25] The stated goal of the 1955 May Festival, for example, was "to make every citizen feel at home in every part of the Art Institute."[26] These open houses were overwhelmingly successful. Reaching millions through the press, they routinely attracted crowds in excess of five thousand people "from every part of the city and every walk of life," all eager to take advantage of Chicago's "biggest bargain in art appreciation and entertainment" by looking at art objects and at the same time taking in living tableaux; demonstrations by artists and flower arrangers; lavish table settings; and performances by such attractions as the popular television personalities Kukla, Fran, and Ollie.[27]

On one occasion, a society columnist went so far as to praise the May Festivals as a "great experiment in democracy."[28] As we have seen, however, these productions, like the Woman's Board's other spectacles, were a far more slippery, interesting mix of elitism and populism than that. By putting themselves on display alongside the museum's art and inviting the city to come watch, the Art Institute's "high-powered ladies" leveraged their own social privilege in the service of the museum's "democratic" goal of serving an ever more diverse and expanding public. Creating occasions that humanized the Art Institute and threw its doors open to the community, they attempted to achieve from the top down—at least for a series of isolated, shimmering moments—the sort of universal accessibility and identification that has been an important, elusive goal of American art museums since almost the moment of their founding.

II."A True Kinship of Effort, a Combined Undertaking"

While the Merry-Go-Round, May Festivals, and the even more inclusive Celebrations of the 1980s constituted a crucial element of Woman's Board activity, it was on the level of the practical, just as much as the imaginary, that the group set out to shape the Art Institute's relationship to Chicago. Getting the museum into the press and the public into the museum was only the beginning of a wide-ranging series of focused experiments—community

associations, an art rental and sales gallery, a volunteer docent program, and a pioneering children's museum—that aimed to strengthen the institution's role in the day-to-day life of citizens, and to convert the groundswell of interest generated by the Emergency Fund Drive into more substantial, concrete change.

In late 1952, as the capital campaign drew close to final success, Chauncey McCormick, president of the museum, announced with great fanfare the official formation of the "Woman's Board of The Art Institute of Chicago." This step, which Rich and the trustees had hinted they might take as early as 1950, was in effect offered as a reward for the "distinguished service" of the Women's Division, which was credited with raising $675,000 toward the museum's total goal. It was also framed, though, as an acknowledgment of "the outstanding contributions made by the women of Chicago to the Art Institute

Figure 8 Chicagoans enjoy a rare tour of the Art Institute's shipping room during the Merry-Go-Round, the May 1953 celebration of the museum's successful Emergency Fund Drive.

Figure 9 At the 1953 Merry-Go-Round, Woman's Board President Margaret Day Blake and Chauncey McCormick, President of the Art Institute's Board of Trustees, announce their common victory: a capital campaign that exceeded all expectations.

throughout its existence."[29] Either way, the decision lent an extra measure of legitimacy and influence to what was until then a rather informal association of women, and situated it firmly within the museum's administrative structure. Indeed, the Woman's Board president was guaranteed a place on the Art Institute's all-male board of trustees, and Margaret Blake, newly elected to that position, became the first woman to break the boundary (see fig. 9).

As the first of its type in Chicago, the Woman's Board was heralded not only as a trailblazing development, but as a prime example of a "matriarchate of the arts" that was seen to include the Art Institute and the Chicago Symphony, and stretch from the Renaissance Society on the city's south side to the Evanston Art Center on the affluent, suburban North Shore.[30] While women had long been active supporters of the Art Institute and other organizations such as the Arts Club of Chicago, which had championed avant-garde works since its foundation in 1916, there is ample reason to suspect that, by the early 1950s, they were moving onto the cultural scene in greater force as both audiences and patrons. For example, in drafting its announce-

ment of the Woman's Board's creation, the Art Institute's administration admitted that it was in fact not innovating, but instead following a larger trend "borne out by the fact that thirty-two museums in the United States have either instituted women's boards or placed women on their boards during the past ten years."[31] At the same time, women across the continent were beginning to identify themselves as members of an incipient museum movement dedicated to making "the lethargic and stagnant atmosphere of many galleries come to life."[32] On the very weekend the Art Institute voted to start its own women's organization, a group of female delegates from eighteen art museums throughout the United States and Canada met in Toronto, where they came to realize that they had "been working, in many cases simultaneously, yet unknown to one another, on a program so similar that it would appear to be a true kinship of effort, a combined undertaking."[33]

While it is unclear whether the founding members of the Chicago Woman's Board attended this conference, they certainly knew of it, and their plan for the group hit upon many of the ideas articulated there. Apart from the prime directive to raise funds through benefit parties, the board singled out a number of "housekeeping" projects—new gallery benches and a members' lounge, to name a few—that it was later able to implement with dispatch (see figs. 3, 10). Other, more ambitious objectives included a "picture lending service," a "volunteer bureau," and a "community relations" initiative that might continue to "increase the institute's warm and human relations with the public."[34] Chartered as a forty-member committee, the board soon filled its ranks with influential women hand-picked from throughout the city and suburbs. Many had worked on the Emergency Fund Drive, but many more had long been active in the

Figure 10 In 1960 the Woman's Board created a Members' Room that offered a place to relax amid fine modernist furnishings and works of art such as a large textile panel designed by Henri Matisse, at left, still in the Art Institute's collection.

Chicago Public School Art Society, the museum's Antiquarian Society, or on departmental committees. Florene May (Mrs. Samuel A.) Marx, Elizabeth Nitze (Mrs. Walter P.) Paepcke, and Muriel Kallis (Mrs. Jay Z.) Steinberg, moreover, had already established independent reputations as important collectors. [35] Adding to the mix a rich diversity of artistic and professional experience were such individuals as Helen Tieken (Mrs. Maurice P.) Geraghty, a talented theatrical producer; the noted sculptor Sylvia Shaw (Mrs. Clay) Judson; Dr. Ann Lally, Head of the Art Department for the Chicago Public Schools; and the "First Lady of Radio," Judith Waller, Director of Public Affairs and Education for the National Broadcasting Corporation. [36] Colleagues and friends, these women forged close relationships, working together with a high sense of fun and drama, and traveling near and far to explore other museums and the world of art more widely (see fig. 11). [37]

As Margaret Blake made clear at the board's first meeting, however, the only way in which the new group could hope to accomplish its goal of "bringing to the Art Institute countless thousands who have not yet shared its rich experiences" was to expand its ranks immediately. [38] To that end, the board began in 1952 to organize the Community Associates, a network of local, autonomous groups that would "extend the activities of the board outside the city . . . to people in the suburbs who, due to modern living, could not make use of its [the Art Institute's] treasures as freely as those who lived nearby." [39] In this endeavor, the board relied on the experience of member Helen Curtenius (Mrs. Robert) McDougal, who previously served as president of the Infant Welfare Society of Chicago, which had formed its own successful system of suburban chapters.

Beginning with the northern village of Winnetka, McDougal and her team studied a map of commuter train lines into the city, tar-

Figure 11 Woman's Board members Babbie Smith and Muriel Newman (at center and right) in Iran with their traveling companion Lucy Lynn, on a University of Chicago-sponsored trip, c. 1953. Photo: Albert Newman.

Figure 12 The membership committee of the Highland Park Community Associates pose for a photograph promoting the group's local activities, 1959. Gathering in the home of Mrs. Albert L. Arenberg (at right), they admire *Night Rising*, a painting by Chicago artist and early Woman's Board member Martyl (Mrs. Alexander) Langsdorf.

geting affluent suburban areas that seemed ripe for cultivation.[40] Their growth fueled by press coverage and word-of-mouth publicity on the neighborhood level, associates groups spread rapidly over the next decade, attracting nearly two thousand people residing in inner-ring suburbs and outlying towns within a forty-mile radius of the Art Institute.[41] The chapters announced their frequent activities in suburban newspapers (see fig. 12), and made modestly priced memberships available by mail to all interested parties. Most of these were educated, middle- and upper-middle-class women who, while less socially prominent than their counterparts on the Woman's Board, also had time and energy to spare, and ample experience as leaders in their own localities. Jane Harshaw (Mrs. Richard) Clarke, a member of the Junior League of Chicago in the 1950s and later a museum educator at the Art Institute, recalls that she and her league compatriots "had the leisure, in a way, to volunteer." "It wasn't even that we had that much money, but we were home, and we never thought of working while our kids were little."[42]

To a great extent, the popularity of the Community Associates, like that of the movement of women into cultural leadership roles more generally, can be seen to have been part and parcel of a much wider wave of community involvement that crested in the two decades following World War II.[43] Americans of all income levels and social strata were allying themselves with a cornucopia of organizations ranging from Kiwanis clubs and the League of Women Voters to town councils and parent-teacher associations. Indeed, it appears as though many younger women emerged from the war years with a renewed sense of public commitment and confidence. For example Sara Wood, a Junior League colleague of Clarke's who later served on the Woman's Board, describes an important difference of experience between her mother's friends and her own: "A lot of women were more liberated, because they'd been either in the service, or rolling bandages, or driving trucks—they were more active, that generation."[44] The Community Associates plan, which brought prosperous, suburban women together to socialize and in the process forward the work of the Art Institute through taking news of its activities to local schools and other interested groups, perhaps succeeded as well as it did because it approached museum support as a collaborative act of civic engagement.

While improving the cultural climate in their own towns and offering a new way to connect with the urban center, the associates groups also offered members pleasures that were deeply personal and intellectual in nature. In 1964 Peg (Mrs. Frederick J.) Keilholz, chairperson of the Community Associates chapter in suburban Barrington, northwest of Chicago, characterized her experience in just such terms:

> We meet to hear about the permanent collection of the Art Institute, special exhibitions, the work of a particular artist or sculptor, or [the] history of some phase of art. We learn to appreciate what we like, open our eyes and minds to things we do not presently understand or like, and have the opportunity to find new interests to enrich our lives.[45]

That year Keilholz and her fellow Barringtonians expanded their aesthetic horizons by attending four lectures in their home town on subjects ranging from the paintings of Chicago artist Ivan Albright to the history of fashion design.[46] Associates took trips into the city to keep themselves abreast of goings-on at the Art Institute, and conducted further study groups according to their own interests (see fig. 13). They were also encouraged to volunteer their time further, and often served as greeters at Woman's Board festivals, sharing the limelight with society celebrities such as

Figure 13 Three members of the Winnetka Community Associates in the Art Rental and Sales Gallery, 1958.

Margaret Blake and Mary Block. Over time a significant number of new Woman's Board members emerged from the ranks of suburban supporters. One of them, Patricia Cooper (Mrs. Robert) Kubicek, describes such transitions as a product of individual commitment more than social ambition: "If you had any talent, and if you were willing to work, it was not about money. It was what you were willing to bring to the table. That's different."[47]

As they brought their energy and skills to that table, many of these volunteers became passionately involved in another of the board's major attempts at audience outreach and art education, the Art Rental and Sales Gallery. The Art Institute opened the facility in 1954, largely in response to a growing climate of anxiety over Chicago's failure to adequately support its own artistic talent. Some artists complained that their most promising colleagues were moving to New York, and that snobbish local collectors were bypassing Chicago dealers and buying in that city, or abroad, instead. Others blamed the problem on what they perceived to be the low level of art criticism in local newspapers, and a consequent lack of aesthetic development on the part of the public.[48] More than a few, though, took the Art Institute to task for its indifference. George Buehr (see Rhor, fig. 10), a popular lecturer in the museum's Education Department, spoke out "as a citizen and a painter" when he admitted that "the institute has been remiss in not showing more Chicago art." "Its first obligation," he maintained, "is to its community."[49]

Chicago's commercial art scene was in fact not completely moribund at this moment, however. In the early-to-mid-1950s, the Benjamin, Fairweather-Hardin, and Allan Frumkin galleries, among others, all sold modern works by respected local artists, and shared the market with many less adventurous competitors located along Michigan Avenue and Oak Street, and in the city's department stores and hotels.[50] The Chicago branch of Artists' Equity had beaten the Art Institute to the punch in late 1952, opening its own art-rental service in the new 1020 Art Center, which housed the offices of *Poetry Magazine* and other cultural groups in a renovated graystone mansion on Lake Shore

Drive.[51] The Woman's Board's initiative, though, stamped with the museum's seal of approval and located within its walls, was a striking development on its own terms, and signaled the institute's commitment to Chicago artists in a clear and public way. Inspired by the success of a similar venture at the Museum of Modern Art, New York, board members scoured the city looking for works to fill the gallery. Muriel Steinberg (later Mrs. Albert Newman), for example, "spent days on the phone. . . . and with Florene Marx's car and driver, visited what seemed like hundreds of artists" in all corners of Chicago.[52]

Although run by a corps of volunteers, the Art Rental and Sales Gallery achieved its success through rigorous professionalism.[53] All works of art were fully insured and carefully displayed, and respected panels of jurors were secured from the ranks of local artists, Art Institute curators, and faculty members from Chicago-area art schools and universities. The gallery (see fig. 13) offered a changing and stylistically diverse selection of paintings, sculptures, and works on paper for prices ranging between five and twenty five dollars for a two-month period, and turned renters into buyers by allowing clients to apply their payments toward actual purchases. From the start, the venture attracted businesspeople such as Arnold Arenberg, an electrical supplier who jumped at the prospect of enlivening his "dull, routine sort of business" with art, and helping employees "get an outlook that isn't strictly commercial."[54]

Equally as compelling, however, was the gallery's appeal to "Mr. and Mrs. Homemaker whose walls are bare because 'We can't afford originals and don't like reproductions.'"[55] By making both abstract and representational work available and economically accessible to a wide audience, the staff of Art Rental and Sales helped their clientele develop their own

Figure 14 This stage set was constructed in 1932 for "A Red Library," one of Dudley Crafts Watson's many lectures on interior decoration. Held in the Art Institute's Fullerton Hall, such seminars were a popular educational offering from the early 1920s through the 1950s.

Figure 15 George Culler, Director of Museum Education from 1955 to 1958, meets with high-school students to choose artworks for display in their schools. This 1956 photograph was taken in the Art Institute's Blackstone Hall.

acute tastes in art, and encouraged them to exercise this newfound discrimination through active collecting. The gallery also performed the critical task of boosting the museum's image with artists and the public, who were even at that moment joining in the general outcry over the Art Institute's proposed Ferguson addition. Most important over the long term, however, was its role in expanding the sense of possibility that ordinary Chicagoans had in respect to the museum—as volunteers; as makers of art; and as inquisitive initiands eager to bring the experience of looking at and living with art closer to their everyday lives.

"What would we have done if we hadn't done this?": Professionals, Volunteers, and Volunteer Professionals

As we have seen, the Woman's Board's early initiatives of the 1950s sprang from an unusually acute sense of how audience relations and a broad approach to art education could be combined to bring the Art Institute and Chicagoans together in new, creative ways. These efforts were also, like the group's members, intimately connected to a wider network of female-run arts and social-service organizations, many of which continued the related, reformist work of the late-nineteenth century Arts and Crafts and Settlement House movements. At the same time, though, Woman's Board programs operated in concert with the formal offerings already in place at the museum itself. Community Associates, after all, were taught by the none other than the museum's curators and lecturers. The Art

Figure 16 Maryette Charlton, the Extension Lecturer for the Chicago Public School Art Society, readies herself for a school visit in the society's new Jeep, 1951.

Rental and Sales Gallery, furthermore, can be understood properly only within the wider context of the Art Institute's longstanding attempts to refine its audiences' sense of design through such seminars as the Better Homes Institute (see Rhor, p. 32) and interior-decoration classes like Dudley Crafts Watson's "Clinic of Good Taste," which had met weekly since 1939 (see fig. 14).⁵⁶ It was the board's later attempt to reestablish a children's museum, and to sustain that facility with a corps of volunteer guides, however, that brought it most fully into contact with the Art Institute's staff of professional museum educators. The story of this relationship, which began to take firm shape in the early 1960s and continues to this day, provides a clear window onto how education for both young and adult audiences played itself out as a richly varied endeavor within the museum's galleries.

In her essay in this volume, Sylvia Rhor describes how, in the 1950s, the museum continued to split its educational work between different individuals and departments, each with their own particular traditions, pedagogical approaches, and spheres of influence. When he reasserted education's place at the core of the Art Institute's mission in 1955, Daniel Catton Rich was attempting to bring these disparate efforts into focus, and to unite them in one department that could pursue vigorously the "great unexplored opportunity for serving a wider public."⁵⁷ It was to that end that he hired as Director of Museum Education George D. Culler (see fig. 15), formerly head of the Akron Art Institute (now the Akron Art Museum) in Ohio. Culler, an artist turned curator and administrator, set about quickly transforming the institute's programming, moving it in a direction consonant with Katharine Kuh's pioneering Gallery of Art Interpretation (see Rhor, pp. 41–44). Speaking to the *Chicago*

Daily News soon after his arrival, Culler announced his philosophy in sweeping terms:

> During the last twenty-five years, we've had a gradual revolution in art museums. In the old days, all a museum had to do was open up and let people look around. Today, getting people to understand what they see has become the museum's central job. It has to make art understandable, not just show it off.[58]

Culler, like Kuh, believed that this understanding could best be achieved not through the traditional lecture format, but by means of more informal, interactive exchanges between curators, educators, and museum-goers. The new director put in place an ambitious series of gallery talks and study and discussion groups that aimed to engage curious amateurs with the basic issues of art interpretation. In late 1955, for example, Culler led a "series of gallery explorations" called the Starting Point, which was "designed to answer some of the layman's most pressing questions," including such heady ones as "What is a work of art, and what is it supposed to do?"[59] He intensified this approach over the next several years, working with his curatorial colleagues at "discussing and sharing aesthetic experiences" on "often neglected" areas of the museum's collection such as medieval art and modern prints and sculpture.[60] Just as crucial, however, was the fact that Culler made more of his department's activities free, and opened them to include the general public. Up until then, gallery tours, art classes, and travel lectures were, to a remarkable degree, the preserve of Art Institute members alone.[61]

This "revolution" was short-lived however, and ended abruptly in 1958, when Culler left the Art Institute to become director of the San Francisco Art Museum, now the San Francisco Museum of Modern Art. Rich and Kuh also departed within the year, leaving in their wake an impressive, innovative record

of adult education that belied the fact that younger audiences had long been left to shift for themselves. Indeed, in the years since the Children's Museum was dismantled and converted into the Gallery of Art Interpretation in 1939, the only in-museum activities for young people were weekly drawing classes geared solely to members' children, and the Raymond Fund lectures (see Rhor, p. 30, fig. 9), which still served large numbers of teenagers from public high schools throughout the city. As in the past, the Chicago Public School Art Society supplemented the museum's limited fare with its own initiatives, which it funded independently and coordinated with the Art Institute's Department of Education. In 1951, for example, these included the purchase of framed reproductions for schools and a free, small-scale guidance service for classes visiting the museum. A new Jeep (see fig. 16) permitted the society's extension lecturer to zip around town, giving slide talks that

Figure 17 Longtime Woman's Board member Suzette Morton Zurcher at home in her Astor Street apartment, Chicago. An eclectic collector, Zurcher brought a creative and unorthodox design sensibility to her work on the Art Institute's Junior Museum.

Figure 18 Director of Museum Education Barbara Wriston (at left) and her colleague Lois Raasch contemplate Sylvia Shaw Judson's *Rain Tree Fountain* (1963) at the opening party for the Junior Museum, February 1964.

explored "every-day visual experiences familiar to the children, such as color at the corner stop signal, line in the roller coaster at Riverview, and form in gasoline storage tanks."[62]

The problem of how to bring children back into the museum itself—and what to do with them once they were there—had occupied the minds of Woman's Board members from as early as 1953. In that year, Margaret Blake gathered a small group of women that, for more than half a decade, investigated volunteer docent and children's programs at museums throughout the continent.[63] It was not until the Community Associates, Art Rental and Sales, and May Festivals schemes were well established, however, that the board was able to devote itself fully to developing new opportunities and facilities for the young. One major inspiration emerged in 1957, when the Metropolitan Museum of Art, New York, inaugurated a sixteen-thousand-square-foot Junior Museum complete with an auditorium; a gallery of original artworks; an art reference library; a snack bar; and elaborate push-button displays designed to capture children's attention. This venture provided a concrete example of what might be done in Chicago, one that, combined with the earlier precedent of Kuh's Gallery of Art Interpretation, gave Woman's Board planners a model they could both imitate and refine. It also helped energize the prospective donors who visited it, among them Mr. and Mrs. James M. Alter, who returned from a 1959 junket to New York determined to help fund a similar facility at the Art Institute.[64]

The individual who was perhaps most instrumental in bringing the Junior Museum into existence was Suzette Morton (Mrs. Victor) Zurcher, a founder of the Woman's Board who in many ways personified the unique combination of wit, creativity, and intelligence that the group managed to consistently attract. Zurcher

(see fig. 17) had great economic and social capital at her disposal—both from her family's Morton Salt Company and her descent from important political figures such as Chicago mayor Carter H. Harrison—and had long exercised them on behalf of the Chicago Public School Art Society and the Art Institute. Trained as a graphic artist and master printer, she had, by 1951, created for herself what was then the only volunteer position on the museum's staff, Designer of Publications.[65]

Zurcher's lone status only begins to suggest, however, how the larger issue of women's volunteerism offered both the key to making the Junior Museum happen, and posed a major challenge at the same time. The Woman's Board realized that in order to achieve its goal of serving large numbers of school children, and using a junior gallery as a starting point for tours throughout the "adult" regions of the Art Institute, it would have to assemble a critical mass of trained, nonpaid guides. During the mid-1950s, an increasing number of women were donating their time at the Art Rental and Sales Gallery, and the Community

Associates presented themselves as ideal candidates for education work, but it was only with the assistance of the Junior League of Chicago that the volunteer effort took flight. The league, a longtime catalyst for social-service and cultural programs in the city, had been, quite coincidentally, searching for a way to turn its substantial financial resources and volunteer force to yet another unmet need: children's art education. Joining heads with the Woman's Board in 1960, her organization helped provide, Jane Clarke remembers, "what the Art Institute needed—money and young women." [66]

In their plan to fund and staff a volunteer guide program and then a Junior Museum, the Woman's Board and its new colleagues were attempting a feat that not even the Metropolitan Museum had tackled. In New York, as elsewhere, children's tours were still the domain of paid professionals. In fact, the growing prospect that amateurs might take over the galleries alarmed many leading museum figures of the moment, including Theodore L. Low, Director of Education at the Walters Art Gallery, Baltimore, who explained that "the fact that we have never used volunteers for teaching is the result of a firm belief that the quality of instruction must take precedence over the quantity of attendance figures." The very informality of his vocation, Low declared, "carries with it a danger of laxness against which museum educators must be constantly vigilant." For her part, lecturer Morna Crawford of the Museum of Fine Arts, Boston, cautioned her colleagues against the temptation to relegate children to volunteer lecturers while continuing to serve mature visitors themselves. "Since the giving of talks to school children is considered one of the most important aspects of educational work," she argued, "this above all should be done by those best qualified." [67]

Figure 19 Lois Raasch lectures to Staff Assistants during a training session in the Art Institute's Asian galleries, 1964.

Figure 20 Architect
Arthur Myrhum's render-
ing of the entrance to the
Junior Museum, 1964.
Tree-trunk benches deco-
rate the sides of the room,
which holds at its center
the *Rain Tree Fountain*
(1963), executed by sculptor and Woman's Board
member Sylvia Shaw
Judson (see fig. 18).

As it happened, the success of the Art Institute's experiment in lay docentry rested largely on the rigorous character of the museum's own education staff, and the hard work and dedication of the many women they trained. If members of the Woman's Board can be seen to have typified the role of the "professional volunteer," Barbara Wriston, who came to Chicago as the new Director of Museum Education in 1961, embodied female professionalism in a different but equally strong way.[68] The daughter of Brown University president Henry Wriston and sister to longtime Citibank chairman Walter Wriston, she arrived with powerful social connections that were matched by a master's degree in history and sixteen years of experience as a lecturer at the Museum of Fine Arts, Boston.[69]

Now, as then, Wriston is characteristically frank about both the role she saw volunteers assuming, and the high stakes of the undertaking.

> I was willing to start the program, but I insisted on standards," she recalls. We wouldn't allow volunteers to speak to adults. We had enough Staff Professionals to give the adult lectures, and not only that—talking to adults is a different horse entirely. I know that some

institutes let Staff Assistants talk to both children and adults, but I happen to think that's a mistake.[70]

As Wriston's remarks indicate, she, like Low, drew a firm distinction between "professionals" and "assistants." The fact that she coined her own terms to describe these roles, however, reveals just how far she and her associates were willing to go in order to reinvent them. Together with her colleague Lois Raasch, who soon assumed a key position as both the chief volunteer trainer and supervisor of children's education, Wriston addressed anxieties about "standards" by, quite simply, treating "Staff Assistants" as serious professionals and encouraging the rest of the museum to do the same.

Promising their new students that they would be receiving in a short burst of intense study "the equivalent of a master's degree in art history," Raasch and Wriston (see fig. 18) began in 1961 the first of many evolving experiments in docent education.[71] Roughly one hundred women, half of them drawn from the Junior League and many of the rest from Community Associates groups, immersed themselves in the world of the museum (see fig. 19). They read widely and listened to lectures by curators; researched individual

Figure 21 Parents and children alike enjoy an artist's demonstration at the 1964 opening of the Junior Museum. Photo: Martin J. Schmidt.

artworks in the Ryerson Library; and wrote a demanding series of essays in which they tested out ways of translating complex art-historical information into conversations that young visitors might actually find intriguing. While a number of these volunteers were art-history majors in college, some of the most gifted had little formal training in the discipline. Ruth Becker Powell, a member of that pioneering docent class and still an active volunteer, describes her experience as a unique combination of intellectual risk, challenge, and reward:

> Even though I didn't have the art-history background many other docents had, I felt that wouldn't deter me. . . . We had to do the job, and were expected to be disciplined. It was demanding. You were on time; you got your papers in when they were due; you were really more disciplined than you ever were in college. Lois and Barbara ran a tight ship—a military-type ship! At the same time we loved it. That's why we stayed.[72]

Some new pupils were not up to the task—Wriston, for example, remembers receiving a few angry phone calls—but those who did stay thrived.[73] After successfully designing their own introductory tour of the museum's collections, Staff Assistants were required to broaden their reach, and create specialized talks on art-historical periods and subjects ranging from Asian to Impressionism, medieval to contemporary. Tape recording themselves in the galleries, they worked to polish their skills as teachers and public speakers, all the while adding to the repertory of objects that they could discuss while moving through the Art Institute, negotiating the crush of visitors and remaining responsive to their young charges, who were inevitably bored by some works yet keenly interested in others.

Figure 22 The Little
Library in the Junior
Museum, 1965.

In explaining her own approach to children's art education, Wriston inveighs against what she characterizes as "an exchange of ignorance" in which school groups are "asked for their opinions when they don't have any information, let alone any knowledge." "When I went out to the schools in Boston," she recalls, "I said only 'I will tell you about these things; then you may ask any questions you want.'"[74] Although some early Staff Assistants remember conducting their own tours in just such a way, Raasch attempted to help her guides achieve an effective balance between lecture and discussion. "I didn't want docents to teach art history," Raasch says:

> I felt that children didn't have any sense of history to begin with, and art history seems to me even more complicated. What we tried to do was to have them look at a picture and talk about what was there—what they saw, conclusions they could draw from that, and how the experience of looking at art can be allied to everyday experiences.[75]

That Raasch's strategy should have been to connect art with the real world, and prompt audiences to look more closely and talk more clearly about what they saw, hints at the extent to which the once radical art-interpretation techniques of Kuh and Culler had been woven, by the mid-1960s, into the fabric of their profession. Indeed, the Woman's Board, in its written blueprint for the Junior Museum, voiced its own desire that a renewed children's program should "lean toward exhibitions based on such fundamentals as form, light, color, and how to see." Such an approach, the board hoped, would help young people "develop concepts which they can apply to all periods of art and to the visual elements of everyday life."[76]

In its own way, the Junior Museum was an important extension of the board's earlier attempts at humanizing the Art Institute, "aiming at an intimacy and freshness designed to render more comfortably the transition between the child's world and big, bewildering marble halls."[77] As with those efforts, the board conjured the facility into being through a clever publicity and fund-raising campaign, bringing in more than $250,000, much of it from donors who had never before been approached for major contributions.[78] The new museum opened its doors in February 1964, boasting an informal, playful look created by the Chicago architect Arthur Myrhum, who worked with Zurcher and other Woman's Board members to build a warm, welcoming environment in a basement space formerly occupied by the Art Institute's kitchens and cafeterias (see figs. 20–23). Salvaged carousel horses, sculpted tree trunks, and Sylvia Shaw Judson's *Rain Tree Fountain* (1963; see figs. 18, 20) were set off by a decorative palette of russet and deep green, and paired with furnishings by famed modernists such as Harry Bertoia, Charles and Ray Eames, and George Nelson.[79] By constructing a veritable gallery of good design, it appears, the Woman's Board aimed to subtly introduce young audiences to the finer pleasures of art and life from the moment they walked in the door.

The Junior Museum was also an eminently practical, full-service art center that enabled the Art Institute to accommodate record numbers of young visitors. In 1964, their first year of joint operation, the Staff Assistant program and the new gallery welcomed nearly seventy-three thousand school children, compared to roughly twenty-seven thousand just four years earlier.[80] Meeting their guides in the Michigan Avenue lobby, groups entered the little museum within minutes; they stowed their coats and lunches, toured the facility, and headed up into the galleries for a fifty-minute guided walk. Returning afterward, they could choose among a number of displays that were designed both to amuse them and help them continue on the path of learning to see for themselves.

A huge "Geo-Physical Relief Globe," for instance, helped children figure out exactly where the art they saw came from, while the Rainbow Gallery introduced the basics of color theory through a sound and light presentation. In the Thoresen Avenue Galleries, they might receive instruction on the differences between making actual paintings and good reproductions, or discover a small show that introduced them to the special exhibition currently installed in the Art Institute's main galleries. They could also flip through an illustrated book in the Little Library (see fig. 22), or wander over to the Crossroads Gallery and inspect works by some of the very artists whose creations hung down the hall in Art Rental and Sales. Beginning in the early 1970s, written gallery games, long a staple of children's museum-education programs, were supplemented by a series of brochures that families could use to take self-guided architectural expeditions through the Loop business district.

While Raasch and her staff routinely conceived more than fifteen small and traveling shows every year, it was in the Junior Museum's main Hammerman Gallery (see fig. 23) that they concentrated their most substantial efforts. For an impressive series of rotating exhibitions, which began with "Color and Light in Your World" (1963–64), "Motion in Art" (1964–65), and "Size" (1965–66), Raasch coaxed original works out of often reluctant curators, and supplemented them with reproductions. By focusing on expansive visual themes more often than historical ones, these displays successfully incorporated objects from all areas of the Art Institute's permanent collection, while at the same time reinforcing the Staff Assistants' attempts to give young viewers a broad aesthetic education. Raasch never self-consciously modeled her own efforts on Kuh's Gallery of Art Interpretation, but did

Figure 23 The Junior Museum's Hammerman Gallery during the exhibition "Sky Blue Pink" (1972–75), which incorporated objects ranging from a nineteenth-century Staffordshire flower holder (at far left) to Marino Marini's bronze *Horse and Rider* (1947, at right).

combine artifacts, photographs, and other sorts of visual information in a similar way, using modernist design and minimalist, interrogatory labels that spurred audiences to look independently and draw their own conclusions.

As a result, the Junior Museum appealed to children and their parents alike, providing adults with, as one observer characterized it, "a graphic explanation of the world of culture they've been embarrassed to say they don't understand."[81] Interested in these exhibitions as well as in every other aspect of Raasch's work, the Woman's Board stayed closely involved with the museum's programs throughout the 1970s, stepping in to endow the facility and fund renovations, repairs, and improvements of all kinds. The group also, as was its practice with the Community Associates and Art Rental and Sales, stood back, and moved on to support the increasingly diverse range of endeavors—benefit galas, collections catalogues, conservation efforts, and major exhibitions—that continue to occupy its atten-

tions to this day. Particularly important was the board's 1975 decision to organize a Volunteer Committee, which built on the success of the Staff Assistants and Art Rental experiments, integrating nonpaid workers into the daily routines of departments throughout the museum.[82]

But through its earlier devotion to the Staff Assistants program and the Junior Museum, the Woman's Board succeeded at nothing less than redirecting the Art Institute's educational focus toward young audiences. As George Schneider, former Associate Director of General Programs, looks back on his work as a lecturer in the 1960s and 1970s, he recalls that since "the emphasis was on children's programs," he and his colleagues "were left alone to do what we wanted to do."[83] While instrumental in implementing the Woman's Board's vision of children's programming, and in the process shaping it on her own terms, Wriston also enriched a varied array of adult offerings that in many ways bore more resemblance to those of the Parker and Watson eras than they did to Kuh and Culler's experiments in art interpretation through informal conversation. An increased battery of travel talks, most of them geared to European destinations, joined film screenings, subscription-lecture series, and a new graduate-student seminar that was designed to heighten the Art Institute's presence in university art-history departments throughout the Midwest. As in earlier decades, television and radio programming was used, much like today's experiments with the Internet, to extend the museum's reach through technology.[84]

At the same time, though, issues of economic and racial diversity were beginning to reassert themselves in respect to the museum's potential publics and the ways in which its programs might serve them more proactively. In the Art Institute's 1969 *Annual Report,* for example, the museum's director, John Maxon, acknowledged that "a problem which has concerned the staff in the past year is how to project the Art Institute and make it more accessible to underprivileged areas of metropolitan Chicago." "This is not easy," he admitted, "because the impetus and interest must not only come from these areas, but must be developed by the staff as a collaborative and meaningful venture."[85] Although it is less than clear exactly who fell into Maxon's category of the "underprivileged," his words suggest the complexity of any effort to expand museum audiences. They also hint that the Art Institute was considering, yet again, how to rearticulate its mission in response to new, increasing pressures from within and without. In the 1970s, these vague rustlings resulted in varied attempts such as those that reached out to Chicago's Latino community by originating Spanish-language extension lectures and gallery walks.[86] But as Robert Eskridge argues in the essay that follows, it was from the early 1980s onward that the museum's work in this direction began to take on an added dimension.

At The Art Institute of Chicago, women have always been in the galleries. At the moment of the museum's inception, the world of art, like that of teaching children, was imagined as an extension of the domestic sphere, and for that reason was open to women in ways that other fields of activity were not. Indeed, the opportunity to actually build substantial careers as museum educators doubtless led individuals from Helen Parker (see Rhor, fig. 10) to Barbara Wriston to cast their lot with the profession. The particular history of the Woman's Board, however, reveals how an elite corps of women who were not "professionals" per se made a place for themselves at the Art Institute, and in the process transformed the museum's public character. In the 1950s and 1960s, the board's members staked their claim to power, and used their privilege in a brilliant campaign to expand the institute's place in the life of the city. At the same time, and just as importantly, they cultivated and cooperated with a wider group of women who, like themselves, had talents and ambitions that they were waiting to realize in new ways. Reflecting on her forty-year career as a volunteer docent, Ruth Powell captures the essence of their joint undertaking perfectly:

> What would we have done if we hadn't done this? I think that our lives would not have been nearly as exciting and stimulating; we ask questions, and we probe, and it's just, altogether, an experience that I don't think I ever could have had in any other life.[87]

Museum Education at the Art Institute, 1980–2003: Expansion, Diversity, Continuity

Robert Eskridge

To view the public as consumers is really a throwback to the museum's more authoritarian past. The customer is encouraged to accept the product that is offered, while a museum dedicated to an educational purpose will encourage a far more complex response. Its goal will be to develop critical appreciation where enjoyment and understanding are combined with the self-confidence to exercise an informed personal taste. The goal of such a museum is not a herd of customers but an individualized public which has learned what it *does not*, as well as what it *does* like.

James N. Wood, 1989[1]

I. Expansion

James N. Wood, President and Director of The Art Institute of Chicago since 1980, delivered these words at a conference organized by the National Bureau of Economic Research. That group, which includes some of the nation's leading economists, invited the officials of America's major art museums to help it better understand the problems and possibilities that museums face as they attempt to fulfill their missions and remain financially viable at the same time. That this gathering was held at all suggests how, by the 1970s and 1980s, museums had come to exist within an increasingly competitive economic climate. In these decades, more museums—and more types of museums—were being built in cities

that, up until then, may have had few major cultural institutions.[2] Public interest in the arts expanded, and museums both cultivated and responded to that interest with more frequent and elaborate exhibitions, education programs, publications, and services. The eminent art historian and museum director Joshua Taylor recognized this trend in 1975, writing: "It is a rare prewar [World War II] institution which has not increased its facilities, enlarged its programs and taken a totally new look at its relationship to the art community and the community at large."[3] These expansive tendencies produced their own financial pressures, however: as operating budgets increased, endowment income, often

Figure 1 In response to numerous requests from visually impaired visitors and parents with young children, the Art Institute opened the *Touch Gallery* in September 2000. Developed in consultation with members of the visually impaired community, the gallery exemplifies the many ways in which the museum continues to broaden its attempts to reach and retain diverse audiences.

Figure 2 A main attrac-
tion at Kaleidoscope and
other family celebrations is
"Artie the Lion," a cos-
tumed character who is a
friendly, fuzzy version of
the two bronze lions that
flank the Art Institute's
main entrance.

a museum's main source of revenue, was able to cover less and less.[4] Understanding the museum visitor, then, had become an economic as well as a social imperative.

Even as Wood's talk of "consumers" and "customers" acknowledged the more overtly commercial tenor of museum work by the 1980s, his mention of "a museum dedicated to an educational purpose" recalls the spirit of a much earlier moment. Indeed, like Art Institute trustee and president Charles L. Hutchinson, whose words to the Chicago Literary Club open Danielle Rice's introduction to this publication, Wood (see fig. 6) voiced his vision for achieving one element of the Art Institute's original mission, that of conducting "appropriate activities conducive to the artistic development of the region."[5] But these two leaders displayed very different and revealing notions about who their audiences might be, and what the museum had in store for them. For Hutchinson, in 1915, it was enough to say that art was self-evidently, broadly "democratic," and that the Art Institute was meant, quite simply, for "the whole community." For Wood, almost a century later, the museum's educational objective was

more explicit and definitely more ambitious: to help foster nothing less than an "individualized public" capable of "enjoyment" and "understanding" with "self-confidence."

Implicit in Hutchinson's and Wood's assertions is the overall worth of museum education, which enhances the aesthetic, intellectual, and emotional awareness that viewers bring to bear on their experience of art. An informed public, it seems, is a "democratic" and "individualized" public—a powerful public. Indeed, art education is central to a liberal, humanistic education, and helps provide the intellectual equipment to comprehend, analyze, and challenge received ideas, an ability that, as classicist Bernard Knox has suggested, every free person needs in order to freely exercise his or her powers of freedom.[6]

Mere exposure to art, however, seldom elicits a profound response. The museum's task, whether fulfilled through publications, wall labels, or educational programs, is to heighten the visitor's capacity for perception. An educator can forge a connection between objects and viewers by offering insights into a work's medium, formal aspects, subject matter, historical context, or the probable intention of its maker—all complementary ways of understanding that an "individualized public" can use to form its own tastes and opinions about art. In a broader way, it is just this sort of active, emotional, and intellectual engagement with objects that helps visitors forge a sense of personal ownership in respect to the museums they visit.

The Art Institute's efforts at public education, like its collection and exhibition activities, continue to evolve and diversify, expanding notions of what counts as significant art, and exploring ways in which that art might be relevant to an audience that reflects the increasingly complex fabric of American culture. For over a century, in fact, the museum and the city of Chicago have created and re-created themselves in response to each other at singular moments. In Hutchinson's day, for instance, the museum established a collection of Old Master and contemporary European works for a metropolis of immigrants, thereby garnering a substantial measure of self-respect and international status for the town known as "hog butcher to the world." Only a few years after the economic crash of 1929, the Art Institute cleared its galleries for one of its most popular shows ever, a loan exhibition of paintings and sculpture that served as a highlight of the Century of Progress Exposition of 1933–34 (see Rhor, pp. 40–41). It was also during the Great Depression, as Sylvia Rhor demonstrates in her essay, that the museum established a formal Department of Museum Education, seeking to better serve the broad public that the exposition attracted. Gregory Nosan suggests here how, in the decades immediately following World War II, when the adjectives "suburban" and "middle-class" suffused our national lexicon, the Art Institute's Woman's Board invented the Community Associates program to attract citizens from the burgeoning suburbs. In the 1960s, moreover, the Department of Museum Education and the Woman's Board collaborated with the Junior League of Chicago to create the Junior Museum, in the process revitalizing the Art Institute as a magnet for students and teachers from all corners of the greatly enlarged metropolitan area.

By 1980 further changes in American culture were underway. As Danielle Rice discusses here, one no longer studied the history of art solely from a Western perspective. In the wake of the civil-rights movement, colleges and universities established new academic departments for the purpose of examining issues of race and gender, and applied critical approaches that continue to exert a strong influence on the study of what is now often called "visual culture." In the last few decades, moreover, the very notion that works of art can have universal value has been all but demolished by both art historians and scholars in other disciplines. For instance, psychologist Mihaly Csikszentmihaly's extensive research led him to assert that "two persons can never be expected to have the same [aesthetic] experience, and the farther apart in time and place they are, the more the details of the two experiences will differ." "Whenever we gaze at an object," he contended, "our reaction to it is historically grounded, inseparable from ideologies and social values."[7] A museum such as the Art Institute, then, with its nearly continuous collection of world art from the past to the present, offers itself as a means to trace those human values and feelings that do endure—an ideal setting for a community of shared traditions and experience. Museums have also, however, come to serve as places where individual and group identities can be challenged. Carol Becker, Dean of the School of the Art Institute, characterized our moment as one in which "art

Figure 3 In an Art Institute gallery devoted largely to works by Abstract Expressionists, educator Susan Kuliak teaches parents techniques of talking with their children about modern and contemporary art.

um's physical plant has been restored and expanded nearly continuously over this period. In addition to renovating various key spaces in the original Allerton Building, and creating collection study rooms and cutting-edge conservation facilities, the museum's administration encouraged many curatorial departments to redesign their galleries and reinstall their collections. The Daniel F. and Ada L. Rice Building (constructed in 1988), expanded the Art Institute's total area by one third, and includes Regenstein Hall, one of the largest and most flexible facilities for major exhibitions in the country. As we shall see, this improved physical setting, together with an larger staff of professional curators and educators, has enabled the Art Institute to display—quite literally—a deepening respect for the cultural contributions of artists around the globe, and to sustain its commitment to encouraging critical seeing and judgment across a wide and growing spectrum of audiences.

II. Diversity

Serving as a cultural institution in a multicultural age is a complex challenge. In Hutchinson's day, it was by building a collection that a new museum could best meet its responsibility of serving the public. Now, however, after a century of filling galleries with exquisite objects, museums are devoting ever more attention to the question of precisely how their exhibitions and interpretive programs meet the expectations and needs of their visitors. In order to better understand the ways in which they and their publics relate to one another, institutions have been turning to sophisticated methods of audience research and evaluation. This process of healthy self-critique has gone beyond simply designing satisfaction surveys, which are geared toward collecting visitor impressions and opinions, to conducting in-depth focus groups that

has become the focus of a much larger debate over who gets to write, to speak, to visualize, to tell their story, who gets to frame and interpret reality, to position their text as part of the cultural mastertext."[8]

Occurring within this wider, dynamic cultural climate—and in many senses responding to it—the work of the last two decades has marked a turning point for the Art Institute in a number of ways. The muse-

explore the very nature and quality of the experiences that audiences have with art objects. The use of such methodologies, originally drawn from the social sciences, marks a significant development in museum management and signals a new willingness to work *with* the public, not just *for* it. Museum educator Lisa C. Roberts aptly described the implications of this last impulse: "Now, the task of education is not just interpreting objects but also deciphering interpretations—in other words, anticipating and negotiating between the meanings constructed by visitors and the meanings constructed by museums."[9]

In 1989, as the first phases of the Art Institute's building renovation were being completed, the museum began a rigorous process of self-assessment that aimed to revisit its public mission and develop a clear vision for carrying it out. In this project, which was directed pro bono by the consulting firm McKinsey and Company, teams of staff wrestled with fundamental questions of

institutional purpose, and channeled their answers into a document that proposed a mandate "to serve more, and more diverse, audiences."[10] In 1992 the Department of Museum Education drafted its own, complementary mission statement, which responded to the McKinsey study and attempted to keep the Art Institute in step with larger changes in the museum and philanthropic communities. At precisely this moment, for example, the American Association of Museums, the organization that represents the nation's museums and addresses their needs, published the seminal *Excellence and Equity: Education and the Public Dimensions of Museums* (1992), its first major report on the educational role of museums. In this document, the association argued that its member institutions should take on a stronger public role, and adopt "an expanded notion of public service and education as a museum-wide endeavor" that involves all staff, who "shape the educational messages museums convey to the public."[11]

Figure 7 The innovative design of "Art Inside/ Out," exhibited in the Hammerman Gallery from 1992 to 1996, accorded interpretive materials such as the Japanese Print series (at left) and "Tang Tomb" (at right) the same emphasis as the wide range of original art works they described.

Figure 8 (opposite, top) An exterior view of the renovated Margaret Day Blake Court in the Kraft Education Center. Photo: Jamie Padgett, Karant + Associates, Inc.

Figure 9 (opposite, bottom) In "Art Inside/Out," educators combined innovative, interactive learning tools with more traditional approaches such as this timeline, which situates art works and cultural developments within an historical arc stretching from 500 A.D. to the opening of the Kraft Center in 1992.

During the last decade, the Art Institute has tried to answer this call by undertaking two major audience-development efforts that have resulted in sustained and evolving relationships with critical, formerly underrepresented publics. The first of these programs, the ReFocus/Resources Initiative (1995– 2000), was led by Ronne Hartfield, the Department of Museum Education's first African American executive director (1992–99), and signified a milestone in the Art Institute's efforts to attract and engage more African American individuals, families, and school groups. Generously funded by a grant from the Lila Wallace-Reader's Digest Fund the ReFocus/ Resources project brought trustees, administrators, curators, and other Art Institute professionals together under the guidance of the Leadership Advisory Committee. Formed with invited representatives from Chicago's African American community, this committee continues to assist the Art Institute in the ongoing process of creating connections with

metropolitan Chicago's 1.4 million black residents. ReFocus/ Resources attracted approximately four thousand new African American members to the museum's rosters, and supported exhibitions; original research on the permanent collection; a teacher manual; and a cornucopia of ongoing educational offerings, including a number of successful performance programs. [12]

Another important product of this initiative is the annual Kaleidoscope: A Family Day, now in its eighth year. With the help of local YMCAs, Boys and Girls Clubs, the Chicago Urban League, and a host of churches, the festival annually draws over two thousand guests, who come to the museum to enjoy art-making activities, gallery talks, artist demonstrations, performance programs, and storytelling sessions by award-winning authors and illustrators (see figs. 2, 4). The Art Institute's Urban Professional Partners group, formed at the outset of the ReFocus/ReSources project, helps recruit audiences for Kaleidoscope celebrations and is indispensable in assisting with the day's activities. Members include African American professionals who serve as Art Institute ambassadors to neighborhoods and community organizations, as program hosts, and as volunteers at various large-scale family events held throughout the year.

Encouraged by the large number of families that participated in ReFocus/ReSources programs, the Art Institute launched a second major audience initiative in 1997, this time focusing on family audiences in particular. The four-year project, called Looking at Art Togther: Families and Life-Long Learning, was funded by a grant from the Pew Charitable Trusts, which supported the effort's goal of increasing both the diversity and the annual number of family visitors. In order to achieve this aim, museum educators worked not just to make families more aware of the Art Institute's existence, but also to render the museum more accessible by teaching parents ways to enjoy its offerings with their children on their own, without the help of official guides or docents. The museum designed Saturday workshops, for example, in which parents explored childhood development with Art Institute educators and leading experts in the fields of education and psychology (see fig. 3). The Pew grant also enabled the Art Institute to create a written guidebook that offers parents tips on preparing for museum visits, and outlines games and activities that help young visitors experience specific works (and the museum itself) in a more familiar, comfortable way. A companion catalogue, designed for museum and early childhood educators, summarizes the scope and curricula of the project, and provides readers with a blueprint they can use to create similar programs at their own institutions. [13] Thanks to the combined efforts of the entire Art Institute staff, by the initiative's

end in 2002 the museum had increased its annual percentage of family visitors from 9 to 15 percent. Indeed, it can be said that, at the Art Institute, family programming now receives as much attention as the planning of major exhibitions. [14]

While these two audience-development initiatives were groundbreaking in and of themselves, the Museum Education Department, under the leadership of Rex Moser (1980–85) and J. Kent Lydecker (1985–90), had

Figure 10 Young visitors explore illustrated children's books and art games in the Medard and Elizabeth Welch Family Room Center.

for some years worked to expand its services to reach greater, more diverse segments of the museum's public in new and creative ways. Since 1980, for example, a media division has produced video introductions to major exhibitions that are routinely viewed by thousands of visitors. A teacher-programs division was launched in 1980, a division of family programs in 1981. Summer internships for university students began in 1987, followed one year later by a regular schedule of performance programs for all ages. From a few modest efforts in the late 1980s, the Art Institute is now one of the most popular Elderhostel sites in the country, hosting groups of seniors for twenty week-long programs each year in collaboration with the national Elderhostel organization (see fig. 5).

III. Continuity

As we have already seen, over the last twenty years museum educators, patrons, and administrators have often sought new ways to make the Art Institute and its collections more present and useful in the lives of an ever-widening spectrum of audiences. They have also, however, worked to refine and expand initiatives—the Junior Museum and children's outreach efforts, school tours, adult lectures and performances, and technology-based programs, to name only a few—that have been in place at the Art Institute for many decades in one form or another, in some cases reaching back to the museum's formative years. While by no means an exhaustive catalogue of what we do and why we do it, the following section suggests the many ways in which current museum educators have built on past successes even as they broaden their reach and intensify their meaning for visitors.

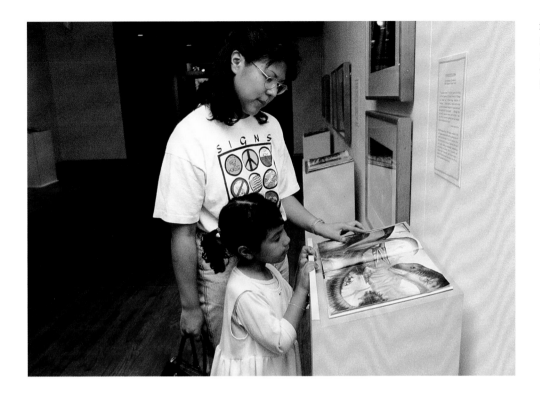

Figure 11 The Richard
Ehrman Thoresen Gallery
regularly showcases the
work of noted children's-
book artists.

The Woman's Board

As the work of museum education has continued to evolve at the Art Institute, perhaps
the greatest force of support and continuity
has been the Woman's Board. Since 1952,
when it was officially founded, the board has
contributed to the museum's general endowment and activities in many departments with
its generous patronage; it has advocated for
education, however, with particular determination, energy, and enthusiasm. Celebrating
the group's fiftieth anniversary (see fig. 6), the
Art Institute's Board of Trustees praised its
"efforts to make the museum accessible and
responsive to the community, especially to
young people." "Members of the Woman's
Board," the trustees continued, "have embraced
the museum's mission to educate, and have
given that mission wings."[15]

In fact, this commitment has taken shape
not just from the top down, but from the bottom up. Following in the footsteps of their
predecessors, many Woman's Board members assume an active, personal role in the life
of the Department of Museum Education.
Some have worked as docents; others have
served on the Trustee Committee on Education,
which helps the Art Institute develop and
refine its educational principles, programs, and
objectives. For example, two board members
have recently chaired the Trustee Committee
back to back: Quinn Delaney (1996–98) worked
as a volunteer docent for twenty-five years, and
Karen Alexander, a docent for ten years, has
presided over the group since 1999. Speaking
from their own experience as educators, these
women and others are able to bring their
familiarity with the museum's galleries and
visitors into the board room itself.

As in earlier years, the group initiates
some programs of its own, and supports others by raising funds and offering much-
needed, hands-on assistance. When it helped
transform the Junior Museum into the Kraft
Education Center (see fig. 8) in 1993, the group
collaborated with the Art Institute's develop-

Figure 12 Art Institute volunteer docent Anne Murphy talks with middle-school students in the Art Institute's galleries of modern and contemporary art, with Grant Wood's *American Gothic* (1930) in the background.

ment, education, and operations professionals, bringing its characteristic intelligence and imagination to bear on every aspect of the planning and building process. While obtaining numerous private donations, the Woman's Board was instrumental in securing the largest corporate gift the museum had ever received, from the Chicago-based Kraft General Foods Corporation.[16] The improved infrastructure of the Kraft Center and the programming it undertakes have made the facility—like the Junior Museum before it—a model for other museums nationwide.

Thanks in large parts to the board's efforts and acumen, the original components of the Junior Museum received a new lease on life through the work of the Chicago firm Weese, Langley, Weese Architects, Ltd. The Little Library (see Nosan, fig. 22), for example, was relocated and renamed the Medard and Elizabeth Welch Family Room Center, and continues to house over one thousand picture books and visual-art games for children (see fig. 10). Complementing this space is the Richard Ehrman Thoresen Gallery, which now displays rotating exhibitions of original artworks created to illustrate children's books (see fig. 11). The Price Auditorium, meanwhile,

was outfitted with new seats, an enlarged stage, and state-of-the-art audiovisual equipment. In addition, the educational programs and services established in the 1980s received their own facilities for the first time. For example, two new studios for art-making activities (housed in the former Picnic Room) are now joined by a small amphitheater that hosts story hours and "meet the author" sessions, while the Elizabeth Stone Robson Teacher Resource Center, named for a member of the original docent class, operates as a satellite office for school teachers.[17] There educators can receive expert advice on integrating art into their lesson plans, and borrow or purchase a host of Art Institute curriculum guides, posters, teacher manuals, and other art-related resources.

Perhaps the keystone of the Kraft Education Center, however, is the renovated Sol and Celia Hammerman Gallery, which has rededicated itself to serving all novice visitors, whether students, families, or adults. The 1992 improvements included conservation conditions that make it possible for the gallery to display virtually any work from the museum's collection for an extended time. The Hammerman Gallery (see fig. 7) remains the Art Institute' principal space in which works of art from many different cultures and eras can be displayed side by side, making it an ideal first stop where visitors can draw connections with objects on view elsewhere in the museum. For instance, "Art Inside/ Out," the gallery's inaugural exhibition, included twelve works from widely different cultures, ancient to modern, with each work surrounded by interpretive, hands-on "learning environments" complete with maps, timelines, and interactive computer programs that addressed the objects and how they were made (see figs. 7, 9).[18]

The Kraft Education Center has been by no means the Woman's Board's only sphere of influence, however. In a program reminiscent of the early-twentieth-century efforts of the Chicago Public School Art Society (see Rhor, pp. 27–28), the group also spearheaded Sears Galleries, a six-year project undertaken with the Art Institute's division of Student and Teacher Programs. Funded by the Sears Foundation, the program successfully distributed ten framed reproductions of artworks from the Art Institute's collection to all six hundred grade schools in the Chicago public school system, as well as to more than one hundred of their parochial counterparts. These examples were carefully selected to reflect the city's diverse population, and teachers were offered resources to help them integrate these images into their classroom activities.

Another Woman's Board-initiated effort, Art Volunteers in the Classroom, has since

1992 extended the museum's influence deep into city and suburban areas. Now conducted by the Department of Museum Education, the program annually serves as many as 1,500 parents through seminars conducted at the museum, where they learn how to discuss art with grade-school classes by using reproductions of works in the Art Institute's collection.[19] The board's other accomplishments include its joint sponsorship (with the Chicago Public Library) of two city-wide summer reading games that reached tens of thousands of children through a program linking verbal and visual literacy.[20]

The Woman's Board has also played a pivotal role in supporting the Art Institute's staff of educators, all the while working to attract young people to the museum profession. In 1994, for instance, the board established an endowment to fund the position of the Executive Director of Museum Education. It also sponsors summer student intern-

Figure 13 On a MAPS (Museums and Public Schools) field trip, Art Institute educator Cori Wulf and fourth graders from Chicago's William J. Onahan Elementary School work on an Art and Creative Writing exercise in the museum's Surrealist galleries.

Figure 14 Art Institute visitors enjoy the opening of "To Inspire and Instruct: Art from the Collection of the Chicago Public Schools." Photo: Cheri Eisenberg.

ships in the education department, as well as a two-year fellowship in which a promising master's degree graduate rotates through each division of the department, gaining a range of valuable professional experience in the process. In these and many other ways, the Woman's Board has continued to have a substantial, enduring impact on education efforts at the Art Institute, and throughout the Chicago metropolitan area as a whole.

Schools

Building on the pioneering successes of the original Staff Assistants program and Junior Museum in the 1960s, the Art Institute now welcomes as many as 150,000 students, teachers, and parent chaperones every year.[21] As a result of the museum's increased array of resources and professional development programs for teachers, the number of self-conducted tours has increased considerably, particularly over the past ten years.[22] Half of all student visitors, however, experience the museum's permanent collection and special

exhibitions accompanied by Art Institute docents (see fig. 12), who may lead them on general gallery walks, or on more specialized tours such as Art and Creative Writing and Seeing Through Drawing, which encourage a close examination of three to four art works in particular. A few docent-led courses—"Art and Stories" and "Museology"—are aimed at small groups of gifted students who meet at the museum one afternoon a week, delving deeply into the Art Institute's collections and inner workings.[23]

Over the past two decades, the work of volunteer docents has grown increasingly challenging in a number of ways. In order to justify the time and expense of museum field trips, school districts nationwide have demanded that what students learn in the galleries be relevant to formal curricula. In response, Art Institute docents work to stay abreast of academic goals and standards, and to design their tours and other programs accordingly. Continuing to refine the museum's rigorous docent training program, education staff have incorporated new art-historical approaches over the years, and drawn freely on the expertise of the museum's curators, faculty at the School of the Art Institute, and other professional educators. Taking advantage of current trends in psychology and learning theory, docents now employ an interactive, inquiry method of teaching, and are encouraged to give equal attention to interpreting the museum's collection and responding to the needs of students. Indeed, they learn to approach teaching itself as an art form, and to experiment with new ideas and methods of instruction. [24]

Not all of the museum's school programming takes place within its own walls, however. Early twentieth-century extension programs involved museum educators traveling around the city armed with fine-art reproductions, and updated versions of this approach continue to succeed today. Since 1987, for instance, the Art Institute has co-organized Art Partners, a singularly effective program geared to 3,500 public elementary and middle schools in Chicago.

Art Partners is produced in collaboration with A.R.T. (Art Resources in Teaching), an independent arts organization that evolved from the venerable Chicago Public School Art Society. In the six-week program, artist/teachers on the A.R.T. staff visit classrooms, conducting an art curriculum that includes two field trips to the Art Institute. Another initiative, MAPS (Museums and Public Schools), is the result of an innovative partnership between the Chicago Public Schools and nine Chicago museums, and has served eight thousand third-to-sixth-grade students and 240 teachers in sixty schools throughout the city (see fig. 13). [25]

Neither are all of the Art Institute's school programs geared toward students. Beginning in 1993, the museum focused with renewed vigor on high-school teachers and students, and began hosting weekly Evenings for Educators, in which art, language arts, and social-studies instructors learned a multicultural, interdisciplinary approach to enriching their curricula. Attending such semester-long

Figure 15 Catherine Klein (left) and her volunteer escort, Teri Danai Vrakas, enjoy the 2001 exhibition "Beyond the Easel: Decorative Painting by Bonnard, Vuillard, Denis, and Roussel, 1890–1930."

Figure 16 Noted dancer and choreographer Arthur Hall performs his signature work "Obatela" in conjunction with the 1990 exhibition "Yoruba: Nine Centuries of African Art and Thought."

courses as "Nature, Society, and Spirit" and "Looking to Write/Writing to See," teachers tested out new techniques by bringing their students on field trips to the Art Institute. Over a five-year period, Evenings for Educators attracted 150 teachers from every public high school on the city, and reached thousands of students in the process. This initiative also inspired the class "Science, Art, and Technology," which helped science teachers from the Chicago Public Schools integrate the visual arts into their work. [26]

Even as they continue to reinvent their

relationship through programs such as these, the Art Institute and the Chicago Board of Education have also, quite recently, looked back and celebrated their longstanding partnership. Between 1995 and 2000, the board undertook the monumental task of conserving the vast art collection housed within the city's public schools. Many of these objects have Art Institute connections: the easel paintings were originally selected from the Art Institute's annual exhibitions of work by Chicago artists, and the murals were executed by students at the School of the Art Institute early in the twentieth century (see Rhor, p. 28). After the process of physical restoration was complete, Art Institute museum educators helped teachers integrate these works in the curriculum.[27] The project culminated in the celebratory exhibition "To Inspire and Instruct: Art from the Collection of the Chicago Public Schools," organized by the Department of Museum Education and held at the Art Institute (see fig. 14). While showcasing the collection's breadth and recalling the pivotal role that art played in public education during the Progressive and WPA eras, "To Inspire and Instruct" also underscored the school board's commitment to preserving this educational resource—one of the strongest examples of its kind in the nation—for future generations of Chicago's children.[28]

Adults

From the museum's earliest years, when children were seldom seen or heard in the galleries, the lion's share of Art Institute visitors has been adults. The Department of Museum Education aims to serve this varied audience, which ranges widely in age, background, and interest, with an extraordinary range of activities that take place both at the museum and in offices and community centers around the city. In ArtExpress, for instance, lecturers present lunchtime talks to downtown-Chicago businesspeople, echoing early-twentieth-century efforts to extend the Art Institute's reach into factories and other commercial concerns (see Rhor, p. 33). The Art Insights program, meanwhile, enables carefully trained volunteer educators to visit senior centers throughout Chicago, discussing the Art Institute's collections with people who are able to visit the museum in person only rarely, if at all. In the Art Institute proper, Escorts for the Blind offers guided tours for visually impaired visitors (see fig. 15), while the annual Senior Celebrations

festival (see fig. 17) welcomes 1,500 participants with gallery tours, artist demonstrations, performance programs, studio activities, and a complimentary lunch, to boot.[29]

Every day, staff lecturers offer visitors free tours of the general collection or more focused gallery discussions about single works of art, while a range of leading artists and intellectuals present topics of interest to both general audiences and specialists throughout the month. On Tuesdays, when the admission to the Art Institute is gratis and galleries remain open until 8:00 p.m., educators have steadily expanded their programs in order to better serve what is perhaps the museum's largest and most diverse audience of the week. Moreover, since the 1980s curators and educators have collaborated closely on exhibition programming, planning an increased number of offerings ranging from Web sites and family guides to scholarly lectures and symposia.[30] At monthly Metropolis programs, for instance, noted Chicago artists discuss their work and often explore objects in the museum's collection that have influenced them. On Study Days, adult learners take to the road on field trips that seek to connect the Art Institute's collections to the city's broader cultural offerings.

It is through witnessing acts of performance as well as those of scholarship, however, that many adult visitors are best able to forge their own relationship to works of visual art.[31] For this reason, ever since the late 1890s, the Art Institute has attempted to interpret its collections and exhibitions through music, theater, and literature.[32] Performance programming continues unabated and features a dazzling array of professional actors, dancers, and musicians, each of whom expand viewers' perspective on art and the creative process in their own way. Beginning in 1989, for instance, the Chicago Symphony

Orchestra has collaborated with the museum on an annual chamber music and art series.[33] In a weekly program called Voices, moreover, actors present staged readings of noted artists' letters, journals, and essays—literary works that help shed light on the writer's oeuvre or historical moment.[34] On other occasions, Kabuki actors have enlivened exhibitions of Japanese prints; a performer in African costume has taught traditional dances to illuminate the ritual function of Yoruba sculpture (see fig. 16); and a figure from an Italian Renaissance drawing has come to life, dancing to the sound of a lute.

IV. Looking Forward

In 1975, the art historian Joshua Taylor stated that, because of the richness of their collections, American museums "hold responsibility to a world-wide constituency."[35] Since then, the World Wide Web has changed profoundly how that responsibility is being discharged, not to mention the ways in which people around the world communicate and learn. In its ability to help the Art Institute store, organize, and visually reproduce "virtual" versions of the objects in its collections, the Internet is helping the museum connect with "more, and more diverse" audiences on a vast scale, whether they are foreign tourists looking for general information, teachers preparing for a field trip, or Chicagoans planning their next outing to a special exhibition.[36] The museum's many education-driven Internet projects include exhibition sites that reproduce signal art works and link them to artists' writings, bibliographies, maps, timelines, and related Web materials. At the present moment, the Art Institute's Web site also features several interactive, multimedia educa-

Figure 17 Visitors make their way up the Woman's Board Grand Staircase during a recent Senior Celebration.

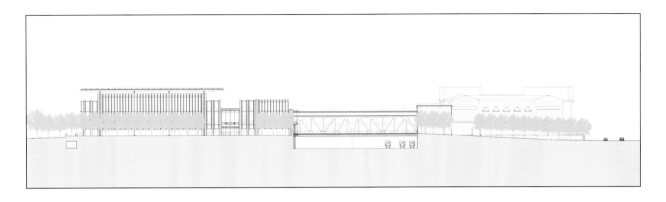

tional projects, and plans are underway to expand the amount of images and interpretive content significantly.[37]

In the midst of this technological revolution, however, architectural historian Victoria Newhouse has identified what is perhaps an unexpected benefit of real, "bricks-and-mortar" art museums:

> In a world that has become increasingly virtual, the museum is an important refuge of reality, making both its concerns and their relation to architecture more important than ever before . . . the experience of seeing original art in the unique spaces designed by Renzo Piano, Richard Rogers, Frank Gehry and others cannot be duplicated.[38]

As this publication goes to press, the Art Institute anticipates the completion of a bold plan to expand its physical presence yet again. The renowned architect Renzo Piano has designed a new building that promises to provide additional galleries for the museum's collections of architecture, Asian art, and modern and contemporary works. Also included in this scheme (see fig. 18) are greatly enlarged education facilities, including a dedicated student entrance, studio spaces, an enlarged teacher resource center, and many conveniences for the benefit of visitors. A majestic new entrance will directly face the Music and Dance Theater and the Frank Gehry-designed Music Pavilion, both situated in Chicago's vast new Millennium Park.

Technological tools and enlarged facilities aside, however, what will best enable the Art Institute to face the ongoing challenge of helping each new generation discover its collection and exhibitions is a highly qualified and ever more diverse staff, and strong leaders with a steadfast commitment to sustaining a clear, purposeful educational mission. The direct experience of art does indeed have the potential to excite, inspire, and renew. Art museums, in constituting a rich history of imagination, can and should continue to serve as playgrounds for exercising the creative power of their audiences—reflecting the past, defining the present, prophetic of the future.

Figure 18 In size and scope, the Art Institute's proposed addition, designed by the Renzo Piano Building Workshop, constitutes the museum's most significant plan of expansion since the construction of the Allerton Building in 1891–93. Courtesy Renzo Piano Building Workshop.

Notes

Alexander, Preface, p. 4

1. Peter F. Drucker, *Managing the Nonprofit Organization* (New York, 1990), p. xviii.
2. Robert D. Putnam, *Bowling Alone: The Collapse and Revival of American Community* (New York, 2000), p. 117.
3. Ibid., p. 406.
4. "Comparing two women of the same age, education, financial security, and marital and parental status, full-time employment appears to cut volunteering by more than 50%." Ibid., p. 195.

Rice, "Balancing Act: Education and the Competing Impulses of Museum Work," pp. 6–19.

1. Charles L. Hutchinson, "Art and Artists," address delivered to the Chicago Literary Club, c. 1915. Charles Hutchinson Papers, Newberry Library, Chicago. I am grateful to Greg Nosan for bringing this to my attention.
2. Henry James, *The American Scene* (New York, 1907; repr. New York, 1987), p. 138.
3. For the history of museum education, see Terry Zeller, "The Historical and Philosophical Foundations of Art Museum Education in America," in Nancy Berry and Susan Mayer, eds., *Museum Education: History, Theory, and Practice* (Reston, Va., 1989), pp. 10–89; and Danielle Rice, "Museum Education Embracing Uncertainty," *Art Bulletin* 77, 1 (Mar. 1995), pp. 15–20.
4. Charles Coleman Sellers, *Mr. Peale's Museum: Charles Willson Peale and the First Popular Museum of Natural Science and Art* (New York, 1980), p. 1.
5. David C. Ward, "Democratic Culture: The Peale Museums, 1784–1850," in Lillian B. Miller, ed. *The Peale Family: Creation of a Legacy 1770–1870,* exh. cat. (New York, 1996), pp. 260–75.
6. Lawrence W. Levine, *Highbrow/Lowbrow: The Emergence of Cultural Hierarchy in America* (Cambridge, Mass., 1988), chap. 2, "The Socialization of Culture."
7. Ibid., pp. 85–168.
8. Quoted in Levine (note 6), p. 150.
9. Michael Conforti, "The Idealist Enterprise and the Applied Arts," in Malcolm Baker and Brenda Richardson, eds., *A Grand Design: The Art of the Victoria and Albert Museum,* exh. cat. (London, 1997), p. 24.
10. See Allan Wallach, *Exhibition Contradiction: Essays on the Art Museum in the United States* (Boston, 1998), pp. 39–56.
11. Ibid., p. 49.
12. Matthew Prichard, correspondence with the board of trustees, Museum of Fine Arts, Boston, 1903, quoted in ibid., p. 52.
13. For an excellent survey of the often paradoxical relationships between art museums and their publics, see Andrew McClellan, "A Brief History of the Art Museum Public," in idem, ed., *Art and Its Publics: Museum Studies at the Millennium* (London, 2003), pp. 1–49.
14. Quoted in Zeller (note 3), p. 41.
15. Quoted in ibid., p. 43, n. 43.
16. Ibid., p. 37.
17. John W. Smith, "The Nervous Profession: Daniel Catton Rich and The Art Institute of Chicago, 1927–1958,"in *Art Institute of Chicago Museum Studies* 19, 1 (1993), p. 65.
18. See Edward S. Robinson, *The Behaviour of the Museum Visitor,* American Association of Museums Monograph, new series, no. 5 (Washington, D.C., 1928); Paul M. Rea, *The Museum and the Community: A Study of Social Laws and Consequences* (Lancaster, Penn., 1932); and Arthur W. Melton, "Studies of Installation at the Pennsylvania Museum of Art," *Museum News* 10, 14 (Jan. 15, 1933), pp. 5–8.
19. Philip Youtz, "Museumitis," *Journal of Adult Education* 6 (1934), cited in McClellan (note 13), p. 24.
20. Quoted in Zeller (note 3), p. 43.
21. Quoted in B. Y. Newsom and A. Z. Silver, eds., *The Art Museum as Educator* (Berkeley, 1978), p. 21.
22. Andrew McClellan, "From Boullée to Bilbao: The Museum as Utopian Space," in Elizabeth Mansfield, ed., *Art History and Its Institutions* (London/New York, 2002), pp. 46–64.
23. For more on the paradoxes faced by museum educators, see Rice (note 3).
24. Thomas P. Hoving, "Branch Out!" *Museum News* 47, 1 (Sept. 1968), p. 15.
25. Steven C. Dubin, *Displays of Power: Memory and Amnesia in the American Museum* (New York/London, 1999), pp. 18–63. As Dubin demonstrated, this pathbreaking exhibition was criticized from all sides: by black artists who felt excluded from both the planning stage and from the show itself; by many Jews for including what appeared to be anti-Semitic remarks in the catalogue (which was, in fact, suppressed, and reissued in 1995); and by art critics who complained that the endeavor was sociological rather than aesthetic, gimmicky and populist rather than respectful.
26. For a comprehensive analysis of the different programs and practices in museum education of the late 1960s and early 1970s, see Newsom and Silver (note 21).
27. Susan F. Rossen in conversation with the author, recalling her days as a museum educator at the Detroit Institute of Arts.
28. Danielle Rice, "Looking into Seeing: What People Learn in the Art Museum," in *The Museum as a Place for Learning* (Ithaca, N.Y., 2001), pp. 42–49.
29. The emergence of feminism encouraged new perspectives on many fronts. Linda Nochlin was one of the first art historians to ask: "Why have there been no great women artists?" See *Art News* 69, 9 (Jan. 1971), pp. 22–39, 69–71; repr. in Elizabeth Baker and Thomas B. Hess, eds., *Art and Sexual Politics* (London, 1973), pp. 1–43. Critics such as John Berger, echoing earlier socialist art writers, criticized museums for mystifying art; his influential 1972 BBC television series, "Ways of Seeing," was published with the same title (London, 1972) and went through numerous reprints. For more about the evolution of art history, see Donald Preziosi, "The Art of Art History," in idem, ed., *The Art of Art History: A Critical Anthology* (Oxford/New York, 1998), pp. 7–25.
30. Kenneth Silver, "Past Imperfect: A Museum Looks at Itself," *Art in America* 81, 1 (Jan. 1993), p. 43. See also Peter Noever, ed., *The Discursive Museum* (Ostfildern, Germany, 2001).
31. Museum educators themselves worked actively to bring these changes about. Examples of these efforts include support for the wider trend toward researching how people learn in museum settings, and the initiation of the influential Getty Focus Group study in the 1980s, which was published as *Insights: Museums, Visitors, Attitudes, Expectations, A Focus Group Experiment* (Malibu, Calif., 1991), with an accompanying videotape composite of some of the focus groups. More recent studies of museum learning include Gaea Leinhardt, Kevin Crowley, and Karen Knutson, eds., *Learning Conversations in Museums* (Mahwa, N.J., 2002); and Scott G. Paris, ed., *Perspectives on Object-Centered Learning in Museums* (Mahwa, N.J., 2002).
32. Gail Durbin, "Connecting with the Visitor at the Victoria and Albert Museum: Moving from Programme Design to Gallery Design," in Donna R. Braden and Gretchen W. Overhiser, eds., *Old Collections, New Audiences: Decorative Arts and Visitor Experience for the 21st Century* (Dearborn, Mich., 2000), pp. 38–49.
33. Housen and Yenawine started an organization called VUE (Visual Understanding in Education). The web site at www.vue.org includes a description of the VTS program, a curriculum for kindergarten through fifth-grade intended for classroom use. Museum projects are also described.
34. See James Cuno, "A World Changed? Art Museums after September 11," in *American Academy of Arts and Sciences Bulletin* 55, 4 (summer 2002), p. 25.
35. E. W. Eisner and S. M. Dobbs, *The Uncertain Profession: Observations on the State of Museum Education in Twenty American Art Museums* (Los Angeles, 1986).
36. See Rice (note 3).

Rhor, "Every Walk of Life and Every Degree of Education: Museum Instruction at The Art Institute of Chicago, 1879–1955," pp. 20–45.

I would like to thank Bart Ryckbosch and Ashley Weinard for their indispensable help in researching this topic. I would also like to thank Jane Clarke, Robert Eskridge, Susan F. Rossen, Barbara McCloskey, and Dr. Charles Pearo for their careful readings of the manuscript. I would like to thank Greg Nosan, in particular, for his limitless patience, astute insights, and professionalism in bringing this project to completion.

1. Constance Drinhaus to Helen Mackenzie, November 19, 1935, Archives of The Art Institute of Chicago. Unless otherwise specified, all references to correspondence, manuscripts, and ephemera are to documents residing in the Art Institute Archives. Drinhaus's is one of many similar letters in the museum's archives written by students in the 1930s and 1940s.
2. These approaches have become so familiar that Will Joyner wryly summed up the history of American museums as "a story about the power, plunder, wacky acquisitiveness and inquisitiveness, the blossoming of the middle class, social posing, romantic notions of democracy and the tension between art and architecture. It wouldn't make a very good movie." See Will Joyner, "A Few Thousand Years of Museums in a Nutshell," *New York Times*, Apr. 21, 1999.
3. See, for instance, Carol Duncan, *Civilizing Rituals: Inside Public Art Museums* (London/New York, 1995).
4. "Education Work in The Art Institute of Chicago," undated typescript, Art Resources in Teaching Papers, Special Collections, University of Illinois at Chicago Library. In 1934 there were also three other divisions of the Art Institute engaged in "education work": the Department of Extension, the Membership Department, and the Children's Museum.
5. Quoted in Donald L. Miller, *City of the Century: The Epic of Chicago and the Making of America* (New York, 1996), p. 387.
6. The charter of the Metropolitan Museum of Art, New York, for example, states that the institution was formed "for the purpose of establishing and maintaining in said city a Museum and library of art, of encouraging and developing the study of the fine arts, and the application of arts to manufacture and to practical life, of advancing the general knowledge of kindred subjects, and to that end, of furnishing popular instruction." Quoted in Theodore L. Low, *The Educational Philosophy and*

Practice of Art Museums in the United States (New York, 1948), pp. 61–65.

7. For more on cultural philanthropy in the Gilded Age and Progressive Era, see Helen Lefkowitz Horowitz, *Culture and the City: Cultural Philanthropy in Chicago from the 1880s to 1917* (Lexington, Ky., 1976); and Kathleen D. McCarthy, *Noblesse Oblige: Charity and Cultural Philanthropy in Chicago, 1849–1929* (Chicago, 1982).

8. See, for instance, Duncan (note 3), p. 56; or Horowitz (note 7), p. 105.

9. Duncan (note 3), pp. 61–65.

10. Hutchinson was actively involved with sixty charitable organizations during his lifetime, including the Auditorium Commission, the Chicago Public Relief and Aid Society, the Chicago YMCA, and Hull-House. The Art Institute, however, remained his primary interest. At Hutchinson's funeral, one of his friends remarked: "In the deepest sense Charles L. Hutchinson *was* the Art Institute." Quoted in Miller (note 5), p. 389. For more on Hutchinson, see Horowitz (note 7), pp. 49–55.

11. Quoted in Low (note 6), p. 51. For more on Hutchinson's role at the Art Institute, see Ernest Poole, *Giants Gone: Men Who Made Chicago* (New York, 1943), pp. 268–77; Miller (note 5), pp. 385–93; McCarthy (note 7), pp. 85–89, and Horowitz (note 7), pp. 51–54. Hutchinson's papers are located at the Chicago Historical Society, though much of his correspondence and many of his personal notes are housed in the AIC Archives and at the Newberry Library, Chicago.

12. Quoted in Poole (note 11), p. 272.

13. Quoted in Low (note 6), p. 51.

14. Quoted in Miller (note 5), p. 391.

15. Hutchinson reportedly reviewed attendance figures daily, an act that reveals his deep interest in public attendance and accessibility, as well as his engagement in the museum's everyday operations. See Horowitz (note 7), pp. 105, 108.

16. Quoted in Miller (note 5), p. 391.

17. Although European museums such as the Musée du Louvre, Paris, played host to nineteenth-century copyists and academic artists, it was post–Civil War America that popularized the union of art museums and art schools under a single roof. Boston's Museum of Fine Arts, the Minneapolis Institute of Art, and the Corcoran Gallery of Art in Washington D.C., for example, began as such dual institutions. The Art Institute of Chicago and the Museum of Fine Arts are unique among them because of their continuing relationship with a sister institution. See Peter C. Marzio, "A Museum and a School: An Uneasy but Creative Union," *Chicago History* 8, 1 (spring 1979), pp. 20–23, 44–52.

18. In 1908 these programs were threatened by detractors from within the school system who dismissed art education as a "frill" and a "fad." Chicago teachers signed a petition imploring William M. R. French, the Art Institute's director, to continue the museum's efforts on their behalf:

We, the undersigned teachers, appreciating the inspirational and educational value of the instruction of the Art Institute, and the help it has been to us in our work with the children in the school room, and desiring to increase our professional efficiency by continuing study under the influence and sympathetic helpfulness and co-operation which we find at the Art Institute, hereby make application to continue therein next year our work toward the attainment of a diploma or a degree.

French replied: "We shall neglect no means to promote the present happy relations between the Art Institute and the public school teachers." See "The Public School Teachers and the Art Institute," *Bulletin of The Art Institute of Chicago* 1, 3 (Apr. 1908), p. 40.

19. The organization was renamed Art Resources in Teaching (A.R.T.) in 1982 and continues to work with public schools and other local arts organizations. For more on the history of the Chicago Public School Art Society, see Caitlin Ann Patterson, "Redecorating a Nation: Creating Democratic Arts from the Settlement House to the New Deal" (Ph.D. diss., University of Minnesota, 1997); and Karen Dawn Finley, "Cultural Monitors: Clubwomen and Public Art Instruction in Chicago, 1890–1920" (Ph. D. diss., Ohio State University, 1989).

20. See "The Public School Teachers and the Art Institute" (note 18); and Julia Wrigley, *Class Politics and Public Schools: Chicago, 1900–1950* (New Brunswick, N. J., 1982), pp. 54–60.

21. Thomas Wood Stevens, "New Fields for the Art Institute," *Midland* (partial copy, n.d.), pp. 9–10. I explore the overlapping concepts of mural making, municipal culture, and public education more fully in my forthcoming "Educating America: Murals in Chicago Public Schools, 1904–1943" (Ph.D. diss., University of Pittsburgh, 2003).

22. Both these murals and those later placed in Chicago public schools under the auspices of the 1930s Federal Art Project have inspired recent conservation efforts, exhibitions, education projects, and research. In 1995 the Art Institute launched "Chicago: The City in Art," a program for teachers and students from schools with restored murals to develop curricula and art projects based on these works. The exhibition "To Inspire and Instruct: Works from the Collection of the Chicago Public Schools" brought many key murals and easel paintings to the Art Institute in 2002. Two recent publications on the subject are Heather Becker, *Art for the People: The Rediscovery and Preservation of Progressive- and WPA-Era Murals in the Chicago Public Schools, 1904–1943* (San Francisco, 2002); and Mary Lackritz Gray, *A Guide to Chicago's Murals* (Chicago, 2001).

23. Dwight H. Perkins, for example, served as architect for the Board of Education between 1905 and 1910 and designed over forty public schools that have become historic landmarks. Carl Schurz High School, Friedrich L. Jahn Elementary School, and Samuel Tilden High School are few of his best-known school designs.

24. The concept promoted by women's clubs and other civic organizations to create public art galleries in the halls and common rooms of public schools prompted great enthusiasm. See Lorado Taft, "Little Art Museums in Schools," *Chicago Schools Journal* 9, 1 (Sept. 1926), pp. 330–33.

25. For more on Buehr's appointment, see "Museum Instruction," *Bulletin of The Art Institute of Chicago* 16, 3 (Mar.–Apr. 1922), p. 29. Ten years later, in the depths of the Great Depression, the Chicago Board of Education abruptly eliminated Buehr's position because its members considered it a "frill." Helen Parker, later Director of Museum Education, wrote to museum director Robert Harshe, decrying the loss of Buehr and the reduction of school tours due to budget cuts. She suggested that public schools be admitted without charge on occasion "so that the [school] work [will not] die out all together." Helen Parker to Robert Harshe, Jan. 18, 1932. See also "School Board Finds it Doesn't Need Any Docent," *Chicago Tribune*, Jan. 16, 1932.

26. The endowment was founded in 1926 by Mrs. Anna Louise Raymond.

27. See Joel Orosz, *Curators and Culture: The Museum Movement in America, 1740–1870* (Tuscaloosa, Ala., 1990), p. 85. Benjamin Ives Gilman set forth his theories on museums in *Museum Ideals of Purpose and Method* (Cambridge, Mass., 1923).

28. John Cotton Dana, *The New Museum* (Woodstock, Vt., 1917). For more on curatorial debates over museums' educational function, see Orosz (note 27); Danielle Rice, "Museum Education Embracing Uncertainty," *Art Bulletin* 77, 1 (Mar. 1995), pp. 15–20; and Terry Zeller, "The Historical and Philosophical Foundations of Art Museum Education in America," in Nancy Berry and Susan Mayer, eds., *Museum Education: History, Theory, and Practice* (Reston, Va., 1989), pp. 10–89.

29. In 1910 the Metropolitan Museum of Art, New York, assured its members of its dedication to both endeavors: "As the Bulletin is constantly filled with illustrations and descriptions of new accessions, readers may easily reach the conclusion that the present chief activity of the Museum is acquisition. Important as is the acquisition of objects of art, it is only one of the educational functions of our museum. Interpretation of these objects is another." See Robert W. de Forest, "Expert Guidance to the Museum," *Bulletin of The Metropolitan Museum of Art* 5, 9 (Sept. 1910), p. 201.

30. "Popular Museum Management," *Bulletin of The Art Institute of Chicago* 6, 1 (Dec. 1912), p. 7.

31. Though Benjamin Ives Gilman coined the term "docent" in 1907 (see Rice, p. 12), Mary Bronson Hart popularized it in her 1910 article on the subject; see Mary Bronson Hart, "Docentry: A New Profession," *Outlook* (Apr. 1910). It appears, however, that the Art Institute was referring to its own lecturers as "docents" as early as 1909. I would like to thank Karen Alexander for this last piece of information.

32. "The Department of Museum Instruction," *Bulletin of The Art Institute of Chicago* 22, 2 (Feb. 1928), p. 26.

33. A nominal fee was charged for most lectures, though the tours and lectures for servicemen were free.

34. For more on Helen Parker, see Violet Meyer, "Art Institute Education Head Finds Use for Varied Talents," *Chicago Daily News*, Feb. 27, 1947. At this time, the lecturing staff also included Anita Willets Burnham and Mary Hess Buehr.

35. By the late 1910s, most major museums offered special children's hours and storytelling sessions on weekends and during school vacations. In 1917 the Metropolitan Museum of Art, New York, also initiated an offshoot of its members bulletin exclusively for children. At first the *Children's Bulletin* pursued the same subjects as the concurrent members' bulletin, altered slightly for "younger readers." Later issues highlight various aspects of the museums collection and stories that were considered particularly appealing to a juvenile audience. See "Children's Bulletin," *Bulletin of the Metropolitan Museum of Art* 12, 1 (Jan. 1917), p. 16.

36. "Youth and Art," *Bulletin of The Art Institute of Chicago* 12, 5 (May 1918), pp. 84–85. An article in the popular journal *School and Society* reveals a different attitude toward children, considering their presence in museums to be impediments to scholarly or aesthetic reflection: "It is, however, not necessary to belong to this thin-skinned fraternity to find the presence of children a hindrance to quiet thought or serious study. . . . The majority will think it a tremendous responsibility, not merely by reason of social obligation, but on even a higher ground, to shut out children from national and municipal collections." See "Children and Museums," *School and Society* 17, 43 (Mar. 24, 1932), p. 333.

37. "The Children's Museum," *Bulletin of The Art Institute of Chicago* 21, 5 (May 1927), p. 61. In the same year, Kate Brewster, President of the Chicago Public School Art Society, warned that if the city's children "know or demand nothing better than an advertiser's garish appeal, what can we expect of future greatness and distinction?" See Kate Brewster, "A Public-School Art Society," *Educational Review* 73, 1 (Jan. 1927), p. 149.

38. The Children's Art Centre in Boston was one of the first of these institutions. Inaugurated on May 1, 1918, the center included reproductions of well-known drawings, paintings, porcelains, prints, and sculptures. The center also offered drawing classes and story-telling, and contained a library. See "The Children's Art Centre," *Museum of Fine Arts Bulletin* 17, 102 (Aug. 1919), p. 43; and Fitzroy Carrington, "The Children's Art Centre," *Bulletin of The Metropolitan Museum of Art* 13, 9 (Sept. 1918), pp. 201–04.

39. See Mrs. Leo Heller, draft letter, n.p.

40. "Youth and Art" (note 36), p. 85.

41. "The Children's Room," *Bulletin of The Art Institute of Chicago* 16, 8 (Dec. 1922), p. 96.

42. The Art Institute of Chicago, *Annual Report for the Year 1924*, p. 13. In 1924 Mrs. Leo Heller asked local women's clubs to fund the Children's Museum, writing: "the women's clubs of Chicago could find no more worthy field for their attention, and no field which would bring them a greater reward, that that of art education and training in art appreciation of the children of their city." See Heller (note 39). The lumber and paper magnate Charles H. Worcester and his wife, Mary F. S. Worcester, were leading patrons of the Art Institute. In 1918 they presented to the museum a major selection of Old Master and Impressionist paintings, which to this day remains in one of the greatest gifts in the museum's history. After they funded the Children's Museum, they continued to buy art, but always with the Art Institute in mind. See Daniel Catton Rich, comp., *Catalogue of the Charles H. and Mary F. S. Worcester Collection of Paintings, Sculpture and Drawings* (Chicago, 1938).

43. *Fighting Boys* left the Art Institute in 1948, when it was given to Chicago's Jesse Spaulding School for Crippled Children.

44. See Kathleen Bickford Berzock, "African Art at The Art Institute of Chicago," *African Arts* 32, 4 (winter 1999), pp. 19–20.

45. "Suggestions for a Letter to be Written by Mrs. Leo Heller," undated typescript, n.p.

46. Robert W. de Forest, "Museum Extension," *Bulletin of The Metropolitan Museum of Art* 14, 9 (Sept. 1919), p. 189.

47. See Horowitz (note 7), p. 157. Advanced students at the School of the Art Institute began painting murals for these facilities, just as their forebears had done previously for public schools. A student circular mentions mural projects for the field house at Sherman Park, for instance. See *Art Institute of Chicago Circular of Instruction* (1912–13), p. 48. Many of these field-house murals are reproduced in Gray (note 22).

48. "Department of Extension," *Bulletin of The Art Institute of Chicago* 10, 8 (Dec. 1916), p. 240.

49. Ibid., p. 241.

50. Ibid.

51. *Christian Science Monitor*, Feb. 3, 1936.

52. By summer 1936, plans were underway to develop similar community galleries in Chicago's Washington and Lincoln parks; these initiatives were not realized.

53. James O'Donnell Bennet, "Open Free Art Galleries; Bar 'Nut' Paintings," *Chicago Tribune*, Nov. 10, 1935.

54. Tanner's *Three Marys* is now in the Aaron Douglas Gallery, Fisk University, Nashville, Tenn. Sparhawk-Jones's *Shop Girls* (1912.1677) remains in the Art Institute's collection.

55. Bennet (note 53).

56. Ibid. *Mount Lovewell* (1921.102) is still in the museum's collection.

57. Ibid.

58. "The Significance of the Century of Progress Art Exhibition," *Bulletin of The Art Institute of Chicago* 27, 5 (Sept.–Oct. 1933), p. 83. See also *Bulletin of the Art Institute of Chicago* 27, 4 (Apr.–May 1933); and Richard R. Brettell and Sue Ann Prince, "From the Armory Show to the Century of Progress: The Art Institute Assimilates Modernism," in Sue Ann Prince, ed., *The Old Guard and the Avant-Garde: Modernism in Chicago, 1919–1940* (Chicago, 1990), pp. 122–23.

59. Malcolm Vaughan, art critic for the *New York American*, quoted in "The Significance of the Century of Progress Art Exhibition" (note 58), p. 82.

60. Ibid., p. 88.

61. Under Rich, symposia and lectures related to major exhibitions increased, and an innovative High School Extension Art project was initiated. See John W. Smith, "The Nervous Profession: Daniel Catton Rich and The Art Institute of Chicago, 1927–1958," *Art Institute of Chicago Museum Studies* 19, 1 (1993), pp. 58–79.

62. "The Gallery of Art Interpretation," *Bulletin of The Art Institute of Chicago* 34, 2 (Feb. 1940), p. 24.

63. Katharine Kuh, "Seeing is Believing," *Bulletin of The Art Institute of Chicago* 39, 4 (Apr.–May 1945), p. 53.

64. At the time, the Armour Institute's architecture classes were conducted in the makeshift classrooms in the attic of the Art Institute. In 1939 the Art Institute exhibited models, photographs, and drawings of Mies's German works. See Franz Schulze, "The Bauhaus Architects and the Rise of Modernism in the United States," in Stephanie Barron, ed., *Exile and Emigrés: The Flight of European Artists from Hitler*, exh. cat. (Los Angeles/Munich, 1997), pp. 225–34.

65. Kuh's exhibitions were greatly influenced by Alfred H. Barr, Jr.'s innovative plan for the Museum of Modern Art, New York, which was itself inspired by the work of Bauhaus designers. For more on Katharine Kuh and the Gallery of Art Interpretation, see Susan F. Rossen and Charlotte Moser, "Primer for Seeing: The Gallery of Art Interpretation and Katharine Kuh's Crusade for Modernism in Chicago," *Art Institute of Chicago Museum Studies* 16, 1 (1990), pp. 6–25.

66. Katharine Kuh, "Explaining Art Visually," *Museum* 1, 3–4 (1948), p. 158.

67. Quoted in Smith (note 61), p. 65.

68. Quoted in Meyer (note 34).

69. Kuh (note 63), p. 54.

Lorado Taft, p. 25.

1. For more on Taft's studies in France and early years in Chicago, see Alan Stuart Weller, *Lorado in Paris: The Letters of Lorado Taft, 1880–1885* (Urbana, Ill./Chicago 1985); and Timothy J. Garvey, *Public Sculptor: Lorado Taft and the Beautification of Chicago* (Urbana, Ill./Chicago, 1988).

2. "Address of Lorado Taft, Sculptor of the Ferguson Fountain," in *Exercises at the Dedication of the Fergsuon Fountain of the Great Lakes, Chicago, Sept. 9, 1913* (Chicago, 1913), p. 26.

3. For more information on early Art Institute lecturers and their subjects, see annual reports and copies of the *Bulletin of The Art Institute of Chicago* from 1887 through the 1920s.

Dudley Crafts Watson, p. 29.

1. While at the School, Watson produced two of the panels in the mural cycle at Chicago's Wendell Phillips High School. One of these was included in the recent Art Institute exhibition "To Inspire and Instruct" (see Eskridge, pp. 86–87). For more biographical information on Watson, see Dudley Crafts Watson, *Interior Decoration, Reading With a Purpose 39* (Chicago, 1932), p. 7.

2. Clarence J. Bulliet, "Artists of Chicago, Past and Present: No. 67, Dudley Crafts Watson," *Chicago Daily News,* June 1936 (see *Scrapbook of Art and Artists of Chicago* in the Ryerson Library).

3. For more on Watson's career as a traveling Chautauqua lecturer, see "Dr. Dudley Crafts Watson Lecture Series" (Chicago, 1944), Special Collections Department, University of Iowa Libraries.

4. Philip Maxwell of the *Chicago Tribune*, and R. H. Blakesley of Chicago, quoted in ibid., pp. 4, 5.

The Better Homes Institute, p. 32.

1. See "Notes: Extension Department," *Bulletin of the Art Institute of Chicago* 13, 4 (Apr. 1919), p. 60.

2. Ibid.

3. See "The Growth of Extension Work," *Bulletin of The Art Institute of Chicago* 14, 4 (Apr. 1920), p. 50.

4. "The Extension Department and the 'Own Your Own Home' Campaigns," *Bulletin of The Art Institute of Chicago* 13, 6 (Sept. 1919), p. 86.

5. Ibid.

Katharine Kuh, p. 43.

1. Katharine Kuh, interviewed by Avis Berman, Nov. 10, 1982, oral history transcript, Archives of American Art, Washington, D.C. The information presented here was drawn from Susan F. Rossen and Charlotte Moser, "Primer for Seeing: The Gallery of Art Interpretation and Katharine Kuh's Crusade for Modernism in Chicago," *Art Institute of Chicago Museum Studies* 16, 1 (1990), pp. 6–25.

2. The most famous of these is *Art Has Many Faces: The Nature of Art Presented Visually* (New York, 1952).

3. Rossen and Moser (note 1), p. 24.

Nosan, "Women in the Galleries: Prestige, Education, and Volunteerism at Mid-century," pp. 47–71.

This essay was, like its subject, a deeply collaborative effort, and would have been impossible without the generosity of many people. Judith A. Barter, Betty Blum, Sarah Bornstein, Sarah Kelley, Debra N. Mancoff, Suzanne Folds McCullagh, Annnemarie van Roessel, Daniel Schulman, and Martha Thorne all lent their expertise, and this work is much the better for it. Bart Ryckbosch and Deborah Webb guided me through the Art Institute's archives with skill and patience. Celia Hilliard, Susan F. Rossen, and particularly Patricia Kubicek, offered firm support, sound advice, and their own rich historical perspective at every stage of the project. Past and present museum-education staff Jane Clarke, Lois Raasch, George Schneider, and Barbara Wriston shared their time, and memories of their work, with grace and good humor. The lion's share of thanks and credit, however, go to the members of the Woman's Board and the Staff Assistants program whom I had the pleasure of getting to know: Joanne Alter, Nancy Gerson, Gina Jannotta, Carolyn McKittrick, Muriel Kallis Steinberg Newman, Zoé Petersen, Ruth Powell, Elizabeth Robson, Marjorie Webster, and Sara Wood.

1. "Memo on Chicago," *Vogue* (July 1952), p. 68.
2. Ibid.
3. Mrs. Walter E. Anderson, Mary Block, Kathleen Harvey, Mary Ward, and Suzette Morton Zurcher, "Suggested Plan for a Woman's Board of the Art Institute," Sept. 19, 1952, p. 2. Archives of The Art Institute of Chicago. Unless otherwise specified, all references to Art Institute and Woman's Board correspondence, and to oral history transcripts and other manuscripts and ephemera, are to documents residing in the Art Institute Archives.
4. The Art Institute made much of its unprecedented decision to approach the general public for money. "Come and look . . . and learn," declared a museum advertisement of January 1952: "The Art Institute of Chicago has said that to all the people of this city for 73 years. Today, for the first time, it asks all the people to help it meet a financial emergency." See Souvenir Program for Sadler's Well's Theatre Ballet, Jan. 21, 1952, Chicago Civic Opera House. For more on the Emergency Fund Drive and Rich's long career at the Art Institute, see John W. Smith, "The Nervous Profession: Daniel Catton Rich and The Art Institute of Chicago, 1927–1958," *Art Institute of Chicago Museum Studies* 19, 1 (1993), pp. 58–79.
5. "The drive was labeled an emergency," reported the *Chicago Daily News*, "because exterior stonework . . . was crumbling dangerously and repairs were needed throughout the rest of the structure." By April 1953, collected funds had been used to tuck-point and restore stonework; renovate, relight, and enlarge gallery space; and repair the heating system and roof. "City Responds Heartily to Art Institute Appeal," *Chicago Daily News*, Apr. 22, 1953. For more on the architectural history of the Art Institute, see *Art Institute of Chicago Museum Studies* 14, 1 (1988).
6. Daniel Catton Rich, quoted in Rita Fitzpatrick, "Art Institute a Living Thing; Kicks Prove It," *Chicago Tribune*, Dec. 12, 1951.
7. "Thalia," "Chicagoans Rally to Aid Art Institute," *Chicago Tribune*, Feb. 10, 1952.
8. Quoted in Fitzpatrick (note 6).
9. The poem was printed in full in "Recorded at Random," *Chicago Tribune*, May 14, 1952.
10. "Thalia" (note 7).
11. Smith (note 4), p. 66.
12. For a brief introduction to the connections between this Progressive-Era ethos and the Arts-and-Crafts atmosphere of women's education more generally, see Wendy Kaplan, "Women Designers and the Arts and Crafts Movement," in Pat Kirkham, ed., *Women Designers in the USA: Diversity and Difference, 1900–2000*, exh. cat. (New York, 2000), pp. 84–99.
13. Quoted in Jane Gregory, "If They Only Had the Time," *Chicago Sun Times*, May 1, 1959.
14. For more on Blake's character and accomplishments, see Kathryn Loring, "Blake Art to Be Shown at May Party," *Chicago Tribune*, May 16, 1954; and Athlyn Deshais, "Mrs. Blake Is One of Guiding Forces at Institute: She Gave Our Art a Soul," *Chicago Daily News*, Apr. 18, 1959.
15. See Athlyn Deshais, "Art on Wheels Her Big Dream," *Chicago Daily News*, May 23, 1959.
16. Woman's Board members Mary Block, Helen Geraghty, Babbie Smith, and Suzette Morton Zurcher, among others, were all committed members of the Chicago Public School Art Society. For more on the history of the Antiquarian Society, which was founded as the Chicago Society of Decorative Art in 1877, see Celia Hilliard, "'Higher Things': Remembering the Early Antiquarians," *Art Institute of Chicago Museum Studies* 28, 2 (2002), pp. 6–21.
17. For more on Blake's collection, see *A Quarter Century of Collecting: Drawings Given to The Art Institute of Chicago 1844–1970 by Margaret Day Blake*, exh. cat. (Chicago, 1970); and Suzanne Folds McCullagh, "Drawings in The Art Institute of Chicago," *Master Drawings* 38, 3 (fall 2000), pp. 241–48.
18. Herself no stranger to ambition and hard work, Block had, many years earlier, succeeded at carving out a role in Lord and Thomas, the firm headed by her father, Albert D. Lasker, who was known as the "father of modern advertising." In addition to her efforts on behalf of the Art Institute and the Chicago Public School Art Society, Block "played a vigorous role" in supporting British War Relief during World War II, the Community Fund, Hull-House, Lyric Opera, and many other Chicago-based arts and social-service organizations. See Athlyn Deshais, "Men Like Fine Art Now, Too," *Chicago Daily News* (c. Apr. 1959). The Blocks' collection is showcased in *One Hundred European Paintings and Drawings from the Collection of Mr. and Mrs. Leigh B. Block*, exh. cat. (Washington, D.C., 1967).
19. Zoé Petersen, interviewed by Gregory Nosan, Sept. 18, 2002, oral history transcript.
20. For a quick introduction to this complex fracas, see "Art Institute's Plans For Addition Bared," *Chicago Sun Times*, Jan. 8, 1955; and "City Gets Right To Oppose Art Institute Suit," *Chicago Tribune*, July 13, 1955.

21. Petersen (note 19). The Masterpiece Ball was the subject of many feature articles in the Chicago press, the most substantial of which are Annette Darling, "They're as Pretty as a Picture," *Chicago Daily News*, May 17, 1952; Athlyn Deshais, "Art Works Breathe as 600 in Costume Dance at the Hilton," *Chicago Daily News*, May 24, 1952; and "It Was a Masterpiece All Right!" *Chicago Tribune*, May 24, 1952.
22. One reporter, for instance, remarked of Chicago's balls: ". . . if you are one of the old guard you can remember some very spectacular ones, such as the great Victory Ball given by the Arts Club at the end of World War I." "Thalia," "Masterpiece Ball Friday to Be Spectacular Event," *Chicago Tribune*, May 18, 1952.
23. Quoted from "Museum Puts a $2,000,000 Show in Shops," *Chicago Tribune*, May 15, 1952. For more on the Merry-Go-Round, see Richard P. Trenbeth, "Art Merry-Go-Round," *Public Relations Journal* 8, 12 (Dec., 1953); and Mary Dougherty, "Mary-Go-Round," *Chicago Sun Times*, May 13, 1953.
24. Patricia Kubicek, for instance, recalls that the living tableaux were "the most popular offerings" at the board's May Festivals, and drew anxious spectators determined not to miss "the great beauties of Chicago who appeared frequently in the social pages." See Patricia Kubicek, "The Community Associates," handwritten manuscript, Feb. 2002.
25. The Merry-Go-Round inspired eight May Festivals held between 1954 and 1966; these were followed by four Celebrations in the 1980s, which were free, two-day events geared to both children and adult audiences.
26. Mary Dougherty, "Mary-Go-Round," *Chicago Sun Times*, May 15, 1955.
27. See, for instance, Marilyn Unmacht, "Art Institute May Festival Proves Breezy and Informal," *Chicago Tribune*, May 25, 1954; "Cholly Dearborn," "4,000 Enjoy Art Festival," *Chicago Sun Times*, May 17, 1955; Barbara Powers, "Plan 'Backstage Tour' of The Art Institute," *Chicago Daily News*, Apr. 24, 1963; and Jane Gregory, "Culture Festival Extends Its Run," *Chicago Sun Times*, May 15, 1966.
28. Mary Dougherty, "Mary-Go-Round," *Chicago Sun Times*, May 17, 1955.
29. Department of Public Relations, The Art Institute of Chicago, press release on the Woman's Board, Nov. 26, 1952. For more details on the personalities and politics of the Woman's Board's formation, see Percy B. Eckhart, letter to Walter S. Brewster, July 17, 1950; Florence Miller, "The Woman's Board of The Art Institute of Chicago," June/July 1967; and Petersen (note 19).
30. Kenneth Shopen, "Where are the Men? Women Taking Helm of Art World," *Chicago Daily News*, June 5, 1953. "Women," continued Shopen, "far outnumber men at art exhibitions, art lectures, and art functions of all kinds at the Art Institute. . . . The box office at Orchestra Hall reports that from sixty-five to eighty-five percent of audiences at symphony concerts are women."
31. See Department of Public Relations (note 29). Chief among these institutions was the Metropolitan Museum of Art, New York, which added Mrs. Vincent Astor, Mrs. Ogden Reid, and Mrs. Sheldon Whitehouse to its board of trustees in 1951.
32. Mrs. Egmont Frankel, "Summary of the Conference of Women's Committees of America," Nov. 12, 1952, p. 2.
33. Ibid., p. 1.
34. Anderson et al. (note 3).
35. For Marx's collection, see Lucy R. Lippard, *The School of Paris: Paintings from the Florene May Schoenborn and Samuel A. Marx Collection*, exh. cat. (New York, 1965). On Paepcke, see James Sloan Allen, *The Romance of Commerce and Culture: Capitalism, Modernism, and the Chicago-Aspen Crusade for Cultural Reform* (Chicago, 1983). Steinberg's holdings were later catalogued in William S. Lieberman, ed., *An American Choice: The Muriel Kallis Steinberg Newman Collection*, exh. cat (New York, 1981).
36. For a catalogue of Judson's work, see *For Gardens and Other Places: The Sculpture of Sylvia Shaw Judson* (Chicago, 1967). Waller's *Radio: The Fifth Estate* (Boston, 1946) was a pioneering study of broadcasting practice.
37. For more on the Woman's Board's many organized trips, see Kubicek (note 24); and Patricia Kubicek, interviewed by Gregory Nosan, Sept. 13, 2002, oral history transcript. A later Woman's Board tradition that sprang from the group's playful, theatrical nature involved encouraging Community Associates groups to present their annual reports in skit form; see ibid.
38. Margaret Blake, "Redraft of Letter to Woman's Board Members," Feb. 16, 1953.
39. "Function of the Associates Committee," manuscript, n.d., pp. 2–3. This was not the first time that such an idea had surfaced at the Art Institute. As early as 1916, for example, the museum's extension programs involved traveling exhibits; lectures to explain them; and permanent community organizations to further the continuance of such efforts. See *Art Institute of Chicago: Thirty-Seventh Annual Report* (Chicago, 1916), p. 35.
40. For more on this technique and its centrality to the program's success, see Kubicek interview (note 37).
41. By 1964, for example, there existed eight Community Associates groups ranging from Lake Forest in the north to Homewood-Flossmoor and Wheaton, to Chicago's south and west, respectively.
42. Jane Clarke, interviewed by Gregory Nosan, Oct. 11, 2002, oral history transcript. For a general sense of whom the Community Associates attracted, see "Cholly Dearborn," "Smart Set," *Chicago American*, Apr. 13, 1953.
43. Robert D. Putnam, *Bowling Alone: The Collapse and Revival of American*

Community (New York, 2000). For an intriguing attempt to explain the Community Associates program as appealing to a new, particularly middle-class appetite for art, see Athlyn Deshais, "Art Has Moved to the Suburbs," *Chicago Daily News*, Nov. 21, 1959.

44. Sara Wood, interviewed by Gregory Nosan, Sept. 4, 2002, oral history transcript.

45. "Colorful Program Palette for Local Art Associates," *Barrington Press*, n.d. (c. Oct. 1964).

46. Ibid. For more on the associates' art-appreciation experiences at the museum itself, see Sylvia Cassell, "Clubwomen Qualify as Art Critics," *Chicago Tribune*, Nov. 29, 1955.

47. Kubicek interview (note 37).

48. See Kenneth Shopen, "Art Patrons Called Snobs For 'Refusing' to Buy the Works of Chicago Artists," *Chicago Daily News*, Oct. 18, 1953; and idem, "Art Climate Here a Bit Cool; Experts Debate Warming It Up," *Chicago Daily News*, Feb. 28, 1954.

49. Quoted in Shopen, "Art Climate Here a Bit Cool" (note 48).

50. On the Chicago art scene in the 1950s, see Franz Schultze, "Art News in Chicago," *Art News* 70, 7 (Nov. 1971), pp. 48–55; idem, *Fantastic Images: Chicago Art since 1945* (Chicago, 1972); Charles A. Lewis and Cynthia Yao, *Chicago: The City and Its Artists, 1945–1978*, exh. cat. (Ann Arbor, 1978); and Lynne Warren, *Art in Chicago, 1945–1995*, exh. cat. (New York/Chicago, 1996). For a brief sampling of the art on offer to Chicago gallery-goers at this point in time, see Eleanor Jewett, "Interesting Little Shows Fill Galleries," *Chicago Tribune*, Feb. 22, 1953; and Kenneth Shopen, "In the Byways of Chicago—Art Is Where You Find It," *Chicago Daily News*, Feb. 12, 1964.

51. For more about the 1020 Art Center and the various organizations that used it, see Eleanor Jewett, "Plan '1020 Art Center' in Chicago," *Chicago Tribune*, June 14, 1953; and Patricia Moore, "An Old Mansion Is Saved," *Chicago Daily News*, Nov. 21, 1953. The Artists' Equity gallery is described in Frank Holland, "Gallery to Open Saturday In Historic Borden Mansion," *Chicago Sun Times*, Oct. 4, 1953; and Kenneth Shopen, "You Don't Need a Fortune to Purchase Original Art," *Chicago Daily News*, Nov. 20, 1953. The Renaissance Society of the University of Chicago, a leading venue for contemporary art on the city's south side, had also organized its own "Art for Young Collectors" sales as early as 1951; see Frank Holland, "Sale On for Under $50," *Chicago Sun Times*, Nov. 25, 1951.

52. Muriel Kallis Steinberg Newman, "The Woman's Board," manuscript, 2002, p. 1. Early in 1953, Margaret Blake herself visited the Museum of Modern Art, New York, where she explored that institution's rental service with Mrs. John D. Rockefeller III, and the museum's director, René d'Harnoncourt.

53. For details on the gallery's complex, changing business arrangements with both artists and a growing range of clients, see Carolyn McKittrick and Patricia Kubicek, interviewed by Gregory Nosan, Nov. 13, 2002, oral history transcript. Art Rental and Sales served Chicago's artists and public until 1987.

54. Quoted in "Art-for-Rent Project Boon to City's Artists," *Chicago Sun Times*, Oct. 28, 1956. Among the many other corporate collectors were Amoco, American Airlines, the *Chicago Sun Times*, and the architectural firm Perkins and Will.

55. Lois Baur, "Women Put Art on Cash, Carry Basis," *Chicago Sun Times*, Oct. 13, 1954.

56. With roots in early-century lecture courses such as Stella Skinner's "Historic Styles and Periods in Furniture in Relation to Modern Homes" (1911), interior-decoration classes began as a Monday-afternoon staple of Art Institute educational programming in 1923, and went by a number of names over the years. Whether called "Practical Problems in the Modern Home" (1925) or "The Development of Taste in the Home and in Dress" (1931), the course's impulse was consistent: to train implicitly unrefined audiences in the elusive art of "taste," and encourage them to create their own everyday, domestic environments with greater aesthetic and historical self-consciousness. The Art Institute's *Bulletin* offers the most consistent record of who taught these classes when, and of what they chose to focus on.

57. Daniel Catton Rich, "Educational Plans, Television," *Art Institute of Chicago: Annual Report, 1954–1955*, n.p.

58. George D. Culler, quoted in Edward J. Snyder, Jr., "Institute to Give Free Art Lectures," *Chicago Daily News*, Sept. 28, 1955. For more on Culler, see *Art Institute of Chicago Quarterly* 49, 3 (Sept. 15, 1955), n.p.

59. *Art Institute of Chicago Quarterly* 49, 4 (Nov. 15, 1955), n.p.

60. *Art Institute of Chicago Quarterly* 50, 1 (Sept. 15, 1956), n.p. For listings of these classes, which included "More Than Meets the Eye," "The Arts in Your Life," and "Theory of the Arts" in 1956 alone, see issues of *Art Institute of Chicago Quarterly* from 1956 through 1958.

61. The numbers make this clear. In 1938, for instance, while the Department of Education reached nearly 27,000 non-members through public lectures and school programs, the Membership and Extension Lecturers Department served an audience of almost 69,000 members; see *Art Institute of Chicago: Annual Report, 1937–1938*, pp. 29–30. For Culler's efforts to change this state of affairs, see *Art Institute of Chicago Quarterly* (note 60) and Snyder (note 58).

62. Suzette Morton Zurcher, "The Museum, the Jeep, and the School Child," *Art Institute of Chicago Bulletin* 45, 2 (Apr.–May, 1951), pp. 32–35.

63. Noteworthy among these were volunteer docent programs at the Kansas City, Mo., and St. Louis art museums. In 1969 Florence Miller appointed an official committee that continued and enhanced the exploratory efforts of the ad hoc 1953 group. For more details on the Woman's Board's early plans for children's education, see Suzette Morton Zurcher and Barbara Wriston, "The Junior Museum of The Art Institute of Chicago," n.d. (c. Jan. 1964), pp. 5–6; and Zoé Petersen, "History of the Junior Museum," typescript, 1991.

64. See Joanne Alter, interviewed by Jane Clarke, Sept. 16, 1997, oral history transcript. The Sol and Celia Hammerman Foundation, established by Mrs. Alter's parents, underwrote the construction of the Junior Museum's Hammerman Gallery and continues to fund exhibits there.

65. For more on Zurcher's background and work at the Art Institute, see "Front Views and Profiles," *Chicago Tribune*, May 15, 1956; "Printing Art," *This Week In Chicago*, June 20, 1956; Eleanor Page, "Her Art Collection Pays Off in Fun," *Chicago Tribune* (March, 18, 1960; and Petersen (notes 19 and 63).

66. The best specific sources on the league's exploratory efforts, and its eventual collaboration with the Woman's Board, are Clarke (note 42) and Wood (note 44). For the history of the Junior League of Chicago, see Judy York, "Celebrating 75 Years of Service to Chicago" (Chicago, 1988).

67. Low's and Crawford's remarks appear in "Volunteers and Part-time Workers," *Museum Education Circular* 5 (June 1953), pp. 7–8. This series of response papers, in which museum educators shared ideas and opinions on a broad range of common concerns, is an invaluable record of the state of the profession in the 1950s.

68. George Buehr served as Acting Director of Museum Education after George D. Culler's departure in 1958. Richard N. Gregg filled Culler's position from 1960 through 1961.

69. For more on Wriston's life and work, see Barbara Wriston, interviewed by Gregory Nosan, Aug. 15, 2002, oral history transcript.

70. Ibid.

71. Ruth Powell and Elizabeth Robson, interviewed by Gregory Nosan, Feb. 10, 2003, oral history transcript. Other prime sources of information about the docent classes include Wriston (note 69); Lois Raasch, interviewed by Gregory Nosan, Aug. 15, 2002, oral history transcript; Gina Jannotta, interviewed by Gregory Nosan, Sept. 23, 2002, oral history transcript; and "Welcome to the Staff Assistant's Corps," typescript, 1965.

72. Ibid.

73. See Wriston (note 69).

74. Ibid.

75. Raasch (note 71). Raasch, of course, adjusted her pedagogical approach over the years. In 1978, for example, she and Staff Assistants incorporated many of the discussion techniques developed by the Chicago-based Great Books Foundation.

76. "Proposed Program for Expanded Junior Educational Activites: Volunteer Training Program, Junior Art Center," Feb. 20, 1961. An important resource on other contemporary museum-education programs for young audiences is Hardean K. Naeseth, "A Study of the In-museum Art Appreciation Program for Children in Four Major American Art Museums," (Ed.D. diss., Pennsylvania State University, 1963).

77. Zurcher and Wriston (note 63).

78. Major donors included Mr. and Mrs. Leigh B. Block; the Chicago Community Trust; the Sol and Celia Hammerman Foundation; the Service Club of Chicago; Mrs. Walter Byron Smith; Mr. and Mrs. Richard Thoresen; Mrs. Medard Welch; Mr. and Mrs. Henry C. Woods; and Suzette Morton Zurcher.

79. A principal in the Chicago firm Arthur Myrhum and Edward H. Bennett, Jr.—Associated Architects, Myrhum also designed buildings for the Morton Arboretum in Lisle, Illinois, and for Suzette Morton Zurcher herself. For more on Myrhum, see Ambrose M. Richardson, interviewed by Betty J. Blum, Feb. 1–3, 1990, oral history transcript; and John Zukowsky, ed., *Chicago Architecture and Design, 1923–1993: Reconfiguration of an American Metropolis*, exh. cat (Chicago/Munich, 1993), pp. 454–55.

80. "First Three Years of the Junior Museum," typescript, 1967, p. 1.

81. Lois Baur, "Wonderful World of Art Opens to Children," *Chicago's American*, Feb. 16, 1964.

82. For more on the Volunteer Committee, see McKittrick and Kubicek (note 53). The Community Associates became a fully independent museum-support group in 1991.

83. George Schneider, interviewed by Gregory Nosan, Nov. 11, 2002, oral history transcript.

84. Wriston and others of her staff appeared on "Questions and Answers on Art," a weekly segment of the "Stock Market Observer" program on WCIU, Channel 26; and on a weekly show produced by WBEZ, Chicago's public-radio station; see Wriston (note 69); Raasch (note 71); and Jane Clarke, "The Department of Museum Education: The Art Institute of Chicago," program brochure, 1978, pp. 8–9. For more on the museum's earlier, unrealized ambitions for in-house television programming, see *Art Institute of Chicago Annual Report, 1954–1955*, n.p.

85. *Art Institute of Chicago Annual Report, 1968–1969*, pp. 4, 6, 49.

86. See Clarke (note 84), pp. 5–6, 25, 29.

87. Powell and Robson (note 71).

Eskridge, "Museum Education at the Art Institute, 1980–2003: Expansion, Diversity, Continuity," pp. 72–89.

1. James N. Wood, "The Museum and the Public," in Martin Feldstein, ed., *The Economics of Art Museums* (Chicago, 1989), p. 57.

2. See Lisa C. Roberts, *From Knowledge to Narrative: Education and the Changing Museum* (Washington, D.C., 1997), pp. 147–48, for more on the advent of nontraditional and thematic museums. See also Bonnie Pitman, "Muses, Museums, and Memories," *Daedalus: Journal of the American Academy of Arts and Sciences* 128, 3 (summer 1999), pp. 1–31, for a summary of statistics on museums in the United States.

3. Joshua C. Taylor, "The Art Museum in the United States," in Sherman E. Lee, ed., *Understanding Art Museums* (Englewood Cliffs, N.J., 1975), p. 47.

4. See Feldstein (note 1), pp. 1–10

5. From the 1869 Charter for the Chicago Academy of Design, which became The Art Institute of Chicago in 1879, as amended: "The purposes for which The Art Institute of Chicago is formed are: to found, build, maintain, and operate museums, schools, libraries of art, and theaters . . . to conduct appropriate activities conducive to the artistic development of the region . . . and to cultivate and extend the arts by any appropriate needs." This founding vision of broad cultural integration was manifest more generally after World War II, when, as Taylor noted, "communities and universities . . . began to plan complexes to accommodate music, theater, and visual arts. . . . The implications of such a center—apart from its philosophical underpinning holding all arts as different manifestations of a similar impulse—is that one looks at works of art in much the same spirit as one goes to the theater or concert and, in fact, that the various experiences enhance one another." See Taylor (note 3), pp. 63–64.

6. "The humanities," Knox stated, "are still today the vital core of an education for a democracy. . . . not that they will make the individual life a richer, deeper experience—though this is true; but that they will prepare the young mind for the momentous choices, the critical decisions, which face our world today." See Bernard Knox, *The Oldest Dead White European Males* (New York, 1993), p. 104.

7. Mihaly Csikszentmihaly and Rick E. Robinson, *The Art of Seeing: An Interpretation of the Aesthetic Encounter* (Malibu, Calif., 1990), p. 17.

8. Quoted in Janet Tassel, "Reverence for the Object: Art Museums in a Changed World," *Harvard Magazine* 105, 1 (Sept.–Oct. 2002), p. 99. The source of this excerpt is Carol Becker, "When Cultures Come into Contention," in Association of Art Museum Directors, *Different Voices: A Social, Cultural, and Historical Framework for Change in the American Art Museum* (New York, 1992), pp. 58–71. For a penetrating essay on diversity among museum trustees, staff, and volunteers, see Lonnie G. Bunch, "Flies in the Buttermilk: Museums, Diversity, and the Will to Change," *Museum News* 79, 4 (July–Aug. 2000), pp. 32–35. See also Neil Harris, "Polling for Opinion," *Museum News* 69, 5 (Sept.–Oct. 1990), pp. 46–53. Harris, a leading historian of cultural institutions, wrote: "Museums have become central forces in the shaping of opinion and are responsible to broader constituencies than ever before in American history." Art historian Carol Duncan stated that art museums "above all . . . are spaces in which communities can work out the values that identify them as communities. Whatever their limitations . . . and however peripheral they often seem, art museum space is space worth fighting for." See Carol Duncan, *Civilizing Rituals* (New York, 1995), pp. 133–34.

9. Roberts (note 2), p. 3.

10. The Art Institute of Chicago, "Museum Strategic Direction for 1990s" (June 27, 1990), p. 7.

11. American Association of Museums, *Excellence and Equity: Education and the Public Dimensions of Museums* (Washington, D.C.,1992). See also idem, *Museums for a New Century: A Report of the Commission on Museums for a New Century* (Washington, D.C., 1984).

12. Exhibitions included "In Their Own Right: Images of African Americans from The Art Institute of Chicago" (1997); "Pass It On: Celebrating Families" (1998); and "Terrain of Freedom: American Art and the Civil War" (1999). For more on the latter, see *Art Institute of Chicago Museum Studies* 27, 1 (2001). An exploration of the Art Institute's collection of art by African Americans was published in *Art Institute of Chicago Museum Studies* 24, 2 (1999). The teacher manual "African American Art," issued by the Department of Museum Education in 1997, was made possible by the Gaylord and Dorothy Donnelley Foundation and the Elizabeth Stone Robson Teacher Resource Center.

13. See "Looking at Art Together: Parent Guide and Process Catalogue" (2002). This two-part publication won the 2003 "Excellence in Practice Publications Award" for best education guide, presented by the Committee on Education of the American Association of Museums.

14. Family Workshops, for instance, combine a thematic gallery walk followed by a relevant art activity in the studios; Drawing in the Galleries gives both children and parents a chance to learn drawing techniques while surrounded by original art; and the Artist's Studio is a popular art-making activity offered almost every weekend of the year. At festive Behind the Lions Family Days, the Art Institute is given over to the entire range of family programs for parents and children to enjoy. Programming support for family programs is provided by the Siragusa Foundation Education Endowment and a generous grant from Kraft Foods. Marshall Field's Foundation supports Art Institute family festivals.

15. Program for "The Board of Trustees Honors the 50th Anniversary of The Woman's Board of The Art Institute of Chicago" (April 11, 2003).

16. The company is now known as Kraft Foods Corporation.

17. Bluhm Seminar Room, named after longtime docent Barbara Bluhm, complements the center's offerings by accommodating professional development courses for teachers.

18. "Art Inside/Out" proved so popular and durable that it was left on view for four years (1992–96), twice as long as originally intended, and served over 400,000 visitors. For a thorough description of the exhibition and its conceptualization, see Ronne Hartfield, "Challenging the Context: Perception, Polity, and Power," *Curator* 37, 1 (1994), pp. 46–62; and Jean Sousa, "Helping Objects Speak for Themselves," *Exhibitionist* 14, 1 (spring 1995), pp. 32–34. The electronic components of "Art Inside/Out" won the American Association of Museums' Muse Award for best interactive program, the first time an art museum was so honored.

19. The program inspired the department to produce "What Do You See?," an educational video that features educator Philip Yenawine. For more on Yenawine and his research colleague Abigail Housen, see Rice (p. 17–18); and George E. Hein, *Learning in the Museum* (London, 1998), p. 141.

20. The "VisionQuest" game was used in the summer of 1995, while "Reading is Artrageous" debuted in 2001. The Woman's Board has also sponsored several symposia, including a five-week lecture series, "World View: The Art and Culture of Christianity, Hinduism, Buddhism, Islam, and Judaism," in which leading scholars spoke in the wake of the September 11, 2001 destruction of New York's World Trade Center.

21. Approximately one-third of all student visitors attend Chicago schools; fifty percent visit from greater Chicago and Illinois, and twenty-four travel from another state. While tours are free to Illinois schools, the museum requires out-of-state school groups to donate an optional amount.

22. Art Institute teacher programs now serve five thousand professional teachers and parent volunteer educators annually through professional-development credit courses, in-service programs in the schools, curriculum consultations, and thematic seminars, all of which take place year-round. These programs stress the teaching of art across the curriculum, and are developed in consultation with the Art Institute's Teacher Advisory Panel, a standing advisory group since 1980.

23. "Art and Stories," designed for eighth-graders, links art and literature through the study of the museum's permanent collection and special exhibitions. In "Museology," high-school students explore all facets of work at the Art Institute, and conclude the course by designing their own mock exhibition.

24. The Art Institute subscribes to the teaching protocol outlined by Carolyn Blackmon, Helen Voris, and Maija Sedzielarz in their teacher manual "Teach the Mind/Touch the Spirit" (Chicago, 1986), published by Chicago's Field Museum. "To use one's expertise," these authors write, "to ask questions that promote observations and reflection is a no less sophisticated means of teaching than to give scintillating lectures; indeed, it may be more so." See p. 9.

25. The program's interdisciplinary curriculum modules of several weeks' length were developed jointly by museum educators, teachers, and curriculum specialists.

26. Evenings for Educators was funded by the Lloyd A. Fry Foundation, and was conducted from 1993 to 1998. Supported by the Polk Bros. Foundation, "Science, Art, and Technology" took place in the 2001–2002 academic year, and was taught by Art Institute educators and conservators, School of the Art Institute faculty, and scientists from other institutions. For a program abstract, see Jennifer Amdur Spitz, ed., *Urban Network: Museums and Communities* (Chicago, 2003), pp. 76–83.

27. "Chicago: The City in Art" was generously funded by the Polk Bros. Foundation; for more on the Chicago Public Schools Art Collection, see www.cpsart.org.

28. The exhibition was organized at the behest of Armando Almendarez, Deputy Chief Education Officer, Chicago Public Schools, and curated by Robert W. Eskridge and Elizabeth Seaton, with Sylvia Rhor. The Chicago Board of Education, with the additional support of the Woman's Board and the Albert Pick, Jr. Fund, sponsored the exhibition. For the Chicago Public Schools collection, see Heather Becker, *Art for the People: The Rediscovery and Preservation of Progressive- and WPA-Era Murals in the Chicago Public Schools, 1904-1943* (San Francisco, 2002); Mary Lackritz Gray, *A Guide to Chicago's Murals* (Chicago, 2001); and Sylvia Rhor, "Educating America: Murals in Chicago Public Schools, 1904-1943," Ph.D. diss.,

Notes

University of Pittsburgh, 2003.

29. The Hulda B. and Maurice L. Rothschild Foundation makes Art Insights and Senior Celebrations possible.

30. During the last two decades, the Department of Museum Education has welcomed a list of eminent authors that includes Nobel laureates Seamus Heaney, Czeslov Milosz, Octavio Paz, Wole Soyenka, and Derek Walcott, as well as writers and intellectuals such as Michael Ondaatje and Susan Sontag.

31. George E. Hein defined the effectiveness of performance as an interpretive mode as follows: "Drama and theater are gripping, powerful media to draw visitors into a scene, make the human connection to objects apparent to some, and allow visitors' imaginations to expand and associate rich meanings with the objects displayed." See Hein (note 19) pp. 168–69.

32. See, for example, an article in the *Bulletin of The Art Institute of Chicago* which reported that the "well-known Donald Robertson Company" was presenting in Fullerton Hall the "standard plays of masters, ancient and modern." "The different branches of art, painting, architecture, drama, and music," the article's author contended, "are fundamentally one." "Dramatic Entertainments," *Bulletin of The Art Institute of Chicago* 2, 2 (Oct. 1908), p. 22.

33. Other musical programs have featured prominent contemporary performers, ranging from such artists and composers as Laurie Anderson, Pierre Boulez, and Philip Glass to traditional musicians from Africa and Asia.

34. Voices was founded with ongoing support from the Lester and Hope Abelson Fund.

35. Taylor (note 3), p. 67.

36. Use of the World Wide Web has grown exponentially: as of the year 2000, more than half of all households in the United States had computers; the number of African American and Hispanic households with computers doubled from 1998 to 2000; and by 1999, 95 percent of the nation's schools had been connected to the Internet. See Rob Semper, "Nodes and Connections: Museums in the Networked Age," *Curator* 45, 1 (2002).

37. See www.artic.edu/artaccess and www.artic.edu/cleo for examples of two Art Institute educational sites. For more on the Art Institute's Web-based efforts, see David Stark, "Docents Online: Computers, Schools, and Museum Docents," *Docent Educator* 8, 4 (summer 1999), pp 10–13.

38. Victoria Newhouse, *Towards a New Museum* (New York, 1998), p. 270.